#1508

P9-CRC-398

BEHIND THE WHEEL

BEHIND THE WHEEL

THE MAGIC AND MANNERS OF EARLY MOTORING

Lord Montagu of Beaulieu & F. Wilson McComb

PADDINGTON
PRESS LTD

NEW YORK & LONDON

Library of Congress Cataloging in Publication Data

Montagu of Beaulieu, Edward John Barrington
    Douglas-Scott-Montagu, Baron, 1926-
    Behind the wheel.

    Bibliography : p.
    Includes index.
    1. Automobile driving—History. I. McComb,
    F. Wilson, joint author. II. Title.
TL152.5.M56   629.28'3'209   76-53318
ISBN 0-448-22676-6

Copyright © 1977 Maurice Michael &
Lord Montagu of Beaulieu
All rights reserved

Printed in England by
Westerham Press Ltd., Westerham, Kent
Designed by Richard Johnson
Assisted by Patricia Pillay

IN THE UNITED STATES
PADDINGTON PRESS LTD.
Distributed by
GROSSET & DUNLAP

IN THE UNITED KINGDOM
PADDINGTON PRESS LTD.

IN CANADA
Distributed by
RANDOM HOUSE OF CANADA LTD.

IN AUSTRALIA
Distributed by
ANGUS & ROBERTSON PTY. LTD.

CONTENTS

Layout of controls for hands and feet—
Oddities of the past—Driving a coach-and-
four—Driving a Benz and a Panhard of
1898—American cars and their controls—
Early engines, their speed control and
gear changing—Governors and accelera-
tors—The early Lanchesters—The 1907
Electromobile—Steam cars—Instruments
and gauges—Warning lights—Automatic
systems of the future

Starting a car in the early days—100 miles
in 16 hours—Roadside repairs—Backfires
and broken wrists—Magneto vs. coil—
Starting devices—Preliminary checks—
Starting a Model T Ford—More roadside
troubles—Tools and spares to be carried
—Brake failures and runaways—Tyre
troubles—Tyre chains and other gadgets
—Getting there eventually

The motor house or motor stable—Looking
after a car—Washing down—Regular ser-
vicing by the chauffeur or owner—Daily

A TYRE IS A TIRE

AN ENGLISH-AMERICAN GLOSSARY

Every human activity has its jargon, without which its devotees could not effectively communicate with each other, but it takes time for such a vocabulary to become established, and the same thing may be known by different names in different countries. When Henry Sturmey founded the first British motoring magazine in 1895, he called it *The Autocar* because that is what he thought the vehicle itself would be called. But he was wrong: the British chose ''motor-car'' instead. The Americans at first rejected *automobile* because it was a French word, and the Chicago *Times-Herald* chose ''motocycle'' as the winning entry in a $500 competition for a suitable name. As late as 1906, *Cosmopolitan* used ''motor-car'' as the generic word. But eventually ''automobile'' became the accepted term in America, while ''motorcar'' lost its hyphen in crossing the Atlantic and remained in use as an alternative.

In a book such as this, to modernize is to bowdlerize. The temptation to up-date motoring —or automotive!—terminology has been resisted because some of the aura of a period is lost when a modern equivalent is substituted for the contemporary word. In most cases the meaning will be perfectly clear from the context, but the following list of differences between British and American usage may prove useful.

Accumulator—Battery
Beaded edge—Clincher rim
Big-end bearing—Rod bearing
Bonnet—Hood
Boot—Trunk
Bottom gear—Low gear
Bulkhead—Firewall
Capacity (engine)—Displacement
Change gear, to—Shift gear, to
Carburettor (carburetter)—carburetor
Cover (tyre)—Casing
Crownwheel—Ring gear
Damper—Shock absorber
Dickey—Rumble seat
Epicyclic (transmission)—Planetary
Estate car—Station wagon
Gear lever—Shift lever
Half shaft—Half axle
Hood (folding)—Top
Indicator—Turn signal
Lamps—Lights
Lorry—Truck

Mudguard—Fender
Overhead valve—Valve-in-head
Paraffin (oil)—Kerosene
Petrol—Gasoline
Propeller shaft—Driveshaft
Saloon—Sedan
Screenwasher—Windshield washer
Shooting brake—Station wagon
Sidescreen—Side curtain
Sidevalve—Flathead, L-head, T-head
Silencer—Muffler
Spanner—Wrench
Sparking plug—Spark plug
Starting handle—Crank handle
Top gear—High gear
Track (width)—Tread
Two-stroke—Two-cycle
Tyre—Tire
Tyre lever—Tire iron
Wind, to—Crank, to
Windscreen—Windshield
Wing—Fender

McCOMB COLLECTION

INTRODUCTION
THE SPLENDID HORSELESS CARRIAGE

"*Today, the motorist enjoys the most luxurious mode of travel that has been devised by man. He is comfortable, he is warm, and he is protected from the rain. . . . In short, from a weird contrivance that was the plaything of cranks, at which boys in the street threw stones and the public stared agape, the motor car has developed into the splendid horseless carriage of prophecy. It stands as the triumph of automobile engineering.*"

A. E. BERRIMAN, Motoring (1914)

This is a history of motoring, not a history of the motorcar. In it the car has been considered in a number of different roles, because, at one time or another, it has been different things to different people: an exciting new invention which aroused the interest of engineers in many countries; an expensive but entertaining toy for the well-to-do; a continual delight to the ordinary family, for whom it was a magic carpet to a whole new world of freedom; the ideal means of exploring one's own and other lands; a form of transportation for the farmer, doctor, tradesman or businessman that in sheer convenience has never been equalled; and, above all, an unparalleled influence on the development of our civilization.

Unparalleled, I say, because it has exercised such a staggering effect on *all* parts of society all over the world—not just on certain specialized groups. This is what makes the motorcar so much more significant an invention than television, for example, or even the aeroplane. There are very few people today whose life style has not been affected, one way or another, by the availability of mechanized transport.

We have looked at the car as a mechanism, of course, because it *is* a mechanism; inanimate, however animated. But that is not the important point. There is a curiously strong link between man and motorcar. No other piece of machinery bears such a special relationship to its operator. And what really matters is not the fact that a once crude mechanism has been so refined and improved over the years, but the way in which that process has altered the relationship.

So it is not enough to study the minutiae of the machinery. We have to think about the way people drive cars now, and how they once drove them; the controls they have had to operate at different periods; the once laborious tasks of starting the engine, mending tyres, or doing lengthy mechanical repairs at the roadside; the ritual of checking, oiling, greasing and overhauling the vehicle; the different items of equipment that have been used to make motoring safer or more comfortable; the way people learned to drive, and what they wore; the roads they travelled along, how they found their way, and where they went.

In order to arrive at a balanced assessment, we have to avoid the pitfall of considering everything solely from a modern standpoint. For many years, some of the popular British newspapers would refer to the historic London-to-Brighton Run as "The Old Crocks' Race." They looked at the cars taking part in it (all of them built before 1905), compared them with modern cars, and found them funny. Their attitude denoted affection rather than ridicule, but it was, nevertheless, a considerable distortion of the truth. Yet one wonders if today's adulation of *all* old cars, regardless of period, quality or anything else, is really much better.

What we have to try to do is to judge the vehicles of any age as they would have been judged in their own time—with the benefit of hindsight, certainly, but without distortion. The only way to do this is by careful selection from contemporary writings, so that ideally we recapture not just the opinions but even the atmosphere of the period. For example, we all know in a general way that most older people were understandably hostile to the motorcar when it first obtruded on their lives, and indeed for years afterwards. But how much more convincing it is to read in Sir Osbert Sitwell's autobiography the extract he quotes from a letter written to him in 1913 by his grandmother: "I think motors are such dangerous, horrid,

THE MORRIS OWNER

Rustic: "I don't 'old wi' them there new-fangled motor cars, whizzin' along the road like 'ornets!"

By the middle 1920s, early motorcars were regarded as merely objects of ridicule by those who had forgotten that, in their day, vehicles such as the 1900 de Dion (BELOW) provided practical and enjoyable transport.

BRITISH LEY

The startling progress made in automotive design during the early twentieth century is revealed by comparing the well-appointed 15/20 hp Fiat-Brevetti limousine of 1905/6 with the first production Wolseley, the primitive 3½-hp open two-seater of 1899 with its tiller steering and single-cylinder engine.

OPPOSITE: *The first production Daimler of 1895 remained very carriage-like, with a two-cylinder engine mounted at the rear and transmission by flat belts. It was, very obviously, a horseless carriage.*

odious things, and always feel ill for days after I have been in one." Poor Lady Londesborough; she could never have become reconciled to the motoring age.

The world's first mechanically propelled vehicle was built in the France of Louis XV— more than two hundred years ago, when George III reigned over North America as well as Britain. Historians now vie with each other to uncover early examples of mechanized carriages: a steam-driven coach was successfully tested in England a decade before George IV became Prince Regent; a petrol-engined vehicle was running in the streets of New York when Ulysses S. Grant took office as President of the United States; and so on.

On the other hand, it was little more than ninety years ago that the motorcar began to assume the form of a convenient and reasonably sized device for the day-to-day transportation of two or more human beings. Many a man alive today was already a toddler, playing in his nursery, when Karl Benz and Gottlieb Daimler began selling their machines to customers on a commercial basis. In short, the complex modern automobile has been developed to its present state of sophistication within the life span of one man.

The date when the motor industry was born in Britain or America is a favourite subject for argument: on one side of the Atlantic the claims made for Duryea, Pope, Stanley or Winton place it anywhere between 1895 and 1898; on the other, the most likely claimants are the Coventry-built (but Franco-German designed) Daimler of 1897, or the production Wolseleys and Lanchesters of 1900/1901. But whatever the date, it is certain that once the motor industry had started, it did not so much expand as explode, and the rate of technical progress almost tran-

scends belief. In December 1898, what was believed to be the fastest car in the world was timed over a flying kilometre near Paris at a little below 40 mph. Almost exactly seven years later (in January 1906), an American car achieved more than 127 mph at Daytona Beach, Florida. We know this to be true because it is vouched for and recorded in contemporary reports—but how can one actually *believe* that this speed was accomplished in a bare twenty years from the day when Gottlieb Daimler tentatively installed an engine in what had formerly been a horse-drawn carriage?

That same year, 1906, the Hon. Charles Rolls won two races with a "Light Twenty" model— one in Britain, one in America—and at the London Motor Show the public saw for the first time the superb vehicle which was to become known all over the world as the Rolls-Royce "Silver Ghost." It was typical of the really excellent machines that were developed during what we in England think of as the Edwardian period: Napier, Fiat, Mercédès, Spyker, Panhard, de Dietrich and Lorraine-Dietrich, Isotta-Fraschini and Hispano-Suiza, with a sprinkling of American cars in the later years—Thomas, Packard and Oldsmobile. They were large, they were powerful, elegant and comfortable—and they were magnificently built to the highest standards of craftsmanship. Perhaps it is not so surprising that Algy Berriman, writing in 1914, expressed the view that the best cars of this Golden Age had reached the pinnacle of engineering achievement.

They were such an improvement over their predecessors of ten or fifteen years before that they seemed an entirely different creation. Yet the cars of ten or even twenty years later had merely changed in detail—and not always for the better.

BRITISH LEYLAND

BRITISH LEYLAND

ORW 769R

The preponderance of Continental makes among the best cars of the period was unfortunate for Britain and America, but it was an inevitable result of the handicaps that the two nations' motor manufacturers had had to overcome in earlier days. In Britain, the efforts of pioneer motorists and engineers were hampered intolerably by a piece of legislation that belonged to the days before motorcars existed. When they attempted to test their vehicles, they were prosecuted under the Locomotive Act of 1865, which called for a speed of not more than 4 mph in the country, 2 mph in towns, and three walking attendants (one of whom, until 1878, was required to carry a red flag). The so-called Emancipation Act of 1896 removed the need for walking attendants and raised the speed limit to 14 mph (quickly trimmed back to 12 mph by the Local Government Board), but this was still absurdly restrictive, even for the modest capabilities of a nineteenth-century vehicle. Less than two weeks before the 1896 act came into force, the French had held a motor race on public roads all the way from Paris to Marseilles and back, a distance of well over a thousand miles. Despite torrential rain and gales which littered the course with debris, all but four of the fourteen finishers had *averaged* more than 12 mph *for the entire distance.*

So at a time when French, German and Italian cars were being rapidly improved to meet the demands of international motor racing, British motorists were still being prosecuted—and, indeed, persecuted—for breaking a law that was out-of-date when it was introduced. Undoubtedly a minority of motorists drove in a way that was careless, inconsiderate, or downright arrogant, but it is no less certain that many of the police involved in "speed-trapping" gave

OPPOSITE: *Unlike the German Daimler on the previous page, the British Daimlers built in Coventry, such as this 1897 example owned by the Hon. Evelyn Ellis, always followed the Panhard principle of an engine at the front driving the rear wheels through a geared transmission system. This is the basis of the vast majority of cars—even the superficially very different Daimler Sovereign of some eight decades later.*

King Edward VII rode as a passenger on several occasions with John Montagu, the present Lord Montagu's father. In this historic picture they are seated in the latter's 1899 Daimler 12, which is still to be seen today in the National Motor Museum at Beaulieu.

false evidence to ensure a conviction, and many magistrates encouraged the practice. Although new and more realistic legislation was urgently needed, for various reasons it was not until 1903 that the Motor Car Act came before the British Parliament. Its aim, originally, was to make a bargain between motorist and legislator: car owners would agree to carry registration numbers so that their vehicles could be identified if necessary, and in return, the speed limit would be abolished.

The rather unenviable task of introducing this bill was entrusted to my father, John Montagu, the first self-appointed public relations man for the industry. He was uniquely qualified to perform the job, having been a Member of Parliament since 1892 and a motorist since 1898. In 1899 his car was the first British-made motor vehicle to race on the continent of Europe, and also the first motorcar of any kind to enter the House of Commons yard at Westminster. He was the only MP to take part in the 1,000 Miles Trial of 1900. Indeed, his job was, simply, to sell and make respectable the motoring age to both the government and the people. He had taken Edward VII out in his car several times, before and after his succession to the throne in 1901, and he had also introduced A. J. Balfour to the joys of motoring. So it was at least in part due to my father's influence that the King and the Prime Minister of England were both enthusiastic motorists at the time the Motor Car Act came up for consideration.

Yet opposition to motoring was still widespread, often bitter, and sometimes malicious. The bill was described as a perfect example of "government of the rich, for the rich and by the rich." It was suggested that motoring helmets and goggles were a form of disguise deliberately assumed by people who "meant to break

Ample Power. Maximum Efficiency. Absolute
Control. Elegance. Simplicity.

Four cylinders, 4½ x 4½. 24-40 H. P.
Three Speeds and Reverse.
Chainless Bevel Gear Drive. $2,500

THE comparatively poor man finds that the SMITH Car brings to him the greatest return for the hard earned dollars he can invest in the field of motordom. And the man with practically no concern as to purchase cost finds that whatever price he may pay in excess of SMITH price brings to him no greater good for his money. When a prospective purchaser is free to choose intelligently—no family connections—son-in-law "influence"—rebate "strings" or the like—and the SMITH is given a demonstration to that purchaser, the vast superiority of the SMITH Cars wins every time.

We don't make so many, but
we do make them good.
Capacity, 200 per year.

MANUFACTURED BY

SMITH AUTO. COMPANY
Topeka, Kansas

KANSAS HISTORICAL SOCIETY

In 1906 the little-known Smith Auto Co. of Topeka, Kansas, replaced its earlier buggy-style cars by a new model built on European lines. At $2,500 it was exactly twice the price of the contemporary Oldsmobile, for example, but the makers claimed that its quality justified the price tag. "We don't make so many, but we do make them good."

the law." One member urged that erring motorists should be flogged. Another recommended imprisonment, which, he said, "would do these flying millionaires all the good in the world." When one considers the prevailing atmosphere in 1903, motorists were fortunate that the 12 mph speed limit was actually raised to 20 mph instead of being abolished, as they had hoped. But scarcely anybody can have envisaged that this overall limit was to remain in force, increasingly ignored for the absurdity that it was, for no less than twenty-seven years.

America, too, had its anti-motorists, but they were soon swept aside because the advantages of the motorcar were more quickly recognized, and so many small-time engineers were fired with the ambition to build themselves a "gas buggy"; it has been estimated that by 1895, some three hundred experimental cars had been built in factories, barns and shacks all over the country. Nor was there the violent class prejudice which inspired much of the opposition that British motorists encountered. A few rich playboys amused themselves with motorcars, certainly, but they were quite outnumbered by the doctors, farmers and businessmen who could scarcely wait to get their hands on a vehicle of their own. In 1900, well over four thousand cars—American-made or imported—were sold. By 1906 there were more than two hundred American makes on the market, and in that year the nation's total output of cars exceeded that of France, previously the world's leading manufacturer.

The only trouble was that having bought a car, the American motorist had almost nowhere to go in it. Most of the roads turned into a mere track, at best, a few miles beyond the town boundary. When in 1897 Alexander Winton decided to drive one of his prototype machines from Cleveland to New York, he had to seek out the best route he could find as he went along. He drove right around by Rochester and Albany, covering eight hundred miles to span what is half that distance on today's roads, and he did well to complete the journey in only eleven days. When my father visited America to study the road system fifteen years later, he found little improvement; and in 1913 Rankin Kennedy was to write: "American roads are very primitive; our [Britain's] worst country lanes are superior to America's best main roads."

The results could be clearly seen in the native American motorcar. It was sturdily built, but light, with large-diameter wheels which were wide-spaced to fit the ruts made by the farm waggons. The engine was a low-revving horizontal unit fixed under the seat, with a simple planetary transmission and final drive by a single chain, and by comparison with a European car of the same period, the American machine seemed like nothing so much as a horse-drawn buggy without its horse.

Yet two of the most typical American cars of the early 1900s, the Ford and the Cadillac, embodied the principles of precision engineering which were to make mass production possible. Each influenced the motoring world in a different way: Ford emphasized quantity with the Model T, and brought the car within reach of almost everybody's pocket; Cadillac concentrated on quality to become "The Standard of the World," pioneering one technical innovation after another. The resources of Detroit grew to breath-taking proportions, and within a very few decades the American car had not merely made up lost ground: in many respects it was superior to its European counterpart. Nowadays, of course, the accumulated knowl-

CAROLINE NOSTRAND HEBB

Much more typical of early American cars is the 1902/3 Rambler runabout with its wide axles, high seating and tiller steering. The "bonnet" is a dummy, for the single-cylinder engine was under the seat. At a mere $750 the Rambler sold in large numbers, and the present American Motors Corporation is descended from its Kenosha, Wisconsin, makers.

Heavy taxation ensured that British popular cars were much smaller than their American counterparts, but the dearly-loved Austin Seven brought motoring within the reach of many thousands between 1922 and 1939—including those for whom car ownership had seemed an unattainable dream. On both sides of the Atlantic the automobile had begun to play its most important role, as the ideal means of transportation for a family outing.

DETROIT PUBLIC LIBRARY   BRITISH LEYLAND

edge of the industry is shared on both sides of the Atlantic, and the Pacific too, so that in the not too distant future the motorcar will probably have shed most of the features that could be described as national characteristics.

In considering the future, however, I find it depressing that in one respect we have made so little progress. A bitter hostility towards the motorist is still to be found in our legislators and their advisers, just as it was three-quarters of a century ago. The car is denounced as a killer, a polluter of the atmosphere, a waster of energy, a symbol of power for status-seeking materialists. This is done in terms that are often grossly exaggerated, or supported by highly questionable statistics which are allowed to go unchallenged. In their determination to draw attention to themselves—and, of course, the opinions they so violently express—the critics would deny absolutely the many ways in which the motorcar has enriched our everyday life, despite the problems that have accompanied its extensive use.

A widely read British magazine recently stated that in the London of pre-motoring days there were "no fumes and no noise." This kind of sugary, false nostalgia approaches arrant nonsense. The noise made by present-day city traffic is nothing, nothing at all, by comparison with the perpetual clitter-clatter of hundreds of horses' hooves as they passed through the streets; why else was it necessary to lay straw in the roads around hospitals? And the fumes of the motorcar, bad as they may be, are a great deal less damaging to our health in general than the filthy, stinking layers of horse dung that once carpeted the streets of London and every other big city, attracting hordes of disease-bearing flies to invade our houses and pollute our food.

At least one writer on economics has declared that private transport should be banned altogether, on the grounds that "the invention of the private automobile is one of the great disasters to have befallen the human race." Compare that wildly distorted definition with one put forward by Sir Colin Buchanan, a man who has devoted years to the study of road traffic: "What a Godsend to the wife—the kids, the shopping, the bathing things, the buckets and spades, the potties and nappies, the gumboots, the macs, the toys, the dog, the picnic meal, the radio, the books—all bundled in as easily as possible. What a blessing is the car as a modest load carrier, what a contrast to struggling onto buses when you are loaded up with children and shopping! What a boon our car has been for all kinds of modest services. . . . Why can't we be less hypocritical, and admit that a motorcar is just about the most convenient device that we ever invented, and that possession of it and usage in moderation is a perfectly legitimate ambition for all classes of people?"

The answer, one suspects, is that economists, sociologists and politicians all too often fail to realize that the humble motorcar is not only a means of individual transportation, but a symbol of individual freedom. Long may it remain so, for all of us.

LORD MONTAGU OF BEAULIEU

KNOBS AND LEVERS

"*The steering wheel is connected to and actuates the front road wheels . . .*"

S. F. EDGE, Cars and How to Drive Them (1903)

It is nowadays quite widely assumed that almost anyone can drive almost any make of car. Nobody in the car rental business expects you to submit to a driving test before they hand over the ignition key. When you drive up to the door of an American hotel or restaurant it is taken for granted that you will let the parking attendant put your car away (and those with conservative tastes will learn, to their cost, what these individuals can do to a non-automatic transmission). Between one American car and another there is now scarcely any variation of control layout: virtually every model has two-pedal control and a standardized arrangement of switches. European cars display more variety, the manual gear change being more widely used, but there is still considerable similarity in the way the controls are arranged. And virtually all cars resemble each other, whatever their country of origin, in the fact that the driver directs them with his hands and controls their speed with his feet.

Why is this so? Though the control layout of today is accepted without question, it is something that has evolved only very gradually during the brief history of the motorcar. There seems to be no particular reason why it should have found acceptance in preference to any other. It is not obviously based on the driving methods of pre-motoring days. It is not clearly related to any special requirement of the human body. Yet every attempt to design some entirely new controls has met with failure. About twenty years ago the world's largest automobile manufacturers, General Motors of America, embarked upon a major research project to examine in all its aspects the amount of effort that a driver must exert in order to operate his vehicle. One of the results was the development of Unicontrol, a device about the size and shape of a cocktail cherry on a stick. Backed by a complex system of "assist" mechanisms, this little gadget replaced all the major controls—even the steering wheel.

With this small stick it was thus possible to control a large and powerful car: push the knob forward for "Go," back for "Stop," and to one side or the other for a left or right turn. A tiny button let into the top of the knob would sound the horn, and a mere twist of the fingers would select the appropriate range in the automatic transmission. There were a few auxiliary switches elsewhere to turn on the lights and so on, but otherwise the entire car was controlled by one small knob that was, literally, operated by the fingertips.

It was not a success. It made driving too easy—or rather, too effortless, so that the act of directing the vehicle became paradoxically *more* difficult. With all the effort taken out of the procedure, car control was transformed into an operation calling for the utmost precision in every movement made by the driver. The engineers had to fit an armrest to help steady and support the hand that worked the little control lever. Then the power assistance had to be gradually reduced to make it harder to move and thus introduce some "feel" into the system. But whatever was done, the designers were faced with the unpalatable truth that an incautious movement of the fingers could send two tons of motorcar skidding sideways along the road, helplessly out of control. It is apparently unwise to oversimplify the task of the motorist.

Fortunately most of us think it no hardship that our cars are controlled by several pedals and levers instead of just one, though a lady of independent views declared that only a man would have thought of three pedals for two feet.

And in 1907 Eustace Watson wrote in glowing terms of the contemporary Argyll: "The system of control common to all Argyll cars, and a system which I believe to be absolutely the simplest in existence, consists of two small levers placed on the top of the steering wheel, one being operated by each hand, the left-hand one controlling the throttle valve . . . and the right-hand one, by means of a suitable arrangement of levers . . . thereby altering the time of firing of the gases inside the cylinder to suit varying circumstances, and two pedals, the left operating the clutch and the right one operating the foot brake. . . . The reader will understand, therefore, that one has a small lever for each hand, and a pedal for each foot, a state of affairs designed to suit a human being, and the user is not called upon to operate three or four pedals with two feet, and two levers with one hand, as on many cars." The Argyll, however, was not *quite* as simple as that. Mr. Watson forgets to mention that like most Edwardian cars it had a hand-operated side lever to actuate the main brake, and the then not uncommon feature of two gear levers.

It is a sort of sophistry to champion two-pedal control as providing one pedal for each foot, because the odd fact is that when the third pedal is eliminated (as in a car with automatic transmission) the driver almost always operates the remaining two with the same foot—the right foot—and does not use the other foot at all. Most people cling quite stubbornly to this practice, yet it is much more logical to use both feet, one on each pedal. That is the ideal way to park or manoeuvre an "automatic" in a confined space, because the brake can be balanced against the throttle. It is the best way to dry out the brakes after driving through flood water, applying them with the left foot while main-taining normal cruising speed with one's right foot on the throttle. A development of this technique is used by some rally drivers, who in certain circumstances will brake with the left foot while still accelerating round a bend with the right.

But many drivers find these tricks difficult to perform. They discover that the left foot, if called upon to operate the brake, is liable to stamp down hard upon the pedal, bringing the car to a noisy and embarrassing halt at the end of four black lines of burnt rubber—and probably in the middle of a highly disapproving assembly of other road users. We are so accustomed to stamping the left foot down to disengage the clutch, or (if we drive an automatic) not using it at all.

So far as hand controls are concerned we are all reasonably ambidextrous. It matters little which side the various switches and levers are placed, and after ninety years of motorcar manufacture their positions have yet to be rigidly standardized. With a few minutes' practice the holidaying Briton learns to drive a Continental or American rented car, changing gear readily enough with his right hand instead of his left—but his feet still perform the same functions as usual. If the pedals had also changed places there would be chaos and mayhem indeed. It is very, very difficult to drive a vehicle in which their functions have been transposed.

It has to be accepted as a fact of human physiology that the feet are less adaptable, less easy to retrain, than the hands. Why is it, though, that the present layout of pedals is universally regarded as "correct"? Many a highly respected car had its throttle pedal in the middle, between the other two, as late as the 1930s. A quarter-century earlier, more than one had its clutch pedal on the right, brake on the

AUTOCAR

The car seen below has a gear lever working in a quadrant on the right, but a separate pedal to engage reverse. Its speed would be controlled by setting the governor, throttle, air and ignition levers—all four of them. There is no accelerator pedal. But on the Lanchester (LEFT) of the same period, the left foot operates an accelerator pedal and the right foot is used to blow the horn.

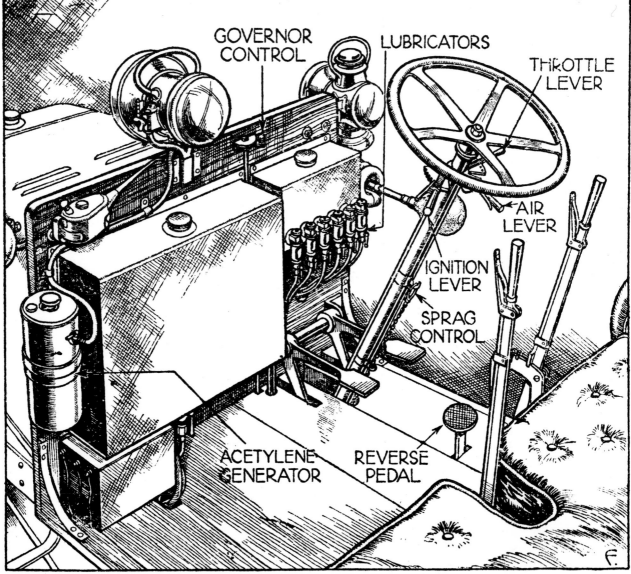

GOVERNOR CONTROL

LUBRICATORS

THROTTLE LEVER

AIR LEVER

IGNITION LEVER

SPRAG CONTROL

ACETYLENE GENERATOR

REVERSE PEDAL

AUTOCAR

left. On many another the clutch *and* brake might both be actuated by hand. The early car makers had none of our preconceived notions about such things, for they were breaking entirely new ground. They simply put the brake pedal or lever, clutch and everything else in whatever position allowed the most convenient mechanical linkage, or perhaps indulged some personal whim and tried to convince their customers of its validity.

At first, then, there was no attempt to standardize the layout of controls, and the man who could drive one early machine well might be quite bewildered by another. It was not uncommon for the manufacturer to provide a course of instruction for the buyer or his "man," and this was certainly desirable at a time when any pedal or lever might do almost anything. In the Lanchester, the left foot operated the accelerator and the right foot had no more onerous task than stamping on the horn bulb. The early Delahaye, too, had its accelerator on the left, but it was pressed to slow the car up and released to make it go faster. If the driver fell out, his wisest course was probably to go away and order a new car; he had little hope of catching up with the old one. Perhaps he would have chosen a Brotherhood-Crocker, whose accelerator pedal had flanged sides and was operated by swivelling the foot from side to side, not up and down. One of the earliest American cars, the Duryea, even anticipated the General Motors Unicontrol system by seventy years: the steering tiller also controlled engine speed and doubled as a gear lever.

The pioneer car designer really did start with a clean sheet of paper when he turned to all the finer points of detail, for he was producing something completely new. Except in broad outline, it bore little resemblance to anything that had gone before. As a device for the convenient transportation of a small number of individuals, the automobile was of course preceded by the many types of horse-drawn carriage which had been in use for several thousand years, and these exerted a strong, easily discernible influence upon its shape during the early years of its development. But nobody expected the controls to be the same (other than one misguided individual who built a motor vehicle that was steered by reins).

And of course nobody foresaw a time when the ability to drive would be an accomplishment of Tom, Dick or Harry. Before the advent of the motorcar, to drive meant "to guide the horse(s) drawing a carriage." Very few people could do it safely and well, and the expert took justifiable pride in his skill. It was acquired by a small number of professionals such as coachmen, and by some—but certainly not all—of those whose position in society was such that they kept a carriage.

To understand something of what carriage work actually involved, consider Major-General Geoffrey White's instructions for driving a coach-and-four:

". . . He has now four reins instead of two to manipulate, and the increase of weight on his hand requires considerable strength of the wrist to support it without tiring. It is of the first importance, moreover, that he should know instinctively the position in his hand of each of the reins, and be able automatically and instantaneously to lay a finger on any one of them. The driver who has to look at his reins to find the off-side leader's rein, or who touches the nearside wheeler's in mistake for it, is in peril of a catastrophe. It is therefore essential that the reins should be correctly disposed between the fingers of the left hand. . . .

"Standing on the ground beside the off-side wheel of his carriage, ready to mount to the box-seat, the coachman, after drawing up his reins till he almost feels the horses' mouths, must then let out about a foot of slack in his off-side reins, in order that when on his seat he may find all the reins as near as possible equal in length in his hand. The reins should then be transferred to the right hand disposed as they will be in the left when ready to start, but one finger lower down; the first finger will then be free to hold on to the footboard in mounting the box. When replaced in the left hand after mounting, the leaders' reins should be separated by the forefinger and the wheelers' by the middle finger. The near-leader's rein will then be uppermost of the four, between the forefinger and the thumb; then between the forefinger and middle finger are two reins together —the off-leader's and the near-wheeler's in the order named; while at the bottom, between the middle and third fingers, is the off-wheeler's rein. It will be found that held thus the reins spread immediately in front of the hand in such a way that each several rein, and each pair of reins—two near-side, two off-side, two wheelers' or two leaders'—can be conveniently manipulated; the proficient driver can instinctively and instantaneously grasp any of them he chooses with his right hand without having to turn his eyes from the road before him to the reins in his hand. . . .

"Then, when he has taken the whip from the socket in his right hand, he is ready to start. This is an operation requiring careful management to secure that the leaders and wheelers start simultaneously, for if the leaders start first they will be drawn up sharply by their bits. . . . The driver should see that his team is going straight. If the leaders and wheelers are not exactly on the same line, this or that rein must be shortened or lengthened as the case may require . . . Practice and considerable dexterity are required in using the whip on the leaders without at the same time touching, or at all events alarming or fretting, the wheelers. . . . No coachman is competent to drive four horses until he is able to touch with the whip any particular horse that may require it, and no other."

To the present-day motorist it suggests some nightmare vehicle whose four wheels are separately steered and controlled by a different hand throttle to each—yet such, in fact, was the essence of the coach-and-four. The man who could drive the four-in-hand may have found an early Benz or Panhard unfamiliar to drive—but surely cannot have thought it difficult, however unaccustomed he might be to the layout of its controls. If he had the "hands" of a good horseman combined with even a smattering of mechanical knowledge, he might well fare better than an experienced modern motorist would do in a similar situation, for the horseman would at least approach the task with an open mind, making no assumptions about the function of each control.

Imagine the modern motorist's reactions to being placed in the driving seat of, say, an 1898 Benz:

"It's very comfortable sitting up here and the visibility is splendid, but there isn't any instrument panel. Where do I find the starter switch?"

"There is no starter switch; the electric starter has not yet been invented."

"I suppose we start by hand, then. Where's the starting handle?"

"There's no starting handle either. You simply turn the engine over by pulling on the rim of the flywheel, and hope for better luck

Engine compartment of an 1898 single-cylinder Benz, showing the drive-belt pulleys on the right, the exposed crankshaft and piston assembly in the middle, and on the left the massive cylindrical carburettor.

The 1898 Benz, with controls as described opposite. This particular example, however, is equipped with the optional (and usually highly unreliable) pneumatic tyres.

than the famous Mr. Koosen who wrote that he had done so '. . . until darkness overtook me. The only result was a pair of worn-out gloves.' Oh, and do retard the ignition first with that push-pull knob behind your legs. There isn't any crankcase, and if the engine should back-fire you don't want to catch your hand in the flywheel. Where *is* the engine, did you say? It's underneath your seat."

"I see, behind these little doors. And there's the crankshaft—oh, and the connecting rod and the piston as well. You know, that's the first time I've seen a piston actually working."

"I shouldn't stop to admire it now that you've got the engine running. Yes, I thought so—you've got oil all down your shirt front. Let's close the doors and get back to our seat."

"Hello, there's only one pedal. Is that the accelerator?"

"No, the engine speed is partly controlled by that lever on the left, behind your legs, and partly by the ignition advance-and-retard knob, and partly by the mixture control lever beside it—the technique is a little tricky. That pedal operates the foot brake, but go carefully with it because it only works on the back wheels, and if you use it when cornering you may spin round. Or you may not—it's only an external contracting brake, so it doesn't work very well. If the final-drive chains have been lubricated recently it probably won't work at all; the oil gets on the brake bands, you see."

"Surely I'll get much more leverage if I just pull on this side-brake lever on the left here?"

"The first thing to remember about *that* lever is that you push it to apply the brakes and pull it to release them again. It actuates the spoon brakes—wooden blocks which rub on the tyres—so they're not much good either,

especially when it's raining and the tyres are wet."

"It seems very odd to have the steering column sticking straight up from the floor like this, and such a tiny brass wheel on the end of it."

"That isn't a steering wheel at all; it's a sort of guard ring which is fixed below the steering lever. You see, this gadget here with the pointer at one end and the knob at the other? You steer by holding the knob, and the pointer shows you where you are going. It's not difficult when you get used to it."

"And these two levers lower down? I suppose one is the gear lever, so what is the other—the clutch?"

"There isn't any clutch. Those are both gear levers. Or rather, they're both change-speed levers, one for high speed and one for low (and don't forget to disengage one before engaging the other). The primary drive is by flat belt, you see—that's why there's no clutch. As for gears, there's an epicyclic gear if you really want it: just turn up that handle facing forward. But that's for starting on a steep hill, and it's such a low gear that you can't do more than about 2 mph in it."

"I suppose there are all sorts of things to check before we set off. Do we go over the tyre pressures, the radiator level, the sump oil and so forth?"

"The tyres are solid, so there's nothing to check there. There isn't any radiator, just a con-denser, which isn't very efficient, so it's as well to pull up and check the level in the water tank from time to time. And there isn't any sump—remember? But we have to stop every five miles to lubricate the big-end bearing in any case. You won't forget, will you? It is rather important."

OPPOSITE: *Karl Benz favoured a horizontal engine at the rear, and obstinately retained this layout even at the turn of the century, when Panhard and Levassor had shown the much greater possibilities of a vertical engine fitted at the front.*

These were the controls of the world's first successful production car in the form they had reached after a decade of development. At that time they were, indeed, much as they had been when Karl Benz first transformed his dream into reality. An essentially conservative man, he saw no reason to make changes when his cars were selling steadily throughout Europe. Why make the mechanism more complicated when the Benz was demonstrably more reliable than its competitors, and a good deal easier to drive? Who needed to go faster than 12 mph or so?

But Karl Benz was wrong; the future lay with other more adventurous designers, and by the turn of the century his cars were to be dismissed as absurdly out-of-date. There was, for instance, the Panhard, which at first looked heavy and clumsy compared to the carriage-like elegance of the German machine. This impression was entirely misleading, as time soon began to tell. The French car had its engine mounted vertically at the front instead of horizontally at the back. Behind the engine was a friction clutch, then a crude arrangement of sliding gears which at first were not even enclosed, then a cross shaft incorporating a differential gear, and finally side chains to drive the rear wheels. The sliding gears provided three or four different ratios depending on the way the pinions were engaged one with another, but it was by no means easy to "change gear," as it was called, and by comparison with the smooth silence of belt drive the *système Panhard* had as much refinement as a washhouse mangle. Yet this was the foundation on which the whole future of the motorcar was to be based; the transmission system that is still to be found in most cars of today. Because of the engine position it was a simple matter to progress from one cylinder to two or more,

one behind another, and thus increase the power of the engine. The early Panhard, with its two-cylinder engine, was 50 percent faster than the contemporary Benz. A couple of years later it had a four-cylinder engine and could travel almost three times as fast as its German predecessor. It is a measure of Panhard's achievement that, broadly speaking, the arrangement of components favoured by that manufacturer has remained the most popular one for three-quarters of a century.

That arrangement brought a control layout that came to be regarded as the norm by European motorists. The clutch was usually actuated by a pedal, and the gears were changed with a long lever that worked in a quadrant normally placed on the right-hand side of the car. A second pedal brought into operation a brake that was incorporated in the drive shaft, just behind the gearbox. The gear-change lever was flanked by another, the side-brake lever, which operated brakes on the hubs of the rear wheels. Motorists learned to use the clutch pedal with considerable delicacy to make the car move off from rest without jerking its occupants unduly or stalling the engine.

Drivers also faced the task of changing gear, which for many years remained the most difficult manoeuvre they were called upon to perform. To quote a contemporary motor manual: "It is absolutely essential that the beginner should carefully cultivate the art of changing his gears correctly if he desires to become an expert driver and to use his motor economically. The sliding type of change-speed gear, which is now almost universal, is, from a mechanical point of view, a brutal system, because, if the driver is not skilful and careful, he is bound to bring the edges of the gear wheels on the primary and secondary shafts into fierce

GEARGUIDE

Give your Gears as many 'lives' as a cat

A simple little arrangement that absolutely forbids your making a misguided gear change, and you know what that means.

Models for all Ball Change Gears may be had from—

LONDON:
L. Whitwam & Co., 31, Gerrard Street, Shaftesbury Av., W.1. 'Phone Regent 2685

LEEDS:
L. Whitwam & Co., St. Ann's Street. 'Phone 25265

MANCHESTER:
Turner Bros., Queen's Chambers, 5, John Dalton Street. 'Phone Central 302

AND ALL MORRIS DEALERS

Worth almost the value of your car and costs but

15/6

Fit Your Morris with one

THE MORRIS OWNER

To those accustomed to the earlier "gate" arrangement, the ball change of the Bullnose Morris was sufficiently unfamiliar for this optional arrangement to be offered as an accessory.

contact whilst they are revolving at different speeds. This will cause great wear, and may even chip off portions of the teeth. The act of changing properly is simply a knack, requiring some experience and a quick, delicate, and sympathetic touch." It was a knack that entirely escaped many would-be early motorists, to whom the careful synchronization of hand and foot movements was something altogether unfamiliar. And as the gearbox mechanism itself became more complex, so did the arrangements for changing gear: there might be a separate lever for engaging reverse, or the number of available speeds might be split up between two gear levers, so that the hapless driver faced the possibility of engaging two gears at once and locking the transmission up solid. A considerable step forward came with Daimler's popularization of the "gate change" on their Mercédès, which had a single lever that moved sideways as well as fore-and-aft to engage the various ratios.

This lever was of course situated on the right-hand side of the vehicle, for apart from the Benz nearly all early cars were furnished with controls on the right side. To a man accustomed to building horse-drawn vehicles, the logical and natural position for a right-handed driver is on the right-hand side, so that he can use his whip freely without inconvenience to his passenger. American auto museums show right-hand-drive examples of such noted transatlantic makes as Stanley, Thomas, Mercer, Pierce-Arrow, White, Winton and Simplex, yet Ford's immortal Model T was a left-hand-drive car from its first appearance in 1908. The better or more sporting European models remained right-hand-drive for many years, even when they emanated from countries that drove on the right, and a central gear lever (allowing the

McCOMB COLLECTION

driver to sit on the left) was long regarded as the sign of a cheap mass-produced vehicle.

In other respects the typical American-built car of the early twentieth century differed considerably from its European counterpart. The high ground clearance (essential in a country that was then almost roadless) resulted in a lofty seating position that seemed curiously antiquated, and suggested a close affinity with the horse-drawn buggy. By European standards such a vehicle (the International high-wheeler, for example) appeared unsophisticated to the point of crudeness, yet it was very well suited to the needs of owners who necessarily considered that reliability and ease of maintenance mattered more than sleek lines and an impressive cruising speed. The curved-dash Oldsmobile, for instance, which may be regarded as the world's first mass-produced car, was a spindly-looking but strongly built machine of which 12,100 examples were produced from 1901 to 1904. The big single-cylinder engine was hidden away under the seat and started by winding a handle at the side. Steering was by a long, curved tiller connected direct to the steering rods (there was no steering box), and

Gear-changing presented no problems for the owner of the American curved-dash Oldsmobile of 1901/5; floor pedals operated the simple planetary transmission. But the European fashion for many years is exemplified by the French 1914 Delage with its right-hand gear lever working in a gate and flanked by the handbrake.

a bulb horn was usually clamped to the upper end. Foot brake and hand brake both acted on the transmission, and did so well enough for a car that was capable of no more than 20 mph. The driver of an Oldsmobile, Model A Ford or contemporary Cadillac—they all looked much the same—had no difficulty in changing gear because the transmission was of the two-speed planetary type, controlled by a simple pedal.

The difficulty that so many early European motorists experienced in gear changing was not entirely the result of unfamiliarity or ineptitude. It was mainly due to a fundamental difference in the car designer's approach to his task at that time.

In the days when the internal combustion engine was merely one of several alternative prime movers (the electric motor and steam engine being favoured just as much, if not more), the man who built a self-propelled vehicle was obviously not an automobile engineer—for that specialized occupation was then unknown—but an engineer in an altogether broader sense. He thought of the petrol engine primarily as a stationary unit which would normally be installed in a workshop or factory to drive some piece of machinery. Such an engine was designed to run at one particular speed, and it was adjusted so that it ran at that speed when under normal working load. When relieved of that load it would progressively speed up until a governor came into action to prevent its rpm from reaching a damaging level. The idea of providing some means of *increasing* engine speed was quite novel, and the car builder at first failed to recognize its desirability when such a unit was installed in a vehicle. Why should a driver want to alter the speed of his engine, anyway? He had a gearbox, had he not, or a system of belt pulleys, providing two or

even three different speeds for the car? To alter the engine speed would introduce all kinds of undesirable complications, like changing the ignition timing and probably resetting the carburettor (if there was a carburettor).

So the nineteenth-century motorist started his engine and kept it running at one speed, endeavouring to adjust his own rate of progress to suit different road conditions by engaging different speeds or ratios as he went along. The engine would run relatively fast and rather unevenly until a gear was engaged, falter and almost stall as the clutch was let in, recover, and resume its syncopated beat at a slightly lower tempo until the next gear change became necessary. As the "tickover" was so fast, some of the earliest cars had a *decelerator* to slow the engine down at times. This was often combined with the brake pedal, or else the brake linkage would be combined with the clutch so that the engine was disengaged as soon as the brake was applied. The progress of such a car was a stop/go affair at best, even when it was handled by a skilled driver.

The importance of effective speed control was still imperfectly understood as late as 1913, judging by the following passage from a motor manual of that year:

"We may require to run the engine at different speeds under any load. To some extent this can be facilitated by the change-speed gear. When the load is normal or light the change-speed gear may be cut out and the engine run direct at its maximum allowable speed, but throttled at the carburettor, and when lesser speeds are required, throttled still more. On an up-grade the throttle can be opened to give more and more power until it takes all the fuel the carburettor can give it, and yet falls off in speed due to the heavy load. The driver can then employ the change-speed gear, throwing on the second speed, thus relieving the engine of the full load and allowing it to speed up. On a still steeper gradient the third speed change gear would be thrown on, so that whilst the car travelled slower the engine could still be run on at or near normal speed. On the level or on a small gradient it may be necessary at any moment to slow down. The most efficient control in this case is to throw in the low gear and throttle down the carburettor.

"It is evident that no automatic governor could perform these operations. Theoretically, the change-speed gear should have a very great range, with an automatically governed engine, the driver operating only the change-speed levers, while the governor keeps the engine at full speed by varying the supply from the carburettor from no mixture to full supply. . . . A governor may be used to maintain the engine at a speed approximately constant while the driver makes proper use of the change-speed gear, the governor throttling fuel supply; but it is found necessary, to meet the many conditions of road travelling, to have also a hand throttle."

The result was inevitable. When the driver was forced by circumstances to "throw on" another gear, he commonly did so to the accompaniment of loud grating from the gear teeth. A silent change on a non-synchromesh gearbox calls for very precise adjustment of engine speed to suit the road speed of the car, and this was virtually impossible to achieve with the extremely unresponsive engines of the early years. Greater flexibility came only with the adoption of mechanically actuated inlet valves, more efficient automatic carburettors, throttle valves and better ignition systems.

Speed control, if any, was effected by altering the ignition timing, changing the proportions of the fuel/air mixture, or by limiting the volume of fresh charge drawn into the cylinder, in one way or another. Some of these ways strike us as a little peculiar today. One was to increase the pressure of the inlet valve spring or, alternatively, to hold the exhaust valve open for some time, or contrariwise to delay its opening (usually by what was called "hit and miss" actuation) so that some exhaust gas was retained in the cylinder. Any one of these manoeuvres would delay the opening of an automatic or "atmospheric" inlet valve, which was closed by a light spring and opened by mere atmospheric pressure as the piston descended in the cylinder. If the inlet valve was mechanically actuated it was common at one time to vary its lift, usually by a sliding cam arrangement. And finally there was the system analogous to that used to control steam engines: to "throttle" the supply of mixture to the engine by gradually closing the induction pipe, usually by means of a butterfly valve.

The governor with which nearly all early engines were fitted would bring into operation one or other of these systems, which were therefore designed to reduce engine speed, not increase it. This effectively protected the engine from damage caused by excessive running speed. It was soon found, however, that the driver of a petrol-engined motorcar needed some means of rapidly increasing engine speed to cope with a sudden increase in load. Consequently car designers started fitting a device that would put the governor out of action. For convenient operation it was usually actuated by a small floor pedal which was known as the "accelerator." Some contemporary motoring writers were curiously given to moralizing about the way it should be employed: "The accelerator lever or pedal should only be used to race the engine under exceptional circumstances, that is to say, when the very highest speed of the car is desired, or when the driver wishes to rush a hill. Many motorists, possessed by the speed craze, habitually race their engines, thus causing excessive wear and tear. It is a great mistake, and results in infinite trouble later on.''

Others took a more practical and reasonable view: ''This piece of apparatus is used when the full power of the engine is required, such as when mounting a hill. It is also most convenient for slowing down and for accelerating the speed of the car whilst threading a way amongst traffic.''

In most cases the action of the accelerator was to prevent the governor from closing the throttle valve, and frequently the latter was also controlled by a separate lever above or below the steering wheel. From this it was a short step to controlling the speed of the car almost entirely by the throttle, setting it for out-of-town running by means of the hand lever and making minor adjustments with the pedal—which to this day is still called the accelerator, although some insist that this became a misnomer when the governor disappeared from the engine. Gradually the hand throttle was relegated to merely setting the tickover speed of a cold engine, until eventually it too disappeared. When the car engine developed into a responsive and flexible unit capable of wide variations in speed, the technique of driving was transformed, and a skilled man delighted in the precision with which his gear changes could be executed. With improved carburation, the mixture control also came to be used only for cold starting instead of needing constant attention. The ignition timing lever remained a control to

be operated with skill until, during the 1930s, an efficient system of automatic ignition advance made it unnecessary.

One of the most widely praised petrol-engined cars of all time offered no very effective means of controlling its engine speed. When Dr. Frederick Lanchester decided to design a motor vehicle he did it *his* way, giving little consideration to the methods of other designers. Consequently almost everything about it was different, not least the controls. As mentioned earlier, the only duty allotted to the right foot was to sound the horn. In an equally unskilled fashion the left foot merely stamped on the accelerator, which was of the ''on'' or ''off'' variety, its action being to cut out the governors on both cylinders. The right hand simply held the steering lever, while the left hand darted from one lever to another in a positive blur of movement to control everything else: two governor levers, two gear levers, the brakes, a petrol pump, a mixture adjusting lever, and more besides.

The engine was started from the right-hand side of the body by winding a removable handle, having first set a starting lever which simultaneously engaged the starting-shaft gear with the engine, retarded the ignition timing, and reduced compression by holding the valves partially open. The steering was by a ''side lever''; it was not the usual bathchair tiller because it pointed away from the driver instead of towards him. One of the pet devices of ''Dr. Fred,'' this was said to make the Lanchester easier to steer than any other car on the market because the right arm lay along the lever and it was simply moved the way one wanted to go. According to the Lanchester manual: ''A car fitted with our side-lever steering tends always to steer in smooth curves, and to over-steer is

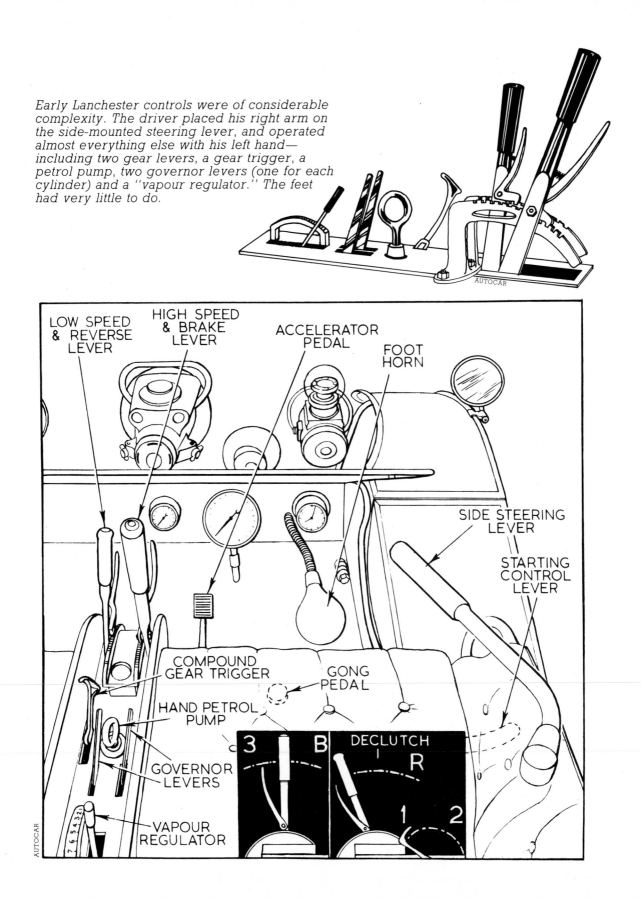

Early Lanchester controls were of considerable complexity. The driver placed his right arm on the side-mounted steering lever, and operated almost everything else with his left hand—including two gear levers, a gear trigger, a petrol pump, two governor levers (one for each cylinder) and a "vapour regulator." The feet had very little to do.

AUTOCAR

LOW SPEED & REVERSE LEVER

HIGH SPEED & BRAKE LEVER

ACCELERATOR PEDAL

FOOT HORN

SIDE STEERING LEVER

STARTING CONTROL LEVER

COMPOUND GEAR TRIGGER

GONG PEDAL

HAND PETROL PUMP

GOVERNOR LEVERS

VAPOUR REGULATOR

3   B   DECLUTCH
                1   R
                        1   2

7 6 5 4 3 2

AUTOCAR

almost a physical impossibility owing to the centrifugal force acting on the driver's body tending always to moderate his steering effort." The manual did not mention that when the Lanchester was travelling at its highest speed the steering lever was hard to move at all, and that a corpulent driver could not go round sharp left-hand corners because his stomach got in the way.

In the centre of the car, between driver and passenger, were all the remaining controls except the accelerator. There was a hand pump which had to be operated at intervals to feed fuel to the unusual wick-type carburettor. There was a "vapour regulator" which adjusted the mixture strength, and this also had to be operated while driving along. There were two governor levers each of which actuated a hit-and-miss speed control, one to each of the two engine cylinders, and as these were not interconnected there was nothing to prevent the driver from putting one cylinder on a different setting from the other, although the foot-operated accelerator did over-ride both governors simultaneously. To the left of the governor levers was another device called the compound gear trigger, and ahead of all this were the two gear levers, the left-hand one controlling the epicyclic low-speed and reverse gears, the right-hand engaging high speed or operating the brake.

The engine having been started with its removable handle, the driver would return the starting lever to its normal running position, climb into his seat and take the steering lever in his right hand. With the other hand he would move the right-hand gear lever forward into its central position to release the brake, preselect low gear with the compound gear trigger, and move the left-hand gear lever forward while putting the left foot on the accelerator. When the Lanchester reached about 5 mph he would move the gear trigger back to preselect second, then pull the left-hand gear lever back to neutral and forward again into second gear. At around 12 mph, top gear was engaged by first putting the left-hand lever into the neutral position, then moving the right-hand gear lever forward. The instruction manual stated that "The gears do not require to be skilfully shot," but a determined attempt to engage top without first disengaging second would probably have wrecked the transmission.

At the opposite extreme from the Lanchester was the typical electric car, the controls of which were simplicity itself. A machine such as the 1907 Electromobile had wheel steering, one lever and one pedal. The lever operated the "controller," on which various tappings provided a selection of forward speeds, a reverse speed, electric braking and a neutral position. The floor pedal brought into action a heavy-duty switch which cut the supply of current from the batteries to the motor, thus checking the speed more quickly than was possible with the controller. Pressing harder on the pedal engaged the mechanical brakes. Consequently the Electromobile was, like most electric cars, exceptionally easy to drive. Unfortunately it was also hopelessly restricted in scope for anything other than shopping and delivery work, and as one enthusiast frankly admitted in *Car Illustrated*, ". . . however much the graceful lines and smooth running of the Electromobile may make it a possession to be coveted for London use, nobody has the slightest desire to drive one himself."

And then there was the steam car. Like the electric car, the steamer is able to exert maximum torque from a standstill, and in both cases

By comparison with the Lanchester, nothing could
have been simpler than the average electric car.
Controls varied, naturally, from make to make.
This is the 1901 Columbia Electric from Hartford,
Connecticut, popular in France and England as
well as in its native America.

Despite its strange-looking controls, the American Locomobile was one of the most successful steam cars ever built; it was sold quite widely in Britain, and Rudyard Kipling was among those who bought one—but his enthusiasm for this fragile device evaporated as fast as the contents of its boiler.

the power unit is not running or ticking over when the vehicle is stationary, so that neither a clutch nor a gearbox is needed—although some steamers have been fitted with gearing for use in exceptional circumstances. Theoretically the only control required is a throttle valve to meter the quantity of steam delivered from the boiler to the engine.

In practice there were rather more controls than this, and they differed considerably from one make to another. The driver of a Massa-chusetts-built Locomobile sat on the right-hand side holding a steering lever in his left hand and the throttle lever in his right. By his right foot was a pedal which operated a rather inefficient transmission brake. A separate lever controlled the link motion to provide forward or reverse movement, another operated a by-pass for the feed water, and there were various stopcocks to be opened or closed at various times. Early White steamers had somewhat similar controls, but later models looked more like petrol cars in their control layout. There were a brake lever and a reversing lever at the right-hand side of the car, and on the floor a foot-brake pedal, a "simpling" pedal (used when starting from rest), and another pedal which passed a supply of air to the fuel tank. In the centre of the steering wheel was fitted a small hand wheel, complete with winding knob, which opened or closed the throttle to control the speed. As a novel form of thief-proofing, the throttle knob was made removable so that the driver could take it off and slip it in his pocket when he left the car.

The later Stanley steamers also resembled petrol-engined cars, for they had wheel steer-ing, side levers and foot brakes, and pedals for reversing and "early cut-off." There was not even the traditional wheel throttle to reveal that

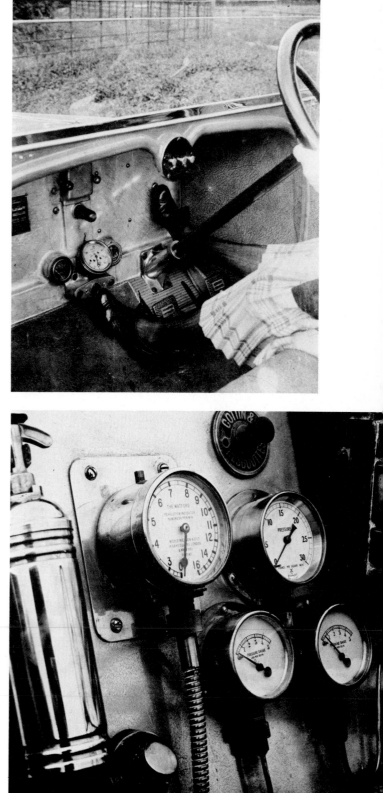

*The 1922 Bianchi (*TOP*) still has its instruments on the bulkhead or firewall, though mounted too low to be legible. The 1911 Cottin-Desgouttes carries very engineering-style gauges high up where they can be seen and read by a driver who, it is assumed, will understand their message.*

they were steam-powered, the throttle being operated in this case by a lever mounted just below the steering wheel, where there was another lever to control the water feed.

Electric cars and steamers were the first vehicles to be equipped with anything resembling instruments—a voltmeter on one, a boiler pressure gauge on the other. One of the things we find most unusual about an early petrol car is the fact that it was seldom fitted with any instruments at all—unless one considers a sight-feed lubricator to be an instrument because it acts as a primitive form of oiling gauge, the number of drops of oil being counted through the glass. For a long time the speedometer remained very much an accessory, and an expensive one at that, to be bought and fitted by the ultra-enthusiastic motorist. The first instrument commonly installed by the manufacturer was a pressure gauge for the fuel tank, into which air was pumped to force the fuel through to the engine if a gravity feed could not be arranged. When simple "splash" lubrication of the engine gave way to pressure-fed oiling systems, another gauge was provided to register the oil pressure. Various types of fuel gauge made their appearance, including the simple sight-glass mounted on the side of the tank, which was perfectly satisfactory when the tank itself was carried in the scuttle and the gauge was therefore readily visible. Another simple but effective arrangement was the fitting of a dial thermometer to the radiator cap, giving a direct reading of the water temperature which was easily seen by the driver. Even at night it could usually be distinguished readily enough against the headlamp beams.

The minimal bodywork of the early car included a simple splashboard or dashboard inherited from its horse-drawn predecessor,

NOTES FOR THE NEW MOTORIST.

An outline of the driving controls and instruments and of the most important points concerning the care of a new car for the first year.

By MAX MILLAR

THE VARIOUS INSTRUMENTS AND DRIVING CONTROLS.

AMMETER.

This instrument shows the amount of current used by the lights and also the rate of charging of the battery by the dynamo.

IGNITION TELL-TALE.

On cars which have coil ignition systems this small light shows red when ignition is switched on and acts as a warning to prevent battery exhaustion.

OIL GAUGE.

Either a gauge or a tell-tale knob is fitted on the instrument board to indicate whether engine oil pressure is functioning.

SPEEDOMETER.

This instrument records mileage in addition to speed on road.

STARTER.

A pull switch for electric engine starter.

CLOCK.

HORN BUTTON.

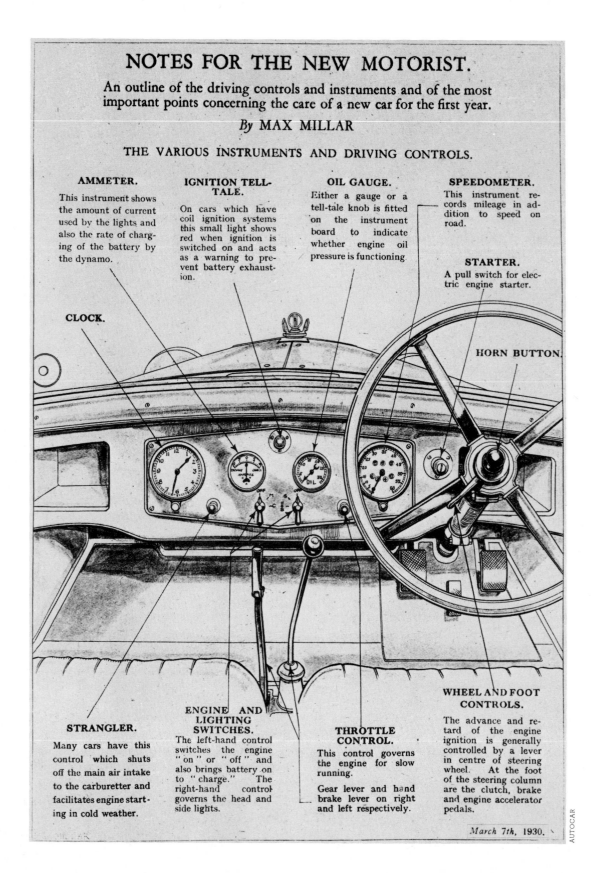

STRANGLER.

Many cars have this control which shuts off the main air intake to the carburetter and facilitates engine starting in cold weather.

ENGINE AND LIGHTING SWITCHES.

The left-hand control switches the engine "on" or "off" and also brings battery on to "charge." The right-hand control governs the head and side lights.

THROTTLE CONTROL.

This control governs the engine for slow running.

Gear lever and hand brake lever on right and left respectively.

WHEEL AND FOOT CONTROLS.

The advance and retard of the engine ignition is generally controlled by a lever in centre of steering wheel. At the foot of the steering column are the clutch, brake and engine accelerator pedals.

March 7th, 1930.

AUTOCAR

The changing face of the dashboard over some two decades: In the 1914 "Prince Henry" Vauxhall (1) the instruments are scarcely visible beneath the scuttle dash, but a rebuilt Rolls-Royce of the 1920s (2) carries a simple and functional display. There are early signs of simplification in a 1921 Chrysler (3), very different from the typically sporting array in a 1934 Aston Martin (4). The 1936 Cord (5) suggests a jukebox with its excessive glitter, and the 1948 Austin A.40 (6) reflects the dismal austerity of its period.

PHOTO-McCOMB

AUTOCAR

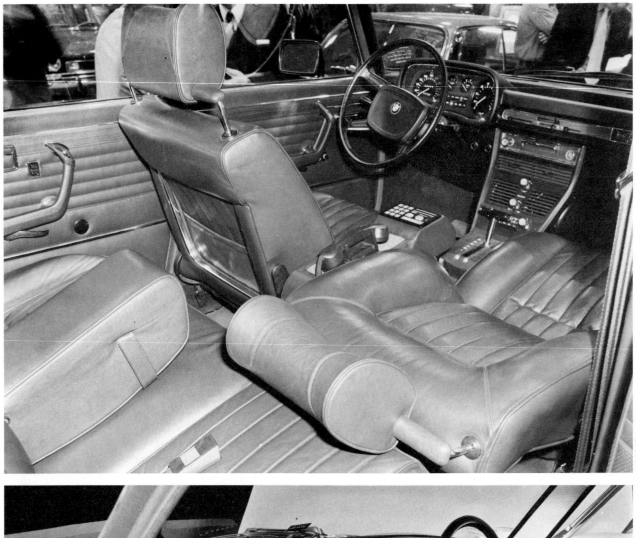

AUTOCAR

AUTOCAR

Two layouts in the modern idiom reflect the personality of the car concerned: luxury for the BMW-driving executive includes a radio telephone, and the manual-change Lotus suggests a more sporting owner.

and it was on this that the first instruments were mounted, for the simple reason that there was nowhere else to put them. When the occupants' legs came to be covered by the scuttle during the gradual process of enclosure, a supplementary panel had to be provided for the instruments. This in turn acquired the name of dashboard, or instrument panel, or facia in modern parlance—a foot-and-a-half of flat surface on which the car manufacturer felt free to express his soul. Instrumentation reached its zenith in the late 1920s, when the builder of a high-quality car would endow it with a polished walnut dashboard and thereon mount an array of a dozen or more handsome dials. Such a machine carried speedometer, fuel gauge, oil pressure gauge, ammeter, coolant temperature gauge, clock and probably a tachometer (indicating engine speed as distinct from road speed). In addition the more sporting car flaunted gauges to show the engine oil level and temperature, possibly the fuel tank air pressure, and the pressures applied to the shock absorbers (front *and* rear) if these were of the remote-adjustment type. A supercharged car would need a boost gauge indicating the pressure in the induction tract, and probably another for the supercharger oil pressure as well, while the unsupercharged car might carry a different gauge to show the inlet manifold depression. Finally, many a well-garnished vehicle has been fitted with an instrument that recorded the state of the battery, or even the temperature of the air outside the car.

With the coming of the mass-production car, cost-conscious manufacturers cleared out most of the instruments and saw to it that the few remaining gauges were made as simply and cheaply as possible. The honest circular dials beloved by engineers were replaced by combined or grouped devices of hideous shape and nauseating colour. Some disappeared because improved design elsewhere made them unnecessary: there was little need for an ammeter when the battery-charging circuit was provided with an effective automatic voltage control unit, or for a coolant thermometer when radiators were so improved that the water ceased to boil on a hot day. Other instruments gave way to warning lights, which were a cheaper and not always equally efficient substitute. Manufacturers justified them by claiming that motorists did not understand proper instruments anyway, or never bothered to look at them.

Since then, warning lights have multiplied to an astonishing extent as they serve to indicate disc-brake pad wear, low hydraulic fluid level, unfastened safety belts or hand brakes that have not been fully released, and on the Jaguar XJ-S, for example, the grand total has reached no less than eighteen. A large number of tell-tales occupies a great deal of space on the dashboard, and some are likely to be missed because they are outside the driver's immediate field of view. Recent research has therefore concentrated on simplifying the presentation of all this information, though this may only be achieved by more sophisticated systems. One arrangement, pioneered by Bosch, allows information to appear on a single panel in front of the driver, priority being controlled electronically so that if, say, brake failure and fan breakdown occurred simultaneously, the former would be advised first because it is more important. There are systems that provide for the driver to call up the information he wants to see. There is the development of "head-up display," which allows speedometer readings and other information to be projected in such a

Futuristic interior is presented by the Lagonda with its gas plasma instruments and heat-sensitive touch switches. A complex electronic system controls the display of information.

ASTON MARTIN LAGONDA LTD.

way that the images appear in the lower part of the screen below the driver's normal sight line.

But from the first boiler pressure gauge to the latest electronically controlled display panel, the purpose of instruments and warning lights has been to inform the driver of a malfunction so that he can take steps to correct it. In some cases it may well be more logical to dispense with the instrument altogether and arrange for the fault to be corrected automatically. Years ago, the simple radiator thermometer told the driver if the engine was overheating so that he could, if necessary, top up with fresh water. Nowadays a somewhat similar sensing device is more likely to switch in an electric fan that will of itself cure the overheating. More systems of this type are likely to be found in the car of the future.

KANSAS HISTORICAL SOCIETY

GOING FOR A DRIVE

"It was impossible to know, when starting out on a journey, when or whether one would return. . . . Personally, I used to become depressed if my car went particularly well, because this always preceded some grand catastrophe."

CHARLES JARROTT,
Ten Years of Motors and Motor Racing (1906)

In an hour the modern motorist covers a distance his great-grandfather would perhaps have covered in a day. A fifty-mile trip is little or nothing to him, just so long as the traffic conditions are reasonable. It is a slightly above-average commuter run to the office. It is a barely significant addition to the day's business mileage so that an extra customer can be fitted in. It is a round trip to a favourite pub or restaurant in the evening.

For a journey of fifty miles—or one hundred miles, or even more—an experienced motorist will allow himself exactly enough time to walk out of the house and start his car, drive off, and travel to his destination at an overall average speed of perhaps 50 mph: faster on motorways, slower on congested roads. No allowance is made for contingencies, no time added to allow for the unexpected, for it is assumed that the unexpected will not occur. The driver takes into consideration the travelling time (based on an estimated average speed for the journey) and on that basis he will leave his starting point at a certain hour, with the confident expectation of reaching his destination within ten minutes or so of the time he has predicted for his journey.

Today's driver does not consider for a moment the possibility that his car's engine might not start at the first or second twist of the ignition key. If his car is regularly serviced, it is very unlikely he will take time to check the oil level, the radiator, the battery or the tyre pressures before getting into his seat and starting the engine. As soon as he has switched on the ignition, the gauge will tell him how much fuel is in the tank, and if he needs more he can stop at any roadside filling station. Somewhere in the car a spare wheel is hidden away, together with a jack, but a puncture occurs so seldom on modern roads that he never thinks of this as a

likely source of delay. He knows that mechanical or electrical troubles are even less likely, and thinks it unnecessary to carry any other tools at all; as for providing himself with overalls or a change of clothing, he would consider that an absurdity.

In fact he probably makes less preparation for the car journey than he would if going out to post a letter at the street corner—for which, in wintertime, he would at least put on an overcoat. This is an extraordinary level of confidence to reach in less than three-quarters of a century. The attitude is now general throughout civilized countries, and of course it is perfectly justified: our cars *do* start immediately; they cover enormous distances without punctures or breakdowns, and journey times can be estimated with considerable accuracy. All this we take so much for granted that we entirely forget what astonishing progress has been made within a span of years that amounts to less than one man's lifetime.

It was certainly not always so. At the turn of the century a motorist might set off in the reasonable expectation of completing his journey, but he would scarcely have dared predict his arrival time, and a year or two earlier he would have been rash to feel confident about reaching his destination at all. Few motorists went to such lengths as Herbrand, eleventh Duke of Bedford, who, when he had to go on an unfamiliar journey by motor, sent one of his men out to make an identical trip a day or two before so that he knew how long it would take. All his cars were maintained in the very peak of condition to minimize the chances of breakdown, the tyres were replaced long before they were worn to any appreciable extent, and every car carried two spare wheels and four spare inner tubes. To make quite sure he would

*Massive and sturdily built, the 50 hp Simplex was
prominent in American motor sport before
World War I. This example receives attention
during an Automobile Club of America event,
while the lady passengers register boredom.*

TROIT PUBLIC LIBRARY

not be inconvenienced in any way during a journey, the Duke also brought a spare chauffeur, for he had once been stranded many miles from home when the unfortunate driver, "swinging" one of the massive 60 hp Napiers favoured by His Grace, had broken his wrist with the starting handle.

The ordinary motorist was scarcely in a position to take such precautions, and his world was full of imponderables. Before the trip even began he had to go through a long list of preliminary attentions to his vehicle, after which came the task of trying to start the engine—a task he faced in the miserable awareness that he had only a fifty-fifty chance: it might start and it might not. Sometimes it would burst into life at one pull of the handle, but at other times it was commonplace for a strong man to be left weak with fatigue after hours of fruitless effort. And the journey begun, no one could say how much tyre trouble, how many mechanical disorders, lay ahead. This was especially true of a long trip, but even quite a short one might call for the utmost patience and perseverance.

One Januáry day in 1898 two of England's most prominent motoring pioneers, S. F. Edge and Charles Jarrott, decided they would take a spin to Brighton and back—the Londoner's traditional run down to the sea. Edge had a Léon Bollée three-wheeler, a lively but temperamental device of uncertain habits, and Jarrott was using a very well-known racing Panhard which, two years before, had successfully completed the 1,000-mile race from Paris to Marseilles and back. They were, at that time, two of the most experienced drivers in all England.

They left London at about 8 am and reached Brighton, some fifty miles away, "at about three o'clock in the afternoon, in time for an un-appetising and spoilt luncheon." During this seven-hour drive both machines had given trouble, so the drivers devoted quite some time to their mounts and were unable to start the return trip until 7 pm. Despite the darkness of the winter's evening they made a race of it, the ever-competitive Edge jumping off his Léon Bollée and running beside it up every hill to keep up his speed. Jarrott had to stop and relight his candle lamps when they blew out at Handcross Hill, but the two of them reached the suburbs of London in a mere four hours.

There, however, Edge's vehicle came to rest when the exhaust valve of its single cylinder broke (not an uncommon occurrence when primitive steels were subjected to the high temperatures of petrol engines). There were, of course, no garages or service stations, nobody they could turn to for assistance who knew more about the mechanism than they did themselves. So, not even bothering to look for help, they stripped out the broken valve themselves and fitted a new one there and then in the mud and darkness at the side of the road. It took nearly four hours. But once the Léon Bollée was persuaded to go again, after a fashion, the Panhard then started to give trouble, backfiring so loudly in the City that a posse of policemen came running to investigate. At 4:30 am the two pioneers at last sat down wearily to a meal at Edge's home. They had been on the road more than sixteen hours, all told, for a total of little more than one hundred miles.

Both these machines used Gottlieb Daimler's "hot tube" ignition system, which was then favoured by several motor manufacturers because it was extremely simple and, in its way, reliable. All it amounted to was a platinum tube (no other metal would stand up to the heat) which was screwed into the upper part of each cylinder and kept red-hot by a flame directed onto its closed outer end. The piston rose in the cylinder, pushing the petrol/air mixture into the red-hot tube. It was ignited, and that was that. The red-hot tube did the work of a spark plug, and instead of a complicated assembly of magneto or battery and coil and distributor, there was just a set of burners, one to each tube, contained in a perforated metal box. (Nowadays one can scarcely imagine driving about with several naked flames under the bonnet of a car; Ralph Nader wouldn't like it at all.) In windy weather the vehicle would often be brought to a halt because the burners had blown out. When this happened, liquid petrol squirting from the jets would gradually spread over the surface of the hot engine and become at least partially vaporized. In that situation, a driver's pulse seldom failed to quicken as he opened the bonnet and burner box, struck a match, and relit the burners one by one. It was a job one preferred to leave to somebody else, while taking a short walk down the road.

Another disadvantage of tube ignition was that if a minor accident led to the car's being overturned—and the high-built vehicles of the period would tip over at the drop of a hat—there was little doubt that it would catch fire and burn to a cinder. Again, there was obviously no way for the driver to control the ignition timing, the moment when the mixture actually ignited. This meant that when swinging the engine with its starting handle, there was every chance of a backfire. Anyone who knew how to hold it properly would usually suffer no more than a fright when the handle was suddenly projected violently in the opposite direction by a backfire, but the penalty for carelessness was frequently a broken wrist or dislocated thumb.

However, before one braved the starting-

PHOTO-McCOMB

This is an 1897 twin-cylinder Daimler engine with genuine hot-tube ignition, now a considerable rarity. Inside the burner box are the protruding ends of the ignition tubes, and beneath each is its burner, which is fed with petrol from a separate tank.

handle routine, there were other things to be done, as the 1900 Daimler handbook tells us:

"It is necessary first to heat the tubes. This is accomplished by lighting a small quantity of methylated spirit below the burners. In the space of half-a-minute, the burners are sufficiently heated to vaporize the petrol. The latter is now fed to the burners from the supply tank. If the tank is placed at a low level, the petrol is forced out of the tank by means of air pressure created by a hand pump, which causes the oil to flow both to the burners and to the float chamber, this pressure being kept up afterwards automatically by the motor when in motion. With gravity-fed engines, it is only necessary to open the supply cock. As soon as the ignition tubes are at a red heat, the motor is started by means of the detachable starting handle which fits on the end of the crankshaft. A few revolutions of the starting handle draw in the first explosive charge, after which the motor will continue to work as long as the supply tank feeds it."

Coming as it does from a manufacturer's handbook, this passage naturally glosses over any little difficulties that might be encountered. Anyone who has lighted a paraffin blowlamp or camping stove will be familiar with the technique, and recognize this as a rather tame account of a procedure fraught with possibilities. Quite a small defect, such as a blocked jet or a failure to warm the burners sufficiently, can introduce so much melodrama to the task that many a hardened camper will have nothing to do with pressurized paraffin stoves, remembering past occasions when he has counted himself lucky to escape with the loss of his eyebrows. And the motorist, remember, was dealing with petrol, not paraffin . . .

Jarrott, in his well-known *Ten Years of Motors and Motor Racing*, recalls the time that he and a friend, Frank Wellington, went to Margate to collect a car and drive it the seventy-four miles to London. It was in fact the old racing Panhard, but this was the summer of 1897, and Jarrott was less experienced then; indeed, he had never driven anything like the Panhard and knew virtually nothing about it. He was therefore delighted when Wellington claimed an expert knowledge of ignition burners—but not so pleased when the courageous Wellington "turned on the petrol tap, flooded the whole of the engine with petrol, turned the tap off, lit a match, dropped it inside the bonnet of the motor, and then ran away. . . ." Jarrott persuaded his friend that such shortcuts were unwise and they warmed up the burners in the conventional way, after which the engine started readily enough and they covered some fourteen miles before 5 pm.

At that point Jarrott made a grave error of judgement, deciding to stop for a meal at a roadside inn. When the two friends were ready to start again, they found that the Panhard was not. "Of course, the usual procedure in starting a car at that time was to 'wind.' If the car did not start you wound again, and if it continued to be stubborn you wound still more vigorously. In fact one's knowledge—at least, our knowledge—did not extend beyond the 'winding' process. . . . If I remember rightly, we wound for at least two hours. The sun set, darkness fell, and we were still winding. At last, poking inside the bonnet with a huge screwdriver (which I had discovered amongst the tool kit of the car), I touched something—and the next 'wind' started up the motor in first-class style. I learnt afterwards that the accelerator chain had got hung up, and that my fortunate touch had knocked it into its normal position. With blistered hands and weary bodies we climbed into the car, having lit our candle carriage lamps, and once more renewed the attempt to reach London."

So, starting a tube-ignition car could be a slow business at times. Steam cars, too, were slow to bring to the boil; as late as the 1920s it took about fifteen minutes to raise a full head of steam on a typical machine such as the American-made Stanley, and owners in that country would leave their pilot burners alight all night to ensure a quick start in the morning—an expensive and rather risky practice.

By the early 1900s almost every manufacturer had turned to electric ignition, but as many of them felt doubtful of its reliability, a tube-and-burner assembly was often fitted as a standby. Writing of the Panhard range in 1903, J. E. Hutton said:

"Now I never stop from one end of the day to another, except for infrequent electric ignition trouble and the occasional punctures, which form a pleasant diversion for a quarter of an hour from the monotony and fatigue of remaining seated in one position for a long time. . . . The new commutator being fitted on the 10 hp cars is a wonderful improvement. The old type used to get dirty and sometimes give trouble, but though I have driven one of the new 10 hp models some 2,000 miles I have not once had to touch the electric ignition system from any cause whatsoever; indeed, so confident am I in the complete reliability of the electric system now fitted that I am almost inclined to say 'Don't have tube ignition fitted at all.' It should be remembered, however, that the accumulators for the electric ignition system require periodically recharging, and if they should run out miles from anywhere it certainly would be useful to have tubes fitted."

Hutton's comments reveal that the Panhards used a battery-and-coil system, which—in a variety of forms—was the type of electric ignition first favoured. But the demands it made on batteries and insulating material were too much for the technology of the time, and drivers came to prefer the magneto. Unfortunately this, while giving a much more satisfyingly "fat" spark at higher engine speeds, was less effective when starting, which led to some of the more expensive cars being fitted with both systems. Eventually the wheel turned full circle, as batteries and coils were so improved that the magneto system was abandoned completely during the 1930s.

It is also obvious from Hutton's words that in the early part of this century it was not the usual practice to charge the battery from a generator—dynamo or alternator—driven by the engine. This is one of the reasons why the electric starter was slow in becoming established. A battery that was recharged only occasionally, from an outside source, could not stand up to the load imposed on it by an electric starter motor. It was only just able to supply the ignition coil, but nothing else—no starter, fan, wipers, lights or horn. Some other means of turning the engine over had to be employed.

Some manufacturers experimented with quite complex systems for starting the engine by compressed air. Such a system festooned the car with compressor, distributor, air reservoir and a mass of pipework, but it could at least be pressed into service to blow up tyres after mending a puncture, or even to operate a pneumatic jack. There were various forms of kick start or hand lever, and the Swiss-built Ajax had a remarkable arrangement of levers by which the driver turned the engine while standing on the running board. There was also

The 1903 Packard (LEFT) was typical of early American cars in appearance, and like most of them, was started by swinging a crank handle at the side. But in 1912, Cadillac (BELOW) set the pattern for all other car makers by adopting electric lighting and starting as part of the standard specification. However, a handle was still provided for use in cold weather.

the starting cord, a device to be viewed with suspicion, despite its simplicity, because if the engine backfired the unfortunate motorist was liable to be pulled into the mechanism before he could let go.

But for years the starting handle remained the normal means of rotating the engine, even on the larger cars of the very well-to-do, so that a rupture became one of the chauffeur's stigmata. The immense labour of swinging a big engine could be eased by the provision of decompression taps, which sometimes doubled as priming cocks through which a little neat petrol could be poured into the cylinders during cold weather. There was even a type of spark plug that incorporated a priming cock. In 1912 Cadillac became the first manufacturer to offer electric lighting and starting as standard fittings, and gradually all the others had to follow suit. But a cold start made such demands on the battery, especially in winter when the oil was thick, that the wise motorist used the handle to free his engine before pressing the starter button.

The de Dion starting instructions for their Edwardian models enumerate some of the duties a driver had to perform before a car of that period could be taken out of its "motor house" (or, as some of the more conservative had it, "motor stable"):

"Prior to starting out, the driver should: (1) See that the crank case contains the proper quantity of oil. This he can do by examining the oil-lever gauge rod, which is marked with maximum and minimum depths. The oil level must on no account be permitted to get below the minimum depth, and for it to exceed the maximum mark is to invite excessive lubrication, engine sooting, leakage and waste. Too much oil will do little real damage, but cause

PHOTO — McCOMB

A 5-foot bar was needed to start the huge 21-litre of the Métallurgique-Maybach raced twenty years ago by Douglas Fitzpatrick. Each one of its six cylinders had a capacity of 3.5 litres!

considerable trouble. Too little will do both.

"(2) See that the gear box and differential casing are filled with oil to the depth marked on the gauge rods, or that of the overflow plugs fitted to them, closed (when not in use) by thumb screws.

"(3) See that all other parts of the car are properly lubricated. It is not suggested that one need make a complete round of every grease cup and oil hole every time the car goes out. If the crank case, gear box, differential casing, grease injector holes, grease cups, lubricators and oil holes are adequately filled they may be left so. Experience is the best instructor as to the frequency with which the lubrication must be repeated. During the first few weeks of ownership the driver will be well advised to make regularly a complete inspection of all lubricating points, to familiarize himself with them and to identify those which require frequent attention and those which only call for periodical replenishment.

"(4) See that the petrol tank is full. This may be ascertained by unscrewing the filler cap and inserting a clean wooden stick or ruler after the gauze is removed, but the greatest care must be observed that no dust or other foreign matter is admitted to the tank.

"(5) See that the radiator, water tank and water jacket are full. This may be verified by unscrewing the water filler cap on the radiator. If the cooling system is adequately filled the water level will be up to the foot of the gauze at the foot of the filler column or tube.

"(6) See that all overflow and drain plugs and cocks are securely shut off.

"(7) See that the petrol cock on the feed pipe (from the tank to the carburettor) is open.

"(8) See that the gear lever is in the 'O,' neutral or out-of-gear position.

"(9) See that the hand brake is 'on,' locking the rear wheels.

"(10) See that the magneto switch on the dashboard is in the 'off' or 'A' position. When 'on,' it will be at the 'M' angle.

"The foregoing details being found in order, if the engine has been standing cold for some time it is advisable to give the crank a few brisk turns before switching on the magneto. This is better than flooding the carburettor, which will often tend to accentuate any starting difficulties that may have arisen. The effect of two or three sharp revolutions of the engine— calling for neither effort nor risk if the switch is left 'off'—with the throttle open, is to set up a wholesome activity of the induction system.

"After the preliminary swing, (1) Move the magneto switch on the dashboard to the 'M' or 'on' position. (2) Push in the spindle of the starting handle (on which it is mounted), turn it lightly and gently in a clockwise direction until its ratchet engages with the ratchet on the fore end of the crankshaft, and then—holding the handle (which should be at the lowest point of its circle) loosely in the crooked palm, keeping the thumb on the same side of the handle as the fingers—give the handle one or two sharp turns. In 90% of cases the engine will fire on the first upward pull of the handle. In the remaining 10% of cases it will do so on the second.

"Now step to the side of the steering wheel and gently ease back the throttle lever until the engine settles down to a nice running speed. Great harm results from 'racing' the engine— that is, allowing it to run at excessive speed— when it is not doing useful work, and there is nothing more offensive to the real motorist than to hear a stationary car's engine running at twice its minimum turnover speed."

In a 1907 motoring manual an even more

cautious approach to a journey is counselled:

"The most certain way of providing against any possible breakdown on the road is to have the car properly overhauled before the run is commenced. A little experience will soon teach the driver what parts need to be examined, and perhaps adjusted, before a long run is commenced. The battery will be tested, the wires and connections carefully looked over, and all terminals and screws tightened where necessary; the induction coils and tremblers will be tested separately; the spark-plug contacts will be cleaned; the carburettor pipes, taps and moving parts inspected; the level of the liquids in the water and petrol tanks measured, and any deficiency made up; the oiling of the various gears attended to; the working of the various levers examined; all bolts, nuts and parts likely to become loose inspected; and finally, when all parts have been examined, the engine should be given a run round for a sufficient time to indicate that the water circulating gear is in thorough trim.

"So far as the tyres are concerned, these ought to have been examined when the car came into the garage, as it would be foolish to leave any overhauling that may be necessary until just before starting out on a run; the hands should invariably be passed over the surface of each of the tyres, if unprotected rubber is used, to find whether there be nails or other foreign material adhering. With protected tyres, a careful examination of the surface which underlies the band should be made after the wheels have been washed down and are clean."

Some cars called for special attention, and it goes without saying that they included that most idiosyncratic automobile, Henry Ford's Model T. One of the homeliest-looking vehicles ever made and assuredly the most exasperat-

Contemporary handbooks and magazines emphasized the need to pull the starting handle instead of pushing it, and to hold it so as to avoid injuring the thumb if a backfire occurred.

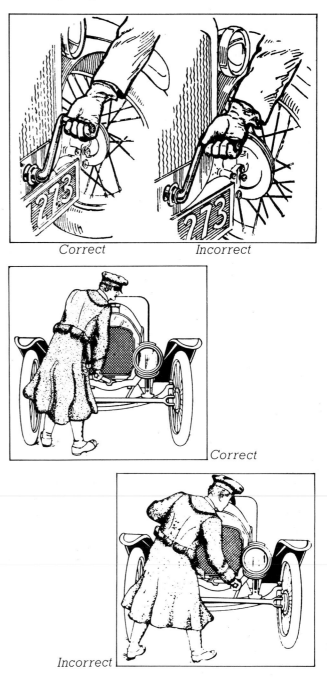

Correct   *Incorrect*

Correct

Incorrect

ing, the Model T was the car that really turned America into a nation of motorists, and well over fifteen million of these minimum-priced masterpieces were built between 1908 and 1927. There is something about the appearance of the Model T, a cross between Mack Sennett and Early Perpendicular, that is inescapably comic, and it remained funny even when it was working extremely hard and performing the most Herculean tasks. It was given to strange whimsies. For instance, the early examples were not normally fitted with a battery at all; their sole source of electricity was a low-tension magneto incorporated in the engine flywheel. At low speed this was barely adequate, so there was some danger of stopping the engine if you blew the electric horn at the wrong moment. Another curious side effect was that the note of the horn and the brightness of the lights both varied with the speed of the engine. This allowed the skilled Model T driver to produce some remarkable effects in *son et lumière*.

In warm weather, starting the engine was just a matter of setting the hand brake, opening the throttle lever slightly, putting the ignition timing lever on "full retard," and closing the carburettor choke. If all the settings were exactly right, the engine would start on the third pull of the starting handle, and it was only necessary to rush for the driving seat before the engine died again—although this also called for a certain knack; there was no door to the driver's compartment, so the quickest way in was to vault nimbly over the side.

Too little choke or too little throttle, and the engine would not start. Too much choke and the engine would flood with petrol, putting the spark plugs completely out of action. Too much throttle, and it would start with a roar that branded the driver as a novice. A little too

much ignition advance, and the starting handle would probably break his arm. The engine was by European standards a big one, almost three litres in capacity, so the winding process demanded muscle power. Not many women were capable of starting a Model T, and fewer still were foolish enough to try.

In cold weather even the menfolk approached the job with some trepidation. A Model T owner knew that unless he observed the correct ritual his Ford would be highly unlikely to start at all, but if it did start it would probably chase him down the road and run him over. This was because the cold oil gave rise to considerable drag in the epicyclic gearbox, and there was no point in writing an aggrieved letter to Henry Ford about it because the other 14,999,999 Model Ts suffered from exactly the same fault. So the first step in the starting procedure was to jack up one rear wheel, chock one of the other wheels, and let off the hand brake so that the jacked-up wheel could spin when the engine started. Next, a kettle of boiling water was poured over the inlet manifold to help vaporize the petrol. If these preparations were followed, it was quite possible the engine would start on the handle.

If not, the inlet manifold was made a little warmer by lighting a small bonfire of petrol-soaked rags under it. The spark plugs, too, could be unscrewed and "cooked" inside the house, then hurriedly refitted in the engine before they cooled down too much. The dyed-in-the-wool Model T man had another trick up his sleeve. Well-worn examples could be especially hard to start because too much end-play had developed in the crankshaft, increasing the gap between magnets and coils in the flywheel magneto and thus weakening the spark. If the jacked-up car was put into high

The Model T Ford's greatest merit was its near-indestructibility. This English-assembled (right-hand-drive) example of Henry Ford's masterpiece went off the road at Stonor, in the Chiltern Hills of Oxfordshire, in 1925, and landed at the bottom of a deep, tree-lined hollow. Yet it was hauled out again, little the worse, without so much as a broken windscreen.

TIMES HULTON PICTURE LIBRARY

Frequent roadside troubles made the motorist wary, so he would carry an ample supply of tools, tyre pump, lifting jack, and as many spare parts as he could conveniently cram into his car. Accessory manufacturers sold special metal containers of spares and tools which could be fixed permanently to the running board.

Your Morris is not complete
until fitted with the

HANDIKIT

THE "**HANDIKIT**" is a neat steel cabinet, 14½"×10"×7" (about the size of an ordinary accumulator box), which is fixed on the running board of a car, and is ingeniously planned to carry the tools, etc., necessary to deal with 90 per cent. of car stoppages. The list opposite shows its remarkable capacity (see also illustration). The divisions between the compartments are specially constructed to hold the contents firmly and prevent rattling, without interfering in any way with easy withdrawal. The lid is fitted with a double rim with rubber watertight joint, and is kept firmly in position by means of a spring catch. It can also be locked if desired, for which purpose two keys are provided.

The "**HANDIKIT**" as supplied comprises a Steel Container, as illustrated, with three compartments and the following equipment :

Tin for one gallon Petrol with reversible spout.   Clips for Plugs, etc.
Cin for half gallon Oil.   Metal Plates and Screws for affixing to step.
Tase for Lamp Bulbs.   *Half gallon Filtrate Oil.
Leather Holder for three tools.   *1 lb tin Solidified Filtrate Grease.

PRICE COMPLETE, AS ABOVE   **49/6**
* or without oil and grease, 48/-

Descriptive Leaflet M   "**HANDIKITS**," Bordesley Green Road, BIRMINGHAM
Post Free from

WHAT THE "HANDIKIT" WILL CARRY.
1. A tin carrying a gallon of petrol, with special reversible spout.
2. A half gallon tin of engine oil.
3. A tin case holding a complete spare set of lamp bulbs.
4. A leather holder carrying wrench, pliers, and screwdriver.
5. A box spanner for plugs, with tommy bar.
6. Four sparking plugs in clips (in lid).
7. Grease gun and connection.
8. Tin of grease.
9. Inspection lamp with flex.

AN IDEAL PRESENT FOR A MOTORIST.

THE MORRIS OWNER

gear (there were only two gears), this would take up the endplay and reduce the gap, thus providing a better spark for starting.

Once started, the Model T was renowned for its reliability and the indomitable way it dealt with all obstacles. Many a more sophisticated and expensive car of the early days gave its owner far more trouble. But the problems that beset motorists in those days were accepted with a fair amount of good-humoured resignation. When J. E. Hutton suggested that punctures and other troubles were merely "a pleasant diversion," he displayed an attitude so philosophical that it was positively saintly. But he was not alone in adopting it. In 1910 Owen Llewellyn wrote in *The Autocar* that: "To be benighted or *en panne* is to be introduced to new sensations. . . . A burst tyre near Sitgés showed us a typical Spanish bathing place and taught us how to drink out of a wineskin six inches off the mouth. A pair of new covers that went to the wrong address showed us a bull fight, Montjuich prison, and several distinct types of Spanish dancing."

The motorist of earlier times expected trouble. Five years after Owen Llewellyn's comment, *The Autocar Handbook* made that quite clear with the publication of two lists which read as follows:

To be taken on Ordinary Runs: Accumulator (spare); Aprons and rugs; Burners for acetylene lamps; Carbide; Complete contact breaker for magneto, with platinum contacts and slip-ring carbon brush; Engine valve and valve spring, etc., complete; Files (round and flat); Gauges for setting magneto contact and sparking plug gaps; Grease and injector; Hammer; Hand vice; Horn; Inner tubes (two, in bags); Insulating tape; Jack; Lamps; Nuts,

On long journeys the early motorist would usually carry his own supply of engine oil in addition to the customary two-gallon can of petrol, necessary when filling stations were few and far between. The Castrol company supplied a "Castrol Caddy" with bracket so that it could be fitted conveniently under the bonnet.

bolts and washers (various); Oils (paraffin and engine); Oilcans (two) for above; Petrol in spare tin (two gallons); Pliers (large and small); Screwdrivers (large and small); Spanners (box and tubular) to fit all nuts; Spare wheel, complete with inflated tyre; Sparking plugs and washers (four); Split pins; Spring washers; Straps; Twine and cord; Tyre inflator; Tyre levers (fork lever for valve insertion); Tyre repair outfit, with chalk and solution; Tyre valve parts; Voltmeter (if batteries are carried); Washers, metal and copper asbestos; Wire (copper 16g, iron 20g and 30g, and high-tension and low-tension insulated wire); Wrenches (large and small).

Additional for Long Runs and Touring: Brass polish; Cleaning brushes, gloves, leathers, cloths and waste; Extra spare tyre cover, or extra spare wheel and tyre complete; Foot muffs (for winter use); Hack saw and blades; Lamps parts; Maps and road books; Overalls; Tin of engine oil; Trembler for coil; Vulcaniser.

Quite obviously, the early motorist's watchword was self-sufficiency, this attitude surviving from the pioneer days of the movement when, if something broke, he mended it, using tools and materials that he had to carry with him. The pursuit of this curious hobby called for considerable mechanical aptitude allied to unlimited patience and fortitude. On one of his many trips to Brighton, S. F. Edge had the bevel pinion of his Panhard slip out of mesh with the crown wheel. To put this right he had to *remove the entire body of the car* and dismantle the gearbox. An incredible sixteen hours later he patiently resumed his drive to the South Coast resort.

And of course the man who had to tackle

CASTROL

To "get out and get under" at intervals was a necessity every motorist accepted, even if it was not a "little machine" but a big 24/32 hp dual phaeton Fiat of 1904. And his lady passenger looked bored, as always on such occasions.

RADIO TIMES HULTON PICTURE L.

jobs like this could scarcely be too fastidious about his clothes or the condition of his hands, so that motorists were often refused admission to the smarter hotels or restaurants because of their bedraggled appearance. It is hard to look the acme of elegance after having to "get out and get under" at more or less frequent intervals. One of the most casual people in this respect was the Hon. Charles Stewart Rolls—of Rolls-Royce fame—whose idea of packing for a journey was to push a razor, some socks and a few handkerchiefs into the pockets of his Norfolk jacket (with an extra celluloid collar for long trips). He would then turn up, oil-smeared and grimy, at some of the very best establishments to the profound embarrassment of managers who dared not turn away the youngest son of Lord Llangattock. Had they done so, however, it would have disturbed him very little. When making one of his motoring journeys he really preferred to eat in the open, beside his car, and often enough he would even sleep all night on the road underneath it.

Charlie Rolls became interested in motoring long before the start of his famous partnership with Frederick Henry Royce, and this naturally led him to visit France many times to investigate the latest developments in the country most actively devoted to automobilism. One of these visits, in the depths of the winter of 1899, was notable for a drive he undertook in an 8 hp Panhard from Paris to Le Havre, a distance of about 140 miles. There is some conflict between different reports of his journey: one says it occupied four days, another three (which seems more probable). Whatever the journey time, it was certainly a triumph over adversity and an indication of his ability to cope with any mechanical problem that came his way.

He had, however, made the mistake of leaving Paris without any tools, and before long he had to borrow some crude substitutes from a blacksmith when clutch trouble made it necessary to dismantle part of the transmission. Lady Shelley Rolls, his sister, waited patiently in the cold while he did so, then: "Some hours later, in order to shelter from the snow, I myself got partly underneath the car. I was just in time to witness the final unbolting of the gearcase. I saw it drop on my brother's chest together with all the black oil the gearbox had contained. He was in a terrible state with the conglomeration of tallow and oil."

So they were not to see Le Havre that night. Next day the clutch began to slip again, but Rolls cured it with a dose of powdered resin. Two flat tyres followed, one after another, and then the Panhard slowly ground to a halt again long after dark on the second day. Investigation revealed that the engine was literally red-hot. In the intense cold the radiator had frozen, stopping the circulation of cooling water and seizing up the water pump. Rolls and his companions poured petrol onto some rags, making blazing torches with which they tried to thaw out the frozen parts. It was a tricky and dangerous business, but they succeeded, whereupon a flood of water showed that the radiator had sprung a leak in two places. Once again Charlie found himself flat on his back in the snow as he applied makeshift patches of canvas and rubber solution to the leaking radiator. It was so cold that the water froze again as it trickled over his leather coat and up his sleeves.

That task completed, he found that one of the ignition tubes had developed a pinhole gas leak which kept blowing out the adjacent burner. Rolls turned his attention to this and repaired it; but by the time he had finished, the radiator had frozen up again.

It was now eleven o'clock of a winter's night, the temperature far below freezing. Rolls and his friends pushed the Panhard to a nearby village where they found a generating station open, for the place—it was St. Romain—was lit by electricity. There they tried vainly to thaw the engine cooling system by pouring boiling water over it. Eventually they managed it, slowly, laboriously and again at considerable risk to the car and themselves, by piling shovelfuls of burning coals underneath it. Once more Rolls started the engine, and once more an ignition tube sprang a leak which had to be repaired. It was 2:30 am when they again set off for Le Havre.

S. F. Edge in *My Motoring Reminiscences* mentions a particularly frightening fault of nineteenth-century motorcars: "If the brakes had to be kept on during the descent of a long or steep hill, they began to burn away, and if this happened one often had to rely on the tyre brakes to stop the car." Unfortunately the tyre or "spoon" brakes were quite likely to rip the tyres clean off the wheel rims if applied really hard, but unless they were applied hard they were largely ineffective. In 1896, only a few weeks after the Emancipation Day run to Brighton, Charlie Rolls had decided to attempt a drive from London to his home in Monmouthshire in a 3¾ hp Peugeot, one of the first cars to be seen in England. "This was considered a very powerful and almost dangerous machine, the most powerful one previously made being 3¼ hp. It was rather a top-heavy vehicle, hung on three springs, and it used to sway terribly when going downhill." Fifty miles from his destination Rolls reached the top of Birdlip Hill in Gloucestershire, and then came the experience that all early motorists dreaded:

"We started cautiously down the first and steepest part of the hill, which was almost like climbing down a precipice. The brakes had to be kept pretty hard on, and while we were still at the steepest part I felt my hand brake lever suddenly yield and go up against the stop—a feather had sheared—and there was an end to the side brakes; that left a miserable foot brake, which I pressed so hard that the lever bent and the pedal sat on the floor.

"That settled it; away went the car down this awful hill. I did not know the road; I did not know what curves there were, or what might not be on the road. There was nothing to be done but to try and keep her on the road and trust to luck. The car kept on accelerating, it swerved terribly from side to side—then came the first corner. She literally jumped round this corner, dashing across the road from one side to the other, and then I hoped the hill was over. But not a bit; there was a long, straight stretch ahead, with a steady down incline. To add to the difficulties we had a canopy, which made the car top-heavy; we also had the front glass down, and this, coupled with the darkness that was just coming on, made it extremely difficult to drive and to see which way the corners went.

"Well, on we sped down this stretch, wondering if we should get round the next corner, when suddenly we caught sight of a light right bang ahead of us. I said to myself, 'Now we're done for!', for we were swaying about the road so much that we could not possibly have got past a vehicle of any sort. We were gathering up speed, waiting for the crash, being by this time quite resigned to our fate, when I suddenly discovered another bend in the road, and the light, happily for us, turned out to be a house on the side of the road. We dashed round this corner somehow, and again came a gleam of hope that we might be saved; but still the road went on, downhill and downhill, until it really became a sort of nightmare, and not until two more stretches were covered and two more bad corners negotiated did we find ourselves at last slowing up, and then it seemed to us miles before the car actually stopped. Such is the hopeless feeling of being on a car with absolutely no brakes of any kind—and when the car did actually come to a standstill we felt a relief which it is quite impossible to describe, for it really was the narrowest escape of our lives.

"I still do not know how we got round those corners; the hill turned out to be a mile and three-quarters in length, and the car literally jumped from one side of the road to the other all the time, but I think it was the fearful swaying of the car that checked its speed to a considerable extent and enabled the turns to be negotiated, which otherwise could not possibly have been got round. On walking up the hill with a lantern afterwards, to look for a bag which had been dropped, I noticed the very wide skid marks which the car had made, and which sometimes went within a few inches of heaps of stones. There was a very strong smell of burning when we stopped, and all the brake leather was burnt up."

Terrifying as it was, an ordeal such as this was not at all uncommon, so that drivers were understandably wary of steep hills and considered them one of the greatest hazards of motoring—as, indeed, they were. On a level road, the speed was such that a skilled driver could usually keep his machine under control, even with tiller or lever steering, provided the surface was fairly smooth. There was, of course, a real risk of overturning if one wheel dropped over the edge of the road surface or into a ditch, and more than one fatal accident occurred when a pothole or a rock jerked the

Steep hills, like the 1-in-3 gradient this 1903 Serpollet is tackling, were not just a difficulty but a real danger for early drivers. Cars often ran away on them, either forwards or backwards.

OWNER (AS THE CAR STARTS BACKING DOWN THE HILL):
"Pull everything you can see, and put your foot on everything else!"

steering out of the unfortunate driver's hand, a thing that could happen readily enough because steering systems were not, in those days, irreversible. But it was the combination of a steep hill and faulty brakes that would be most likely to raise the vehicle's speed to a level far beyond the ability of its operator. Even Charles Jarrott, an experienced racing driver, admitted to fear on one occasion when he tackled Westerham Hill, in Kent, with a 4 hp Panhard phaeton. Knowing it to be dangerous he decided, nevertheless, that in such a light vehicle the descent could be made safely if he went about it cautiously, so he set off slowly with his foot brake hard on. Alas, at the top of the hill the brake rod snapped, "and in a second we shot away. My side brakes operated shoes directly onto the rubber tyres, and I knew that to apply these would have the effect of wrenching the tyres out of the rims and would probably result in a bad accident. I had a lady companion with me, and calling to her to sit tight and hold on, I decided to attempt to reach the bottom in safety, minus brakes. We took the whole width of the road to get round the first corner. . . ." Like Rolls, Jarrott experienced this brake failure in a high-built machine that was short in the wheelbase, distinctly unstable at speed, and not provided with wheel steering. In both cases it was only by the courage and skill of the driver that disaster was averted.

The other problem presented by hills was, of course, that the car might not be able to climb them at all, and in the early days passengers became adept at leaping out at the right moment to reduce the load—and, maybe, to add their muscle power to the failing efforts of the engine. If the engine stalled or the drive belt broke on a hill, however, it was quite possible that the car would begin to run backwards down it again, the brakes being usually even less effective in reverse. To meet this situation some private cars, many commercial vehicles and all army lorries were fitted with a sprag—a rod or bar pivoted from the chassis at one end and pointed at the other. The quick-thinking driver would "let down the sprag" the very moment his car came to rest, so that the pointed end would dig into the road surface. Then, if he managed to get going again, he could raise the trailing sprag by pulling on a piece of string. To be slow in letting down the sprag was a serious matter, for the car would have gathered speed backwards down the hill and might well pole-vault over it, reversing the sprag so that it became ineffective and possibly causing the car to overturn as well.

But the greatest burden of all for the motorist of the past was the behaviour of his tyres. They were the weakest link, giving more trouble than all the rest of his vehicle put to-gether; a continual exasperation which nobody could escape, and the one factor that for years most hindered the development of the auto-mobile as a trustworthy means of transport. As early as 1908, two out of every five cars racing in the French Grand Prix were estimated to be travelling at over 100 mph on the straights, but they were doing so on tyres that could not pos-sibly stand up to the strain. The race lasted almost five hundred miles, but the tyres lasted barely fifty, and at the end of almost every lap the drivers came rushing into their pits for a complete new set to be fitted to their non-detachable wheels. The winning car that year, Lautenschlager's Mercédès, was fitted with nine new tyres in the course of the race—but the highest-placed French car had *nineteen* new tyres fitted. One unfortunate crew, Cissac and his riding mechanic, were killed when a tyre

came off a wheel as they were travelling at full speed in the closing stages of the race.

The first cars were shod with tyres of iron or solid rubber. This was not because pneu-matic tyres were unknown: the first tyre of this type (made of leather) was patented forty years before the motorcar came into existence. John Boyd Dunlop made some for his son's bicycle in 1888, and the horse-drawn buggy raced by Harvey S. Firestone at Grosse Pointe, Michigan, in 1893 was fitted with pneumatic tyres. On lightweight buggies and bicycles they were capable of giving perfectly satisfactory service, but they were considered too unreliable—and rightly so—for use on the heavier horseless carriage, with all the weight of machinery it had to carry.

Solid tyres were reliable, though by no means entirely trouble-free. Indeed, the pioneer motorist found them far from ideal for his pur-pose. On a rough surface his vehicle became almost unsteerable at anything much above a walking pace, because of the continual shocks transmitted to the steering wheel or tiller. For the occupants, the ride was appallingly uncom-fortable, and the car was liable to be damaged by all the jolting. So solid tyres had to give way to pneumatics, and they did so, unfortunately, at a time when the pneumatics were not suffi-ciently developed—in either design or materials —for the job. Slow-moving lorries and other commercial vehicles continued to use solid tyres for many years, accepting discomfort for the sake of reliability until good enough tyres were designed for them. But the ordinary motorist had to face more than two decades of trouble, expense and inconvenience before his tyres even began to measure up to their work.

It almost goes without saying that S. F. Edge was one of the first to have his old Panhard con-

DETROIT PUBLIC LIBRARY

On an unsealed road surface, jacking up and mending punctured tyres was a filthy business, but it had to be done on the spot when wheels were nondetachable. This picture also reveals the softness and flexibility of early tyres—one of the reasons for frequent punctures and blowouts.

verted to take pneumatic tyres instead of solid. This done, he set off from London one morning, accompanied as usual by his friend and rival, Charles Jarrott. At first all went well, and the two friends were enjoying the smooth and jolt-free ride until, about 11 am, one of the tyres burst with a loud bang. Investigation showed that the thin tube had been "pinched" between cover and wheel rim, making a line of tiny holes all around which had to be patched with long, thin strips of rubber. While they were doing this a second tyre, suffering from the same fault, collapsed in the heat of the morning sun. They finished repairing the first, started on the second, and then saw the first tyre go down again because their patches had given way. They went back to repairing the first one all over again. As they did so, they heard the hiss of escaping air as a third tyre started to go down.

They mended it, started the engine and drove off. Before half a mile had been covered, tyre number four collapsed, so they had to stop. While they were repairing it, tyre number two quietly expired again. So it went on all day and much of the following night. At half-past one in the morning they were finally able to restart and drive the car gingerly into the nearest town. Neither of them had had any food since breakfast the previous day.

The pneumatic tyres that came into general use during the early part of the twentieth century were only a little better than this. Their poor quality, the rough roads of the period and the prevalence of horseshoe nails virtually ensured that when a motorist went for a drive he would have a puncture or a blowout. And as the wheels of his car were not detachable, the damage had to be made good before he could continue on his way. This was not an enviable

S. F. Edge, the pioneer British motorist, lends a hand with tyre repairs on his Napier during the 1,000 Miles Trial of 1900. Again the predominant atmosphere is of mud and discomfort, and the usual lady passenger waits in the usual chilly misery.

In rural America a river bridge provides a convenient firm surface for jacking up an early Model T Ford.

KANSAS HISTORICAL SOCIETY

task. Most tyres were of the type known in Britain as "beaded edge," in America as "clincher." Around each edge or rim of the cover ran a shaped moulding of rubber (the "bead"), and on each side of the wheel rim there was a matching groove. When the tube was inflated, the two beads were forced outwards into the two grooves, and this is what held the tyre on the wheel. But it had to be blown up really hard—not the 25 psi or so of today, but anything from 50 to 90 psi or more, depending on the size of the tyre. It was only the air pressure that kept the tyre in place. If a weary motorist failed to pump his tyres up hard, one of them would probably be ripped off the wheel as soon as his car gained any speed, and the tube—if not the cover, too—was likely to be torn to ribbons.

When a puncture occurred the car had to be raised, usually with a simple screw jack. (The wise motorist also carried a length of stout board for use on a soft road surface.) Then the rubber bead had to be forced out of its groove all round one side of the wheel rim, and laboriously stretched over the rim, with tyre levers, to give access to the tube. The tube was pulled out, the puncture located and patched, and the tube refitted, carefully persuading the valve stem back through its hole in the rim. This was not easy when rims and tyres were narrow, and there was little space for the fingers. It was even worse if security bolts were fitted—as they often were—to prevent cover creep. When the tube was back in place it was time to lever the cover over the rim again, using enough force to stretch the beads but taking immense care not to nip the tube with one of the tyre levers. And then came the worst part of all, as the American writer, Bellamy Partridge, reminds us in *Excuse My Dust*:

"With one of Tom Hunter's tire forks I could disrupt a rusted clincher from the rim in a matter of minutes, sometimes seconds. I could raise the bead, insert my hand, and draw out the tube. I could as quickly slip in another, or remove the casing if need be. I was equally swift about getting the tire back on the rim. Then came the real test of strength—pumping up the tire by hand. Sometimes this would take fifteen minutes of back-breaking labor, sometimes more. Pumps were temperamental. They did not always work equally well. The delicate leather washers wore or dried out. A pump that worked beautifully today would do badly tomorrow. You not only had to know your pump, you had to know how to repair it. Tom had taught me to take care of my pump and had furnished me with a set of spare washers. So I felt that I was ready for any eventualities; and I needed to be, for one night on the way home from Rochester I had seven punctures in the thirty-three miles.

"I was carrying only two spare inner tubes,

A British Crossley comes to rest with tyre trouble in France, and a French Renault (with classic taxicab body) is rescued by the Automobile Association in Britain. Notice how road surfaces have improved between the first picture (1906) and the second (1919).

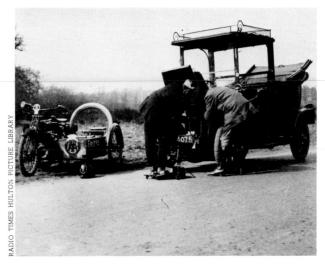

RADIO TIMES HULTON PICTURE LIBRARY

One of many gadgets aimed at reducing the continual tyre troubles which made early motoring so tiresome: a spring-loaded wire scraper intended to remove nails from the cover before they could penetrate it.

and had to put on five patches by matchlight. Patching a tube took time, perhaps half an hour per puncture. When I got home that night, there were blisters on my hands from pumping."

Motorists were as philosophical about tyre troubles, however, as they were about mechanical derangements during the course of a journey. Partridge was even more so, as he goes on to explain:

"In the early days of motoring a puncture, while not especially welcome, was at least something that the motorist could understand. It was not like having your motor begin to miss or perhaps die entirely for no apparent reason. There was nothing mysterious about a puncture. It came because the air had gone out of your tire. And all you had to do was to get some air back inside and keep it there. But not only were we stoical about punctures, we were positively boastful about them. My seven-puncture trip home from Rochester kept me in material for conversation for days and days. In fact, it was one of the best stories in town, until somebody eclipsed it one night by having fourteen punctures in the eighteen miles between Geneva and Canandaigua."

So widespread was the tyre problem that a mass of gadgets and inventions flooded the market. There were Stepney and Captain rims which carried a complete spare cover and tube, inflated ready for use. If one of these was clamped to the offending wheel, the job of mending the puncture could be postponed until later, though the man who was "coming home on the Stepney" naturally lived in dread of having another puncture before he got there. There were "puncture-proof" bands of heavy rubber or leather to fix outside the tyre in the hopes that no nail would penetrate them. Alternatively there were "self-sealing" tubes containing some material—one manufacturer used a mixture of sticky paste and small feathers— which was intended to fill up a hole as soon as it was made. Some people considered that, as air was so difficult to keep inside the tyre, a sub- stitute would be better, and various semisolids were tried with little success. S. F. Edge tested a gelatine mixture on one occasion, and bowled along in fine style—if somewhat bumpily—to cover a remarkable fifty puncture-free miles before putting his car away for the night. Next day, however, when he set off down the road everything felt very peculiar indeed. During his drive the tyres had heated up, melting the gelatine mixture, and overnight it had solidified again in the garage to make a substantial "flat" on each tyre.

A few motorists carried containers of com- pressed air or carbon dioxide to ease the task of tyre inflation. Some of the better hand pumps were double-acting, working on the "up" stroke as well as the "down," and some were provided with three barrels in which the air was progressively raised to a higher pressure before passing into the tyre. There were several kinds of engine-driven tyre inflators, and a four-cylinder pump which could be clamped to the running board and operated by turning its handle, instead of having to push it up and down.

The adoption of detachable wheels took much of the urgency out of tyre trouble, for the car owner could then carry two spare wheels, complete with tyres, and reasonably expect to complete most journeys without actually having to repair punctures by the roadside. The detachable wheel made its appearance in 1906 and was adopted fairly quickly in Europe (though it was not used in the 1908 French Grand Prix because the organizers banned what they

Another accessory marketed as an aid to the motorist was this miniature air compressor which could be mounted on the car and used to operate a pneumatic lifting jack, to inflate tyres, or even to blow the horn. American-made, it was also being sold in Britain in 1910.

To the smooth and rounded surface of the early twentieth-century tyre tread, steel studs were sometimes fixed in the hope of reducing the tendency to skid. Predictably, they were not very effective in doing so.

considered a dangerous device). In the USA, however, the preference was for detachable rims on a nondetachable, wooden-spoked wheel. Long after wooden wheels had disappeared from most European cars, they surprisingly lingered on in America.

Early tyres had a short life, manufactured as they were from natural rubber with a zinc-oxide filler (which made them light grey or white in colour, not black) and woven cotton reinforcement. A motorist counted himself lucky indeed to get two or three thousand miles out of a cover before it had to be thrown away, but a stone cut or sidewall damage would bring it to an early grave. So the expenditure on tyres was considerable—higher, usually, than any other running cost, and an owner who went in for extensive touring with a powerful car could spend several hundred pounds a year on this item alone. Even with quite a modest-sized car, an *Autocar* correspondent is quoted as having spent approximately £65 on fuel (at less than £0.06 per gallon!) but £106.25 on tyres during the years 1909-1912 inclusive, his mileage totalling 20,176. Nowadays, at the end of this distance, a typical motorist would probably have spent nothing at all on his tyres. They would still be the original ones fitted to his car at the factory, and there might easily be some usable tread left on them.

Most of the early tyres were almost completely round in section when fitted, and the tread was smooth. Having no pattern at all, it was rather prone to puncture, and positively encouraged skidding in slippery conditions. So instead of a "puncture-proof" band the motorist might strap on a set of "detachable non-skids," which were leather bands dotted with steel studs. If the car *still* skidded it would do so to the accompaniment of a spectacular show of

TOP: *A motorist demonstrates the fitting of tyre chains to an Austin Seven for driving in mud or snow.*
BOTTOM: *Even Cadillac, so often a pioneer, followed American practice where wheels and tyres were concerned. This 1922 model is still fitted with nondetachable wheels and bolt-on rims.*

sparks. The tyre makers then tried moulding a row of studs or knobs into the rubber itself, all around the circumference, which started the development of the patterned tread. As the mechanism of skidding was not really understood, manufacturers felt free to indulge their fancy at will, and many strange tread patterns appeared. Some consisted of the maker's trademark repeated all around the tyre. Some had their own name moulded into the tread so that it was imprinted in reverse again and again as the car was driven along.

Tyre chains, still used today in thick snow, were at first wrapped around the smooth covers of the period in the far-fetched hope that they would prevent skidding. Even more unlikely to succeed was an arrangement mentioned in the *Motor Manual* of 1912, which, it said, "simply consists of a steel chain hanging loosely on the road, and on the inside of the wheel, and close to the tyre, so that any sideways motion of the wheel results in the chain being trapped under the tyre and thus checking the skid."

In retrospect, it is difficult to understand why motorists put up with so much tyre trouble for so long. The answer to most of their problems lay in a form of tyre construction which had been known since 1890: quite simply, forming the "beads" of the cover around inextensible wire rings instead of moulding them in rubber alone. This meant that the beads would not stretch, so the wheel rim had to be altered in design in order that tyres could be removed and replaced. But this was not in the least difficult, and it put an end to the one massive disadvantage of the beaded-edge or clincher-rim tyre—that it was held in place by air pressure alone. Once that hurdle was overcome, tyres could be made much fatter in section and

TOP: *A motorist demonstrates the fitting of tyre chains to an Austin Seven for driving in mud or snow.*
BOTTOM: *Even Cadillac, so often a pioneer, followed American practice where wheels and tyres were concerned. This 1922 model is still fitted with nondetachable wheels and bolt-on rims.*

inflated to lower pressures. With the coming of the "balloon" tyre in the early 1920s, the pathway to further development was open. Slow at first, progress gradually speeded up as manufacturers competed fiercely with each other to produce tyres that would last longer, grip better in wet or dry weather, and call for little or no attention from the motorist.

Freed then from the fear of tyre trouble or mechanical mishap, the driver of today—while giving his car not much more attention than his wristwatch—enjoys the facility to travel far and fast in comfort, and at a moment's notice. It is arguable, however, that in achieving this he has also lost something of value, though it is a loss he seldom has occasion to perceive in the course of his motoring nowadays.

For all its many faults, the car of half-a-century ago inspired a certain confidence in its ability to surmount obstacles, external or internal. If it did break down more often, it was infinitely easier to repair, even at the roadside and with the simplest of hand tools. More than one modern motorist, immobilized by some complex derangement of a "sealed-for-life" component of his modern car, has sent up a fervent prayer for a Model T Ford or "Bullnose" Morris Cowley. The chassis frame might flex a good deal, but it stood up to astonishing abuse, and an unexpected encounter with a rock or kerb-stone usually meant nothing more than a bent wheel or axle which could be straightened, with any luck, or at the worst replaced. In that respect, such a vehicle needed no pampering, and the ability to get through adverse conditions depended mainly on the skill of its owner. Rough terrain, floods and river crossings, deep mud or thick snow—none of these things held any real terrors for the competent driver of a sturdy and rugged car with big wheels and ample ground clearance. The journey might take longer than he expected, but he would get there eventually, and do it without having to beg assistance from others.

TENDER LOVING CARE

"The hours I spent on that automobile, and the others which were to follow it, if diligently devoted to any profession whatsoever would undoubtedly have placed me near the top."

BELLAMY PARTRIDGE, Excuse My Dust (1943)

Before the coming of the automobile the only privately owned means of transportation was the horse. This is so blindingly obvious that we have to keep reminding ourselves of it, for it is a fact that is continually overlooked. Only if we keep harking back to the horse can we even attempt to reach a true understanding of the early days of motoring. Otherwise we fail, for we would be assessing the vehicles and their performance falsely, by the standards of a later and altogether more technological age, which would necessarily find them crude, clumsy, or merely funny.

Almost without exception the people who bought the first cars were people who kept a carriage. Their attitude to the new "automobilism" was entirely shaped by their experience with horses. These people—with some notable exceptions, of course—knew nothing of mechanics or electricity. They lived in houses heated by open coal fires, lit by coal gas or oil lamps, and containing (other than clocks and watches) no mechanism more complex than a mangle or a hand-operated mincing machine.

They knew that horses had to be housed, fed, groomed and shod. They might assume that the motorcar, too, would require attention like their horses and carriages, but they had no notion what that attention should be. Somehow or other—and indeed, one wonders how!—they came to terms with this utterly alien machinery, learning how to operate it and maintain it in something approximating correct running order. A few who had a natural aptitude for the work learned to do it themselves, and even enjoyed it. Others left it to their servants, and many a harassed coachman or groom cursed the day the new-fangled horseless carriage was invented. To such a man the automobile was infinitely incomprehensible.

Nor was there a friendly local garageman to put things right when they went wrong. That came later, when the blacksmiths and bicycle menders had adapted themselves to a new era. Meanwhile the wise car owner devoted much attention to the care of his vehicle. This was something the medical profession appreciated sooner than most, their need for reliable transportation being self-evident. In an article entitled "Motors for Medical Men" which he wrote for *The Car* of June 11, 1902, Dr. H. E. Bruce Porter made this clear as he studied the advantages of the motorcar over the horse:

"In my case, the cost of a pair of horses and brougham, with rented stables and coachmen, came to about £320 a year and was roughly made up in this way: nearly everyone now jobs horses as it is much less bother, and if the horse goes lame the jobmaster finds another to match the sound one. I paid 80 guineas [£84] for the hire of a pair, and 80 guineas for their forage, etc. Stabling here is very expensive and costs, rent and taxes, £40 per annum, coachman's wages being £1 10s. [£1.50] a week and rooms, etc., and if the carriage is out often he must have a stable helper. The interest on the cost of the carriage, renewing tyres, painting and varnishing, etc., would at the least cost £20 per annum, the odd money going in repairs of the stables, gas, etc.

"My first motor was a Daimler 6 hp station omnibus with removable top, my intention being to let my coachman drive the machine. I soon found, however, the delight of controlling one's own machine, so sold this car and had a mail phaeton built instead. This cost, with extras, about £475. I have had it in constant use for over two years and a half, and have driven it at least, I would think, about 18,000 to 20,000 miles. . . .

"I have had less trouble than most owners

N TRANSPORT EXECUTIVE

In Piccadilly Circus just before World War I, the motor taxicabs and the solid-tyred B-types of the London General Omnibus Company have almost completely ousted horse-drawn vehicles, and the scene is positively restful compared to that a decade earlier, if we may believe the artist's impression of Piccadilly Circus on page 81.

LONDON TRANSPORT EXECUTIVE

of cars because I have always taken as much interest in the machine as I did in horses, and when any bearing showed signs of wear I put it right. No one would think of driving a horse day after day without having its shoes renewed, the harness overhauled and the axle-caps, etc., greased occasionally, yet lots of people buy a motorcar and do not take the trouble to find out where it requires oiling. They seem surprised when the steering gear gets stiff or a bearing seizes. If the doctor is keen on mechanics, he will find motoring a very interesting amusement.

"Going back to the cost of upkeep, I may say that the man who cleans mine is able to do other things about the house. I've been able to let the stables, and I have put up a car house in the garden. This is more convenient, as when called at night I am able to start at a moment's notice, whereas, when depending on horses, I had to wake my man first. The horses then had to be harnessed, and it would always take quite half-an-hour to get under way. When the motor is not in use it can rest in its house for an indefinite period without being any the worse, whereas in the case of horses exercise is required.

"To sum up the cost of a motor in a few words: wages of man, same as coachman; petrol, lubricating oil, grease, cleaning rags, etc., £50; odd repairs (and these depend entirely on the amount done by the man who cleans the car), not more than £6; rent of lock-up coach-house or interest, etc., on the cost of a house in the garden, £10; overhauling at the works, renewing tyres, painting car, etc., £40; this is estimated on their being done every year and a half; reckon the car to require renewing at the end of four years, not because it is worn out but because you will want a more up-to-date one, and this gives a total of £305 per

No gentleman who wanted to maintain his car properly would be without a "motor house" for its storage and regular maintenance, with a covered area where it could be washed down after every journey.

annum, meaning that you will own your machine, that it will do the work of six horses, and that you will save £15 a year on the cost of a pair.''

Not only doctors ''put up a car house'' in the garden. Other new owners soon realized that if they did not garage their own motorcar they were depriving themselves of its main advantage—immediate availability for use. Unfortunately most of them found that the buildings they had ready and waiting on their premises, stables and coach houses, were the two types least suitable for the purpose. Stables always seemed to be the wrong shape for a motorcar, even when the stalls and fittings had been cleared out, and the doorways were usually too narrow. Coach houses were too small, too dark, and inadequately ventilated, being merely somewhere to store the carriage safely out of the weather. A car required varied attentions when in its abode. A coach was just pushed into its coach house *after* it had been washed down, cleaned out and polished.

Anyway, said another motoring writer of the period, ''it is best to retain the stables for many reasons, even if the horses have to be dispensed with, and construct a convenient and useful store for the more modern means of locomotion.'' He considered that ''the wealthy owner of a 'stud' of cars of varying power and for various purposes'' would as a matter of course provide ample accommodation ''not only for storing the vehicles, but for engineers' shops fitted with lathes, forges, and all that is necessary to carry out repairs of a more or less serious nature, in addition to the living requirements for the staff of drivers and mechanics.''

For the owner of only one vehicle he suggested more modest arrangements, but still with the facility for carrying out fairly extensive work at home:

''The motor house should be well provided both with light and ventilation, with blinds or shutters to keep off the rays of the sun. An ordinary gable roof with top light will be found the most practicable, and an overhead arrangement of pulleys on runners is almost a necessity either for removing the body when the necessity arises, or for lifting the engines or other parts and carrying them to the engineer's bench, which should be fitted in all stores in a well-lighted and convenient position. The floor should be of cement, sloping to the centre (so that the rubber tyres do not stand in the oil dripping from the car), with a slight fall to one end and without a drain. The latter would only prove a snare and delusion where oil or petrol has to be dealt with. Nothing will stop a drain quicker than continual oil dropping, and, should a serious leakage of petrol occur, the collection of vapour in a drain may prove a serious danger.

''When a store is properly ventilated the chance of fire is, of course, very small, even though a leakage of petrol is taking place. Nevertheless, it is always a mistake to enter a motor house with a naked light after it has been shut up for any length of time. Electricity is the ideal medium for all lighting. A wall plug conveniently placed, with a hand lamp and long flexible wire, is always useful both in the store and in the pit, and the current can be used for charging accumulators in connection with electric ignition. Artificial heating is not advised unless hot-water pipes can be used. It is better in very cold weather always to empty the water out of the car before leaving it for the night. This is not much trouble, and is not often necessary.

''The most necessary adjunct to a motor house—the inspection pit—should be placed near the entrance, with a good solid wooden cover made in pieces easily lifted by a man. In the bottom and at one corner, with the floor sloping towards it, should be a small sump-hole with an iron grating, where any wet or dirt will collect and be easily removed. This is infinitely preferable to a drain, which is always liable to get stopped and cause trouble. A glass roof, with open sides, over the pit and extending some distance to the entrance of the store and directly in front of it, will be found a great luxury and convenience, more especially for washing cars during wet weather. The floor of the covered way should fall away from the pit and towards the drain, the latter being provided with a self-cleansing trap and movable mud pan, into which the dirt deposits itself and can be emptied from time to time.''

In regard to dimensions the car owner was advised not to skimp things in any way:

''When building a motor house for one car only it would be advisable to make it a trifle longer than is absolutely necessary so that, on an emergency, an additional small car or *voiturette* might be accommodated. . . . The width of the building should be not less than 10 feet, which would, in the case of a 12 or 16 hp car, give a clearance on either side of about 2 feet. The length of such a car, including head lamps, will be found to be a little over 11 feet, so that if only one car is to be provided for, the length of the building should be (if an engine bench is to be included at one end) about 18 feet. If the engineer's bench is dispensed with, however, from 14 to 15 feet should be ample room.

''A very good plan would be to make the building 18 to 20 feet long with a movable bench at the far end, as in this case, should two cars have to be stocked, the bench could be

SCIENCE MUSEUM, LONDON

Even the Hon. Charles Rolls (who later gave his name to Rolls-Royce) had a workshop where he would maintain and repair his own cars in the early days. In fact, the truth is . . .

. . . that Charlie Rolls liked nothing better than messing about with machinery, and soon dismantled his first car, a Peugeot he imported from France in 1896.

SCIENCE MUSEUM, LONDON

temporarily removed. When two cars are always kept the best way is to have the store built to hold the cars side by side. For this the building should be from 17 to 18 feet wide and the same length as given for a single car. One of the size described will stand from 5 to 6 feet high, or with a covered top about 8 feet. The building therefore should be about 9 feet in height to the eaves, the roof being an open one, so that the top of the car, or the body, as the case may be, could be raised and the carriage taken in and out under the same if desired.''

All this sounds impossibly elaborate by the standards of today, but it was thought no more than adequate by the enthusiastic car owner of the early twentieth century, who accepted without question that his vehicle would be maintained and repaired at home. As late as 1915, the *Autocar Handbook* favoured a similarly lavish design for the motor house:

''The house should be large enough to provide a space of at least 4 feet all round the car. If a glass-covered yard can be arranged as an addition to 'the house, this will prove a great convenience. There should be large doors at each end of the house if space permits, so that the car may be run in one way and out the other. This will save a lot of time and trouble in reversing. . . . A good supply of water should be laid on for cleaning purposes, and the soft rainwater falling on the roof should be collected in a covered tank, as soft water should always be used in the radiator if possible.''

And again, in the *Motor Manual* of about the same period:

''Sliding doors may sometimes be introduced with advantage, and in any case, except where the building is of very large dimensions, a separate doorway for each car should be provided. Ample cupboard and shelf room is quite indispensable. One large cupboard, with suitably arranged racks for tyres and inner tubes, should be fitted up. It should be made quite dark, under which condition rubber is best kept. The racks should be arranged out of curved pieces of wood so that tyres and tubes (which latter should be kept partly inflated) can be supported upon them for, say, 2 feet of their circumference.''

The same publication recommended that if electricity was not available, a small paraffin-operated charging plant should be installed so that naked lights would never need to be employed. The properly equipped motor house was not considered complete without its stout bench, vice and anvil, lathe, drilling machine, grindstone, soldering outfit, battery charger, lifting jacks, axle stands, and a full supply of hand tools.

But however elaborate the equipment provided, the tool most frequently used by every car owner was a good hose. Up to the 1920s, vehicles were ''coach-finished,'' the bodywork carrying coat after coat of flatted-down oil paint with a final coat of varnish on top. In good condition, this traditional finish had a lustrous depth which no cellulose or synthetic paint has ever equalled, but it was extremely soft, easily scratched, and quickly deteriorated if neglected. The earliest cars had comparatively little bodywork, but on the unsealed roads of their day they stirred up clouds of dust in summer, or a great deal of mud in winter, and the paintwork soon dulled if this dirt was not washed off regularly. Later cars spattered less mud about because the wheels and tyres were more effectively shielded, but on the other hand they had more bodywork to be cleaned.

There was quite a technique to car washing. With the vehicle placed on its well-drained

If you are laying-up until March

"Dusout" Regd.

CAR COVER

will keep your car spotless

THE MORRIS OWNER

If you are not taking out your licence until March 31st, lock after your car meanwhile. Three months' exposure to dust will do irreparable harm to paintwork and polish. Cover the car with a DUSOUT Cover and keep it spotless until you need it.

SIZES AND PRICES.

	"Dusout" W'rp'f Covers.	"Dusout" Dust Covers.
15ft. × 9ft. for 2 seaters	45/-	26/3
15ft. × 12ft. for 4-seater Cowleys	60/-	35/6
18ft. × 12ft. for Coupés and 4-seater Oxfords	72/-	42/6
18ft. × 15ft. for Saloons, etc.	90/-	53/6
Carriage Paid.		Delivery by return.

THE "DUSOUT" WATERPROOF RUG

Double Texture black waterproof material, with 8in. lap at bottom. Will not peel or crack. Lined finest quality camel fleece. Ideal for bonnet cover in frosty weather. Sizes : 5 × 4ft. 37/6 ; 6 × 4ft. 45/-. Carriage Paid.

Every " Dusout " Cover is sold on the understanding that if you are not satisfied and return the cover within 7 days your money will be refunded. You are fully protected by this guarantee. Send your order (with cash) and the Cover will be despatched by return.

Dusout Manufacturing Co.
43F, Blackfriars St., MANCHESTER
Telephone : 4024 Central.
Telegrams : Dustless, Manchester.

Coach paint, unlike modern cellulose or synthetic finishes, was extremely soft and easily damaged The careful owner would keep his car covered up if it was out of use for a time.

THE MORRIS OWNER

DAVID BURGESS WISE

patch of concrete there would be less chance of further mud splashes from below, and ideally the recommended glass roof would protect it from above. The driver would make ready a hose, two buckets, two large sponges, two brushes and three chamois leathers. Of these, one bucket, sponge, brush and leather would be set aside for the chassis, and the remainder reserved for the coachwork alone. The secret was to flood all the clinging mud with water so that it was thoroughly softened and could be gently stroked off the body with a sodden sponge—but this had to be done without wetting the interior of the car, not an easy task if the body was an open one. The underside of each mudguard was washed completely free of mud, then each wheel jacked up in turn for the same treatment, with help from a spoke brush if necessary—another tricky job if they were wire wheels. All the chassis parts were washed down with water to which a little paraffin oil was added to help remove the grease.

When every trace of mud had been removed—and not before, or the surface of the varnish would be hopelessly scratched—the car would be rubbed down again with a clean sponge and "leathered off" with a chamois to prevent the varnish from drying with a spotted finish. Spotting could also result from specks of tar, if left too long on the paintwork, so these had to be dissolved one by one with a tar remover. When all else was done, it was time to polish up the brass or nickel plating, brush out the mats from the floor and clean all the leather —including, if one was fitted, a massive leather hood.

Done properly, this dismal chore occupied a good four hours of a competent man's time, and it might have to be performed by a weary chauffeur every night. Only then could he relax after the day's driving, praying that not a drop of wash water had found its way into the carburettor, magneto or ignition coil to put the engine out of action. No wonder the *Autocar Handbook* suggested an alternative for those who were not paid to do such work:

"The owner-driver who looks after his own car will find that the washing and cleaning become rather a trouble. To avoid this, and if a man for washing is not available, it is advisable to have the car painted a light grey or some other dust colour. The dust will not show on the car, and it can be cleaned in instalments. For instance, the tops of the mudguards and the bodywork and the bonnet can be cleaned, leaving the wheels and the interior of the mudguards to be done at leisure. If this were done with a dark-coloured car the appearance would be very bad. To avoid continual brass polishing it is a good tip to use lamp covers, which can be obtained from any accessory maker, or the lamps and other removable parts can be carried inside the car in wet weather."

Washing was only one of several attentions that the car required every day: the full list of them enumerated in a 1908 motoring handbook occupies 4½ pages of small type preceded by the stern warning that "This daily overhaul should not start on the day on which a car is required for work, but on the previous evening, when as soon as the car is brought in for the night it should be carefully examined." It was advisable, for instance, to feel the brake drums immediately on arrival to make sure the brakes were not binding and overheating. To distinguish between water loss due to overnight leakage and that caused by overheating when running, it was wise to check the level of the radiator (if any) at night, and again in the morning. Serious oil leaks, too, would be easier to detect when a period of running had just ended. Sometimes the driver would lay sheets of paper beneath the car overnight to help him trace a particularly elusive leak to its source. On some models, Rolls-Royce included, the sagacious operator made use of a specially trimmed piece of wood to hold the clutch pedal in the disengaged position overnight, knowing that if he did not, the clutch would probably be jammed solid in the morning. Petrol and oil pipes were often fitted with cocks that one had to remember to turn off—failing which, the results could range all the way from being merely messy to downright calamitous. When Jenkins was told to bring the motorcar round to the front door immediately, he was expected to do just that. It was useless trying to explain to His Grace that the entire oil tank had emptied itself into the engine during the night, or that the contents of the petrol tank were spread all over the motor house floor.

Tank levels would of course be checked before every run; and if there were sight-feed lubricators, these, too, demanded attention to ensure that the oil was passing through each one at the correct rate. The exact procedure varied from one car to another, sometimes calling for a great deal of inspired guesswork. In the 1907 edition of *Cars and How to Drive Them*, very precise instructions are given for the lubrication of the contemporary Hotchkiss:

"The crank chamber is divided into two parts, one of which contains the two front cranks and the other the two rear cranks. The oil does not pass freely from one crank chamber to the other. The object of this arrangement is to prevent the oil from running to one end when on a hill, but makes it necessary to provide for the lubrication of each compartment separately.

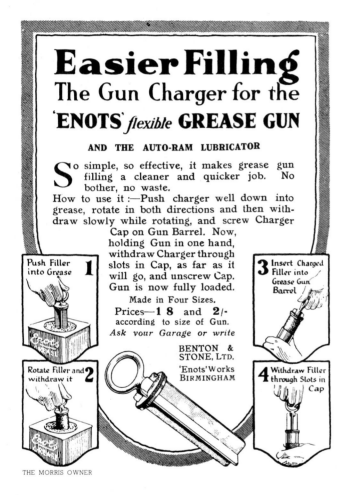

Easier Filling
The Gun Charger for the
'ENOTS' *flexible* GREASE GUN

AND THE AUTO-RAM LUBRICATOR

So simple, so effective, it makes grease gun filling a cleaner and quicker job. No bother, no waste.

How to use it :—Push charger well down into grease, rotate in both directions and then withdraw slowly while rotating, and screw Charger Cap on Gun Barrel. Now, holding Gun in one hand, withdraw Charger through slots in Cap, as far as it will go, and unscrew Cap. Gun is now fully loaded.

Made in Four Sizes.

Prices—**1 8** and **2/-** according to size of Gun.

Ask your Garage or write

BENTON & STONE, LTD.
'Enots' Works
BIRMINGHAM

Push Filler into Grease **1**

Rotate Filler and withdraw it **2**

3 Insert Charged Filler into Grease Gun Barrel

4 Withdraw Filler through Slots in Cap

THE MORRIS OWNER

"Beneath the crank chambers will be found two taps. Turn these taps on and pour oil into both the front and rear crank chambers through the vertical tubes which are fitted on the left side of the motor. When the correct quantity of oil has been poured in, it will run out of these taps. If the crank chambers are empty it will take 2½ pints of oil for each.

"Fill up the automatic lubricator on the dashboard and set the drippers which lead to the crank chambers to drip at the rate of sixty drops a minute. The approximate number of drops is stamped on the three small hand pumps. The two sight feeds on the left lead to the crank chamber, and the one on the right to the driving spindles of the magneto and pump. This latter dripper should run at the rate of about fifteen drops a minute. A motor should never smoke, but should always be just on the point of smoking."

The final sentence, it may be mentioned in passing, recalls the engine oiling arrangements on the Model T, which was fitted with two trycocks—one for the maximum oil level, one for the minimum. Best results, said the handbook, were obtained by maintaining the oil level halfway between the two.

As a basic rule of thumb, one manual advised that every morning the driver should apply oil to every component of the car that was provided with an oil hole, and at mid-day, if the run was a long one, he should oil them all again. These components were: "Spring shackles, the joints of the levers and connecting links operating brakes, the bearings in which the brake levers and the change-speed lever oscillate, and the links and levers which connect these up to the brakes and change-speed gear respectively. Also the bearings in which the clutch pedal operates, the links with their joints which

connect it to the collar of the clutch, the heads
of the steering pivots about which the steering
wheel moves, the links with their joints and
levers which connect the steering wheel to the
road wheels, and such exposed shafts as the
shaft driving the pump, the magneto, the fan,
the lubricating system, etc." Screw-down grease
cups were to be given a turn or a turn-and-a-
half every day, and about once a week they
would probably have to be refilled. The
patrician Rolls-Royce 40/50 hp, better known as
the Silver Ghost, had sixty-three grease cups to
be refilled weekly.

This frequent lubrication was required
partly because the oils and greases used were
of such poor quality, little removed from the
animal fats that had preceded them. Partly, too,
it was because so much of the mechanism was
completely unprotected from dust and dirt. Old
grease left in a bearing would quickly turn into
a species of grinding paste when combined
with flying road grit, and had to be flushed out
by applying fresh lubricant before it did more
harm than good. Exposed driving chains, for
instance, were a constant headache: if lubrication was inadequate they would be noisy, wear
rapidly and perhaps break; if excessive, the
grease would spread and probably put the
band brakes out of action. Some drivers kept
two sets of chains so that ample time could
be devoted to their laborious cleaning and
greasing. Drive belts, too, had to be kept clean
and dressed at intervals with castor oil to keep
the leather supple. In both cases the adjustment would need checking to make sure the
chains or belts were running neither too tight
nor too loose. Likewise the brakes had to be
tried out, preferably before every run, to see
if adjustment was required and to detect
faults before they reached serious proportions.

Keep Oil at Home

*An important message to the
Morris Owner with a home garage*

Morris Oiling Chart
Free!

Morris Owners who have
not yet received one of our
Morris Oiling Charts can
obtain one on request. This
chart, which is suitable for
hanging up in the Home
garage, clearly indicates every
lubrication point on both
Morris-Cowley and Morris-
Oxford chassis and shows the
correct grades of Mobiloil
to use.

Now is the time to see that an adequate home
supply of Mobiloil is on hand in your home
garage.

With such a home supply of Mobiloil you form
the valuable habit of attending frequently to the
oil in your crank-case—at the same time that you
inspect your tyres, the petrol supply, and the
water in your radiator.

Certainty of correct oil always, convenience,
better operation and economy are direct advantages of installing a 10 or 5-gallon drum or
4-gallon can of Mobiloil in the home garage.

In buying Mobiloil be sure that you get the
correct grade Gargoyle Mobiloil "A." For 1924
and earlier models of 11.9 h.p. use Gargoyle
Mobiloil "Arctic" in winter as approved by
Morris Motors Ltd.

GARGOYLE

Mobiloil

Make the Chart your Guide

HEAD OFFICE : Caxton House, S.W.1   BRANCH   *Belfast   Bristol   Dublin   Liverpool   Newcastle-on-Tyne*
WORKS : Birkenhead and Wandsworth   OFFICES: *Birmingham   Cardiff   Glasgow   Manchester   Sheffield*

VACUUM OIL COMPANY, LTD

THE MORRIS OWNER

LOOSEN CLAMPING SCREW

One reason for the continual attention that early cars demanded was, in a word, vibration. Until one has actually seen one of these vehicles running, it is difficult to believe that they vibrate so much. When the engine is going they quiver all over like an excited puppy, mudguards bouncing and shaking on their mountings, the lamps, horn and mirror a mere blur of polished brass. When one adds to this commotion the vibro-massage imparted through solid or high-pressure tyres and stiff suspension systems by rough-surfaced roads, the effect on the mechanism was extraordinary. Firmly tightened nuts slackened off as if turned by an invisible spanner, carburettors and the like fell apart before one's eyes, and small screws disappeared forever. The struggle to keep things together was a battle constantly waged but never actually won.

As for the tyres, these were so troublesome that the motorist treated them like newborn babes, pandering to their every need. Each morning before a run the pressures had to be verified—not after a run, when they were hot and the pressures had risen. Flints or nails were removed from the covers, and careful note made of cuts which had to be filled and vulcanized before water could penetrate and rot the canvas. Weak spots would be patched or fitted with gaiters before they developed into bulges which might burst. Spare tubes, before being taken on a journey, had to be folded up in a special way to prevent chafe, and refolded at intervals so that no cracks would be encouraged to appear. The *Autocar Handbook* counselled that: "When the car is to be left out of use for a long period—for, say, anything in excess of four weeks—it is advisable to jack up all four wheels so as to give the tyres a rest. A special jack is now being sold [it raised the four wheels simultaneously] for those careful motorists who like to give their tyres a rest frequently."

Once a month the conscientious motorist would embark on a more thorough examination of his car. One writer conceded that "if only used occasionally such an overhaul can be left for a longer period," only to add: "The oftener it is made, however, the better a car may be expected to run, and the longer will be its life." The motorist was advised to check the compression of the engine, replacing any faulty compression taps or plugs, grinding in the valves and refitting with new springs if necessary, and setting the tappet clearances. Carburettors were to be cleared of sediment, the jets checked, also the float, and the needle valve ground in if required. The water-pump gland was to be repacked if leaking and its drive, by friction or belt, checked for slackness. The radiator was to be disconnected and flushed out with water. All pipes were to be tested for leakage, taps also, and repaired or ground in as necessary. Every portion of the braking system was to be studied for worn pivots, bands, shoes or linings.

Attention to the ignition system would depend on the type fitted, of course, but would embrace checking the spark plugs (for cleanliness and correct gap between the electrodes), the electrolyte level in the battery and its specific gravity, the state of all wiring; cleaning the distributor and contact-breaker or contact-maker points (with attention to their gap); and inspecting the trembler coils, ignition coil or magneto.

Once again lubrication would occupy a lot of time. It was usual to drain the engine sump and flush out with paraffin oil before refilling with fresh engine oil. The gearbox and dif-

MAIN NUT

LOCK NUT

The owner-driver of the 1920s was well acquainted with the technique of setting tappet clearances, fan-belt tension, checking the front axle U-bolts for tightness, and doing all such maintenance work for himself.

ferential casing or worm drive were given similar treatment. Old grease would be cleaned out of screw-down lubricators and any other nooks and crannies before refilling, while sight feeds also had to be washed out, their needle valves ground in if necessary and re-adjusted. Road springs would be pried apart so that grease could be applied between the leaves, and wheels removed to clean out the hubs and repack them.

The one bright spot for the owner-driver who tried to do his own maintenance work, contemplating the seemingly endless catalogue of attentions to be given to his vehicle, was that he could at least get at it. Ample clearance underneath, lift-up wooden floorboards and well-placed inspection traps made most parts readily accessible, especially if the owner had followed the advice of the motoring manuals and provided his motor house with an inspection pit. Under the mudguards there was adequate space to work at hubs, brakes, road springs and steering connections once the wheels had been removed. The bodywork was regarded as a separate entity, fixed to the chassis by six or eight bolts and usually easy to remove if there were additional helpers or lifting apparatus to take the weight. The gear-box of most such cars was not integral with the engine but quite separate, driven by a short shaft from the clutch, so neither it nor the clutch was particularly difficult to dismantle for re-pair. Axles could be unbolted from their springs if need be. The very chassis frame itself, if damaged in an accident, could be laid bare and straightened, or even replaced by a new one from the manufacturer if it was beyond repair.

Exhaust systems were not welded up in one piece, all the way from manifold to tailpipe.

They were bolted together so that any one por-tion could be renewed when necessary— which was seldom, for they lasted ten years and more. Steering boxes, shock absorbers, gener-ators, magnetos, pumps—all the mechanical and electrical sub-assemblies—could not only be unbolted from the car, but themselves be dis-mantled in order to clean, adjust, or recondition them with the use of replacement parts that could be readily obtained at reasonable cost. The idea of making a unit disposable at the end of a couple of years—of manufacturing a car-burettor or starter motor in such a way that it had to be part-exchanged for another at sub-stantial cost instead of stripping it out for cleaning—would have been thought positively immoral. If a headlamp bulb failed, the motorist fitted a new bulb, not a complete new headlamp unit.

Components were made so that they could be removed and dismantled with the ordinary tools that would be found in the motor house, not factory-assembled with hydraulic presses and other machinery that no owner-driver possessed. It was simple enough to grind in a set of side-by-side valves in an afternoon, when each one could be reached by unscrewing a valve cap above it. There was no great hard-ship about replacing a faulty electrical lead if it was connected to screw-type brass terminals, instead of ending in brittle push-on connectors which were neither replaceable nor reliable.

Cars built in this way, in what is commonly called the "vintage" manner, had their short-comings. In general they were heavy, they were not very fast for their engine size, and they used a lot of fuel. Continual flexing of the frame was inclined to cause rapid deterioration of the coachwork, and body timbers suffered greatly from rot. Though the running chassis seemed immortal if properly looked after, frequent engine overhauls were commonly required: every 3,000 to 4,000 miles the top end had to be decarbonized and the valves ground in; every 30,000 miles or so the cylinder block would have to be rebored, and new pistons and valves fitted; at perhaps 60,000 miles the crankshaft would need regrinding and most of the bearings would call for attention. Fortunately the makers of even the cheapest cars met this need by providing an excellent parts service.

When the earliest motorists wanted a new part for the engine, transmission or running gear, they either made it themselves, if they could, or called on the services of a professional engineer to do it for them. Metallurgical knowledge was limited; components that were hardened inadequately—or not at all—had only a short life; and replacements, made to fit a particular car, might or might not fit another of identical make and type.

It was Henry M. Leland who changed all this for the ordinary motorist. During the American Civil War, working for Springfield and Colt, he had learned the importance of fine tolerances and interchangeability of parts in the firearms industry. When he turned to building Cadillacs in 1903 he stuck to the same principles—though in those days the Cadillac was an inexpensive machine, cheaper even than the contemporary Ford.

F. S. Bennett, Cadillac's first British importer, hit on a unique way to emphasize the quality of their spares service. In 1908 he arranged for representatives of the Royal Automobile Club (RAC) to pick out three brand-new single-cylinder models from the London showrooms. They were tanked up with petrol and driven to the then new Brooklands racing circuit, where they were tried out on the track and then put away in three locked garages.

Next morning, two mechanics were admitted to one shed and proceeded to dismantle that car completely, leaving not a single component attached to any other; every nut and bolt was removed, every ring taken out of its groove in the piston. The garage was locked up, they went to the next, and dismantled the second car. In the same way they dismantled the third. Then the RAC officials carried the parts of all three cars to a fourth locked-up garage and jumbled them so thoroughly that nobody could tell one from another.

That done, the mechanics were instructed to build up a complete car, using only simple hand tools and components picked from the pile at random by the RAC officials. At the end of two days they were standing in front of a finished Cadillac, which started at the first turn of the handle.

Two days later they had completed another, once again drawing on the jumbled collection of parts in the fourth garage. This, too, started up and ran successfully. At this point, however, the RAC observers removed forty components from the remaining heap and substituted replacement parts taken from the Cadillac spares depot in London. Using this collection, the mechanics set to work and completed another car, after which all three were taken out on the track and successfully put through a variety of performance tests. For this remarkable demonstration of full interchangeability, the Cadillac Car Company was presented with the Dewar Trophy, one of the RAC's highest awards.

As mentioned elsewhere, the pioneer motorist normally topped up the fuel tank of his motorcar at home before setting out on a journey. Sometimes when he had done so, he might be seen fitting a potato into the exhaust pipe and winding vigorously with the starting handle. This did not indicate that he had suddenly taken leave of his senses: merely that his car was of the type in which the fuel was fed to the carburettor by the pressure of the exhaust.

His stock of fuel was kept in a separate small store, some distance from the motor house. In Britain the law allowed him to store up to sixty gallons, but no more, so he had to arrange for it to be replenished at regular intervals by his supplier. Usually the fuel was sent by rail in metal cans, which, at the nearest station, would be loaded on to a horse-drawn cart and delivered to his home. It was a great nuisance and a considerable expense, but there was no alternative for the man who wanted to use his car regularly. He could not stop to tank up at a local garage because no such thing existed, and if he tried buying fuel haphazardly from hardware stores or paint shops, he was likely to run into trouble very soon.

The trouble was that hardly anybody knew *what* to pour into the tank of an "oil motor carriage." Oil, yes—that was obvious. But what kind of oil? There were so many of them to choose from by the end of the nineteenth century, and they had such bewildering names. This was because the oil industry is quite a lot older than the automobile. William IV had only just succeeded to the throne of England, and Andrew Jackson had not been long in the White House, when a small London company was established to manufacture a tallow substitute for candles. The founder named the firm after his aunt, a Miss Price, so that his friends would not realize he was doing something so ungenteel as engaging in trade.

After a time, E. Price and Company also began making petroleum-based lubricating oils (previously, most lubricants were made of animal fats or vegetable oil), and took a firmer hold on the illumination business by producing a lamp oil as well as their candle wax. This oil was known to the British as paraffin, to the Americans as kerosene, and it soon became one of the company's most important products—in fact they succeeded in selling no less than 10,000 gallons of it to the United States in 1859, the year that Edwin L. Drake made his famous discovery of oil in Titusville, Pennsylvania. Once the American oil producers got going, however, they quickly outstripped their competitors, and the petroleum industry grew by leaps and bounds. In 1888 John D. Rockefeller's Standard Oil Company was able to set up a British subsidiary, the Anglo-American Oil Company, to sell *in Britain* a product that was poetically described as "American Lamp Oil— an exceedingly beautiful oil in appearance, being absolutely colourless and as clear as the purest spring water."

But a whole array of lighter oils came as an unavoidable by-product of lamp oil manufacture, to be sold as solvents, cleaning fluids— anything—to anybody who could be persuaded to buy them. So another London oil-refining company, ironically named Carless, Capel and Leonard, must have been delighted to receive an inquiry in 1890 from Frederick Simms, an English business associate of Gottlieb Daimler, who was having difficulty in finding a suitable fuel to use in a Daimler engine. Carless produced a light benzine (or benzoline) and named it "petrol," borrowing from the French word *pétrole* which so confusingly means kerosene or paraffin oil. A few years later they marketed a more volatile spirit which cost a little extra, but was advised for use in cold weather; this they named "gasoline." By that time another English engineer, Frederick

Lanchester, was experimenting with an engine which he, like Simms, tried out in a motor launch. But as Lanchester worked for a coal gas company he ran his engine on a coal-tar derivative called benzole (or benzene).

The result was hopeless confusion for all but the most knowledgeable. A particularly well-informed motorist at the turn of the century would be aware that, with suitable adjustment, his engine would run on either benzine or benzene, which sounded exactly the same but were, in fact, entirely different. He would know that benzoline (or benzolene) was the same as benzine, and benzol (or benzole) the same as benzene, and he might even have read somewhere that benzoin was neither of these, being a sort of frankincense obtained from a tree. He knew that he should ask for petrol in Britain, even though this was really one company's brand name for its product—like Kodak. But in France the right word was *essence*, and if he asked for petrol there they would sell him paraffin, the lamp oil (but if he wanted to fill the lamps on his car it was better to use colza oil, made from a kind of cabbage). In America if he asked for paraffin (or even paraffine) he would end up with a white waxy substance used in making candles, not the paraffin oil which was known there as kerosene, but if he wanted petrol he had to ask for gasoline, or gasolene, or gas. And the latter, he might well reflect, was derived from the Greek word for chaos.

Inevitably, then, the early motorist was frequently in trouble with his car because somebody supplied him with the wrong fuel. On one occasion Charles Jarrott, having stayed overnight at an Oxford hotel, sent to "the nearest oil-shop" for four gallons of petrol, with instructions to have it poured straight into the tank of his Panhard, out in the stable yard. There

followed a long and wearisome session with the starting handle before he discovered that his tank had been topped up with paraffin, which so exasperated Jarrott that he emptied the lot out onto the ground. It is easy to guess what happened when another hotel guest strolled into the yard at that moment, lit a cigarette, and threw the match away. Jarrott, of course, had to pay for all the damage.

If extra fuel was required during a journey it was much wiser to seek the aid of a local chemist, who would probably supply benzine in glass jars. Carless at first sent their petrol out in ten-gallon drums made of steel (they used wooden casks for their paraffin oil), but the British railway companies were not satisfied; they refused to handle the dangerous new liquid until it was packed in stout wooden crates, each holding two four-gallon cans. But the safety regulations for home storage called for cans of only two-gallon capacity, indelibly marked "Petroleum Spirit–Highly Inflammable." So Carless started delivering in cylindrical two-gallon cans, painted blue. In 1899 they published a list of agents—1,200 of them, including Harrod's—who sold petrol in Britain.

Not everyone accepted petrol as the most suitable motor fuel. A Bristol firm tried to sell benzole in two-gallon cans at a much lower price, but few motorists bought it. In France the government wanted to encourage motorists to use alcohol fuel, and thus help to dispose of a huge surplus from the sugar-beet crop, so in 1902 they organized a race for cars running on alcohol. This attempt also failed. In 1904 another substitute was tested, using an early Peugeot fitted with a metal box instead of a carburettor. The box was filled with mothballs (which are made from naphthalene, a coal-tar derivative), and when heated by a pipe from the exhaust they propelled the old Peugeot in fine style. It did 2.82 miles per pound of mothballs, but the smell of the exhaust was rated abominable.

Meanwhile the Anglo-American Oil Company had gone into the petrol business, issuing a booklet and a map of depots where "Pratt's Motor Spirit," as they called it, could be obtained in green, square-cornered two-gallon cans. Within five or six years they had become the biggest petrol suppliers in Britain, holding three-quarters of the market—and by 1907 Britain was the biggest consumer of petrol in Europe. All this petrol, about 100,000 tons of it, was sold in the sealed two-gallon cans which were becoming very well known, and by a curious anachronism most of them were still being transported by open, horse-drawn carts. Road tankers were not favoured at all, and when the first of them began to appear, they, too, were drawn by horses.

For years the British motorist filled his car's tank from a two-gallon can that was painted green (Pratt's), red (Shell), green with a yellow shield (British Petroleum, known simply as BP), blue-and-red (Redline) or some other colours, denoting the various products of the different petrol companies. There were special brackets available so that they could be fitted to the running board to provide a reserve supply, and as the cans were stoutly made they stood up to any amount of hard use. The screw caps were of heavy brass with two lugs on top, and could be opened with a tyre lever or by jamming the bottom of another can between the lugs. There were spoutlike gadgets that could be fitted to the mouth of the can so that it poured better, but the experienced motorist took pride in handling the can without spilling a drop, and scorned the use of such things. As the cans were sealed by the fuel company, he felt

A familiar object to the British motorist for many, many years was the two-gallon petrol can. In this picture there are Shell cans on the left, BP cans on the right.

The "Angloco Victory" manually operated petrol pump was sold in Britain by the Anglo-American Oil Company, and the fuel dispensed by Anglo-American was known as Pratts Perfection Spirit until 1935, when it was renamed Esso, which owed its name to the initials of the mighty Standard Oil company.

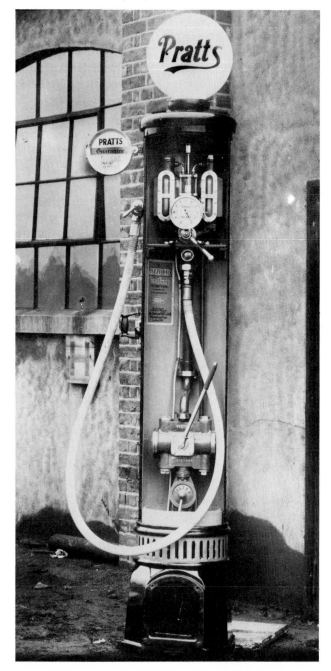

confident that he was buying a full two gallons of clean petrol—and cleanliness mattered to a man who had sometimes lain on his back under a car searching for the elusive foreign body that had brought him to a halt, dismantling and blowing through the fuel pipes, knowing only too well that the foul taste of petrol would be with him for hours afterwards.

In America, where petrol cost much less, refuelling was a fairly casual business, usually accomplished by filling a spouted measure from a tank or barrel and tipping it through a strainer into the car. The wise man used a chamois as well, knowing that this would filter out water, too. He had to take it on trust that the measure really did hold a gallon. But when the first hand-operated pumps came into use, a little before World War I, he had mixed feelings about this new mechanism which transmitted petrol all unseen from an underground chamber to his car's tank. He felt doubtful about the quality of the invisible fluid (some years passed before the oil companies started sealing the underground tanks), and a tiny dial with a pointer inspired no great confidence in the quantity, either.

During the war Pershing's American Expeditionary Force introduced the new *fontaine à essence* to France, and a few years later the first manual pumps were installed in Britain. But for some time the French continued to use their five-litre *bidon*. The English motorist was even more reluctant to abandon his beloved two-gallon can.

Another type of manual pump carried two large glass containers on top. The operator pumped petrol up into one container with an oscillating handle, then emptied that into the car's tank while pumping up the other, and so on. This, too, was a slow method of refuelling, but there was a certain satisfaction in watching the precious fluid (it cost around £0.05 per large British gallon) as it bubbled its way into the transparent containers and then gurgled out again. For a time some of the companies marketed coloured fuel: BP Plus was blue, Pratt's Ethyl was red, and there was a green alcohol blend called Koolmotor marketed by the Cities Service Company (later renamed Fina). This added greatly to the entertainment value of the glass-reservoir petrol pump, and the automatic electric pump which succeeded it in the early 1930s was, by comparison, a very dull device. Anglo-American recognized the sales appeal of the visible product, and in 1934 made a great furore on the British market by selling an engine oil (it was called Essolube) in tall glass bottles. This move brought the Esso brand-name across the Atlantic, and the following year the familiar Pratt's was renamed Esso.

During this time the local garage, with its two or three petrol pumps in front, had become a familiar sight in the smallest towns. The proprietor might be a refugee from the world of steam who had taught himself something of internal combustion, or merely a repairer of bicycles who hoped his customers knew even less than he did. He might be an ex-soldier who had cut his teeth, so to speak, on army lorries in wartime Flanders. The building from which he operated was seldom palatial: an old wooden shed, maybe, with a greasy inspection pit in the floor, an assortment of tools hung around the walls, and beneath the massive workbench a jumbled hotch-potch of part-used components which "might come in useful one day."

The man who ran an establishment like this frequently had to improvise for lack of tools or equipment, and he was not to be observed studying a manufacturer's service sheet or

Many motorists were a little doubtful of the new-fangled petrol pump after buying their fuel in sealed two-gallon cans. Shell, for example, found it necessary to reassure the customer that pumps did deliver the correct quantity from those invisible underground storage tanks.

OVERLEAF: *The archetypal small garageman at the turn of the century: a bicycle repairer with ambition. The signs indicate approval by the Cyclists' Touring Club for bicycle repair work, a Pratts Spirit agency and a dealership for Ariel, who made motor tricycles and quadricycles until 1904. Two newly delivered bicycles are in a crate on the pavement; a Benz and a Panhard are parked outside.*

KANSAS HISTORICAL SOCIETY

By the early 1920s the roadside filling station, already well established in the USA, had become an increasingly familiar sight in Britain. George Thyfault of Tribune, Kansas, who also did some blacksmith work on the side, sold "Filtered Gasoline" by Gargoyle Mobiloils. The much smaller British establishment offered a choice of Benzol or Pratts, by far the biggest-selling motor fuel in the UK.

workshop manual, but he hated to admit defeat. He would tackle the most extensive mechanical derangements, or painstakingly beat out crumpled bodywork after a crash. He worked extremely long hours in great discomfort, charging so little for his services that he could afford neither to keep his premises in reasonable condition nor to heat them adequately in winter. His assistants, too, were likely to be very young and horrifyingly inexperienced, as Douglas Armstrong reminds us:

"There used to be a village butcher in my area who didn't want to know about a proper delivery van. He had a 1921 Lagonda that he had converted to a van, and used to blast around the countryside delivering his wares as though he was competing in some sort of carnal Grand Prix.... The Lagonda was of course on beaded-edge tyres, and one day our cheerful butcher had mended a puncture, and he hared off to the local garage to borrow the air-line and inflate the thing. The poor little blighter of a garage-boy was told to 'Blow it up hard,' so he put nozzle to valve and pressed the trigger. The pressure went up to 40, 50, 60, 70 psi, and each time the lad asked the butcher if it was hard enough, he would answer, 'Just a bit more.' The pressure was just up to 110 when there was the Father and Mother of an explosion as the tyre was blown to pieces. The lad and butcher were blown over backwards, and neither of them could hear anything for a couple of days."

Specialization was almost unheard of, and the archetypal small garageman was just as willing to mend a bedstead as a Buick—or, indeed, a Bugatti, if anyone was foolish enough to let him try. He could be found in every country where motorcars were driven, and what he achieved with minimal resources was beyond comprehension.

By the late 1930s, however, the era of the "reconditioned replacement" had begun. The original manufacturer of a car could offer a rebuilt engine, say, in exchange for a worn one, at a price the ordinary garage could not match. More and more components were assembled in a quite different way. It might be to simplify manufacturing methods, or to improve design, or merely as part of a deliberate cost-cutting policy, but it put their repair beyond the scope of the ordinary man; all he could do was to unbolt them from the car and fit a new or re-conditioned part in their place. It was an in-evitable development, but the long-term result was that many basic skills were lost. Garages came to be staffed by men who were motor engineers, but they were not engineers; they had no idea how to "scrape in" a bearing, and some of them could barely use a chisel, hack-saw or file. They had, however, been trained to perform certain highly specialized tasks, usually with the aid of complex and costly equipment. Three or four decades ago, the repairman trying to cure a flat spot or misfire might spend hours checking the carburettor jets, the contact breaker and spark-plug points, the tappet clearances and ignition timing. His successor could carry out these tests in minutes with an electronic "workshop pulpit." Indeed, some cars are now being manufactured with a built-in diagnostic socket wired to various key points on the engine and chassis. They have only to be connected up to the appropriate "diagnosis station" for a direct reading of engine rpm, ignition timing, advance curve (centrifugal and manifold depression), battery voltage, contact-breaker resistance and dwell angle, and so on. One type even checks the steering geometry and gives a tape read-out in computer fashion.

It is a far cry indeed from the days when a contact-breaker gap was normally quoted as "the thickness of a visiting card," and the modern motorist has been relieved of virtually all the chores that were once so inescapable and burdensome a part of car ownership. He no longer checks the radiator every day; it is either a pressurized cooling system which uses little water, or it needs no attention at all be-cause it has been turned into a sealed system. It is not necessary to check the tyres daily or even weekly; synthetic rubber is less porous than natural rubber, so it holds air better than an old-type tube. More probably there is no tube at all, and that is better still. Now that the charging rate of the generator is governed by a very accurate regulator, the battery level hardly ever needs to be topped up, and only an old engine needs its oil level to be checked frequently—a good one may go 2,000 miles without using more than a pint of oil. Brakes call for very little adjustment now that the front ones, at least, are usually of the disc type, and hydraul-ic operation has put an end to all the rods and cables that needed oiling.

Engine maintenance has been transformed by improved metallurgy, better oils and fuels, effective filters and air cleaners. It can be literally years before the power unit requires any adjustment at all, and those who change their cars at the 50,000/60,000-mile point have pro-bably forgotten what the word "decarbonize" means, if they ever knew. As for major recon-ditioning of the bottom end, this may not be needed until twice that mileage has been achieved.

Gearbox lubrication is equally undemand-ing, and rear axle casings are sometimes made without drain and refill plugs at all, on the assumption that the original factory-fill oil will last the final-drive gears for the entire life of the vehicle. Chassis lubrication, once such a messy and time-consuming task, is almost entirely a thing of the past. The greasegun has become a curiosity to be mercifully forgotten, most modern cars having no greasing points whatsoever. Thanks to the cunning use of rubber bushes, today's suspension systems need no lubricating, and the many small mechanical controls and linkages that needed oil have been designed out of existence.

As we have said in the previous chapter, there is a price to pay for these conveniences. If it is true that the driver no longer finds it necessary to work on his car, it is equally true that he no longer finds it possible. On the one hand this puts him almost entirely at the mercy of the local service station, whatever the quality of its workmanship, for the regular maintenance of the vehicle. On the other, when a roadside breakdown occurs nowadays, the chances of carrying out a repair are almost nil. A tubeless tyre can only be repaired by a skilled man with the appropriate garage equipment. While a broken spring leaf could usually be jury-rigged to get a driver home, today a collapsed fluid suspension system leaves him helpless. Hydraulic brakes scarcely lend themselves to quick repair in an emergency, and without test equipment there is little hope of tracing a fault in present-day electrical components or their wiring. So when a modern car breaks down, there is not much that anyone can do but telephone the nearest garage and wait for the tow truck to arrive.

Yet there are signs of a possible change in the policy of some motor manufacturers, at least. Porsche of Germany, for example, have studied this question very closely, and the president of the company, Dr. Ernst Fuhrmann, has recently made this statement:

"For too long, designers of manufactured products have been thinking in terms of replacement, rather than repair, because manpower has become expensive while materials remained abundant and cheap. Nowadays, materials are no longer cheap and they are becoming less abundant. We must no longer manufacture something in such a way that it cannot be repaired, be it a radio, a refrigerator, or a major component of an automobile. It must be made to last—as it was half-a-century ago! There is no reason why a modern automobile should not be built in such a way that it will last for ten, fifteen, even twenty years. If it were properly made of high-quality materials, it would very seldom need to be repaired at all. And if it were designed appropriately, its equipment could be updated at intervals, if necessary, exactly as we update the equipment that we have in our own houses when technological developments make it desirable to do so."

JACQUES LARTIGUE

BEHIND THE WHEEL

"*I have had several men in my service for a number of years driving and looking after my horses, and I am altogether unwilling to turn them adrift and to engage mechanics in their place. . . . Can one's coachmen be trained to drive a motorcar?*"

LETTER TO **The Car** (1902)

Once upon a time, "motor driving" was a hobby, like playing tennis or croquet. People did not go out in a car because they looked on it as a means of transport; rather they said to each other: "Shall we go motoring this afternoon?", just as they might have said: "Shall we go sailing?"

Perhaps this was why the attitude towards the actual procedure of driving the car was, in a way, exceedingly casual. At first it was not taken particularly seriously—that is to say, it was somewhat like riding a bicycle: it was a pleasant and amusing thing to do once the knack of it had been acquired, but if it proved too difficult, well, one could always fall off and no great harm done. Or possibly the technique of driving a car was being assessed, as usual, by people who were more familiar with horses. If they equated the early motorcar with something on the lines of a mere governess-cart, as they may have done because of its appearance, they may well have concluded that the task demanded no special skill or aptitude. When the driver of a small one-horse carriage got into difficulties, nine times out of ten these could be overcome by simply leaving it to the horse to sort things out.

The horse, as Rudyard Kipling once pointed out, did much of the work his driver was paid to do—even to the extent of pulling a cart home when its driver was too drunk to care. The horseless carriage was not quite so accommodating. You did not steer it by offering occasional guidance to a docile animal out front; you steered it directly by turning the front wheels, and when you stopped steering, the thing was no longer under control. Admittedly this was also true of the bicycle (which you might have encountered a decade or so earlier), but there was one notable difference.

If, when riding a bicycle, you chose to adopt a policy of masterly inactivity, then by ceasing to pedal you deprived the machine of its motive force, so that eventually it stopped (that, of course, was when you fell off). This was not true of the motorcar. It kept on going. In fact it kept on going until you did the right thing to make it stop. At such a moment as this, the word "automobile" tended to acquire a whole new vista of meaning for the novice driver, who began to wish he had taken up fishing or making lamp shades.

One man who found himself in just such a situation was Harry Forster, later Lord Forster of Lepe and governor-general of Australia. He was a boyhood friend of John Montagu, and in 1890 the two men became brothers-in-law when he married John's only sister, Rachel.

Early in the new century, Harry decided to take up motoring and asked John, the expert, to order a car for him. Shortly thereafter, having just returned from a trip abroad, the couple called on Rachel's parents at Palace House, Beaulieu, the Montagu family home, and Harry was told that his new car, a de Dion Bouton, awaited him at John's house in the village. He hurried off to see it and, undeterred by the fact that he had never driven a car before, had the chauffeur start the engine for him.

Back at Palace House, Rachel and her parents saw through the library window that Harry was driving proudly by, smiling and waving to them. Minutes later they saw the de Dion pass by again, its driver still waving, but his expression now a trifle strained, they thought. The Montagus made their way outside just in time for Harry's third appearance, when he whizzed past the family shouting desperately: "I can't stop – I don't know how to stop it!"

The lady at the wheel of this handsome mid-1920s A.C. two-seater is dressed very much in the fashion of the times, and fur trimmings must have been welcome when most cars were still open.

Lady Montagu, however, knew exactly what to do. She rang for the butler and said: "Pleasant, go and stop that car at once." "Yes, m'lady," said Pleasant. When the de Dion appeared for the fourth time, he leapt nimbly aboard and brought it to a halt.

Harry Forster was lucky in that assistance was available, and Pleasant perhaps more versatile than most butlers of his day. Some novices found learning to drive a most harrowing affair, like a certain vicar, as related in *The Scarlet Tree* by Sir Osbert Sitwell:

"Shortly after, in 1906, poor Mr. Gramble, in order to cope with the parochial work deputed to him (he had obtained a curacy not far away), learnt to ride a bicycle. Alas, his experiment coincided in time—and, as it proved, in space—with one conducted by his vicar, who, also with an extension of activity in view, was learning to drive a motor. But the elder man had not yet mastered the machine, and one day, meeting Mr. Gramble on the drive, near the lych-gate, in an effort to put on the brakes, instead accelerated, and ran over and killed poor Mr. Gramble."

Many early motoring writers seemed to suffer from the delusion that they could teach people to drive by means of written instructions; also that once the handling of the controls had been understood, there was nothing more to learn. Mrs. Edward Kennard, writing in 1902 about "Motor Driving for Ladies," was one of the few exceptions:

"The increased interest displayed by the fashionable world undoubtedly is partly owing to its feminine members. Wives urge their husbands to buy a motorcar; daughters leave their fathers no peace until they promise to go in for one. Probably, the ladies possess vague enough notions anent motoring in general at

McCOMB COLLECTION

Here the ladies enjoy a drive in a 1922 six-cylinder Buick through the Hertfordshire lanes. Although a comparatively expensive car, the Buick was popular in Britain for many years.

the start, but they are convinced in their own minds that it is the 'right thing.' And when a woman forms that opinion, as in the case of cycling, an immense impetus is at once given to the movement. She coaxes, she reasons, she pleads, until she attains her end. In process of time the coveted car is purchased.

"But is she content at having achieved her wish? Oh dear no! Very soon she aspires to sit at the helm herself. She mostly imagines that the art of driving is quite easy, and can be acquired in a couple of hours. Her confidence in her own powers is unbounded. Only a few weeks ago I read a flourishing account in one of the motor journals written by a female novice, who triumphantly recorded how she had thoroughly mastered the first car she had attempted to drive in the short space of a single half-hour.

"I confess I entertained sentiments of the profoundest admiration for that lady, and looked enviously upon her as a phenomenon. But in face of such enthusiastic epistles, a word of caution may not be out of place, especially as they are apt to prove misleading in the extreme to less highly-endowed mortals. In my humble opinion, if ladies really wish to go in for motor-car driving, two essentials are indispensable. They must be patient and they must be humble. Because a person can steer a devious course on a wide highway she need not jump to the conclusion that she is an expert.

"A great many qualifications are required to make a really good driver, and it is not everybody who possesses them. Nerve, judgment, prompt decision and a cool head are all indispensable. They are gifts of nature, but their fortunate owner still wants practice and experience. An actor does not usually consider he knows his part merely because he can say his words off by rote. That is but the foundation, to which all the little refinements and delicate touches that give distinction to his performance are gradually added. So it is with motor driving. The rudiments count for nothing. Even when the novice has mastered the steering, and flatters herself she has attained to a wonderful pitch of perfection, she makes a great mistake. She does but stand at the outside portico of knowledge."

This was unusually sound advice in the early part of the century, when the typical article on driving consisted of a frequently tedious catalogue of levers and pedals, like a manufacturer's handbook. In writing of the Ohio-built Winton in its 1903 twin-cylinder form, for instance, Major-General Colville left no stone unturned:

"If the reader will place himself in imagination in the driving seat in rear of the steering wheel, he will find at his right hand, outside the car, a small brass lever which regulates the air valve, and immediately under the seat the ignition lever, the two-way switch and the silencer cut-out. To his right front are the two speed levers, the outer or right-hand one being for top speed, and, as will be explained later, for an emergency brake, and the inner or left-hand one for low speed and reverse. Under his right foot is the accelerator, and under his left the brake, while between the two, held by clips, is the starting handle, which when required is fitted into its place at the right-hand side of the car. In front of the dashboard, under the bonnet, are the petrol and oil tanks. The parts which I have mentioned are all that a passenger on the car would see, and (assuming that the concealed parts are in working order) all that he need concern himself with for the moment should he wish to take a place on the driving seat and see how he likes her. . . .

"As soon as the motor is started the spark is slightly advanced, and the driver can take his seat. As I have said before, under his right foot is the accelerator pedal and in front of his right hand the two speed levers. As he takes his seat he will hear a very low throbbing sound which tells him that the engine is just running. We will imagine him in a garage opening into a narrow street out of which he wishes to turn as slowly as possible. Placing his foot on the accelerator pedal he slightly depresses it, thus increasing the speed of the engine, and at the same time pulls the left-hand lever gently towards him till the car begins to move. Turning his steering wheel round to (say) the left, and playing with the lever so that the clutch only momentarily engages, he allows the car to creep on till the right front mudguard almost touches the opposite wall of the street or mews. If she has been going a little too fast a squeeze of the brake pedal with the left foot will bring her to a standstill, but if the driver has regulated his pace nicely he will only have to move his left lever gently through a vertical position, into an inclined one forward, and then, without any of the usual fumbling for clutches, or anything else (I speak for myself), the car glides backwards as smoothly as she advanced, and the next backward pull of the lever will probably take him into the main street, at about three miles per hour if the accelerator is not pressed."

The "air valve" referred to was a peculiarity of the Winton, in that the variable-lift inlet valve was provided with a compressed-air control. But the band-engaged gears were typical of early American practice. While a European car of the same period would be more likely to have sliding-gear transmission, it might or might not have an effective means of altering engine speed. There were still some very conservative designers who held to the view that a car engine should run at a fairly constant speed, the pace of the vehicle itself being altered by engaging different gears. It was a notion derived from workshop practice and wholly unsuited to a moving vehicle, but for some years it exerted a considerable effect on driving techniques, on what was written about them, and the terminology used. Major-General Colville said of the Winton that: "By keeping the spark lever moderately retarded and the accelerator free, the slowest omnibus or waggon can be followed with the high gear in, while if an opening presents itself in the traffic a touch of the accelerator pedal will shoot the car ahead like an arrow." But Mrs. Kennard, writing enthusiastically of the Napier, used the expression: "She answers to the change-speed lever as does a high-mettled hunter to a touch of the spur."

There is more here than a different taste in simile. Mrs. Kennard was following the older convention by which motorists did not talk of gears, but of speeds; she did not say "changing gear" but "changing speed," because that, in the earliest days of the constant-speed engine, is what they were doing. Of the 1905 Itala, F. R. S. Bircham noted that it was quite a good idea to change down to "third speed" when driving in traffic at about 9 mph, otherwise one would (in top gear) have to slip the clutch to prevent the engine stopping. And in a feature on starting and stopping technique published in *The Car* during 1902, this passage occurs:

"The practice of putting a sudden strain on the machinery when starting has deleterious effects upon the transmission gear, and possibly also, with an engine of great horse-power, on the tyres as well. In the case of a high-powered petrol engine it is advisable to start with the throttle slightly closed, in addition to letting your clutch grip gradually, as a more regular strain results in all the cylinders being put into operation at the same time, and a steady pull instead of a jerk is thus secured. In stopping, it should be remembered that the less the brakes are used the better, and that a good driver hardly ever uses his brakes really hard in an emergency. . . . It is not at all a bad plan to gradually stop your car when coming up to a door by means of the throttle, which, when the car has ceased to move, can then be adjusted so that the engine just runs and no more."

To the driver of today it seems nothing less than ludicrous that anybody should need to be *told* that he ought to change down in traffic, open the throttle and engage the clutch gently when starting from rest, and ease off the throttle in order to slow down. But at the time it was published—when some cars still had governed engines—it actually needed saying; it was not a statement of the perfectly obvious.

Again, one hesitates to think what an advanced driving instructor would say on reading the advice, published seventy-five years ago, on negotiating corners:

"So far as the latter are concerned, he has merely to reduce his speed to a degree sufficient to counteract the centrifugal force, so as to be able to steer round the corner without a wide outward sweep. To do this he has only to press down his clutch-pedal in advance—practice will soon tell him the right moment—and apply the foot brake slightly if he has taken out the clutch too late. Once round the corner he can remove his feet from the pedals, being particularly careful to let in the clutch as gradually as possible."

However extraordinary this seems today, it was the way many drivers had to go round a sharp corner when their cars had constant-speed, governed engines. Driving technique made little progress until engines became responsive and flexible enough to deliver their power over a wide range of rotational speeds. Until then, indeed, merely changing gear was a major achievement, and in 1903 Dr. Dawson Turner bluntly commented that he found it "difficult to understand how anyone can be found to prefer gearing (except for racing purposes) who has once made a fair trial of a good belt drive. The belt drive is noiseless and elastic, and a child can change the speeds."

The driver of an early motorcar was kept very fully occupied doing a great many things that are now done automatically, or that the modern driver performs with such consummate ease that he is barely aware of doing them at all. So far from resenting this, some people looked on it as an added attraction of the hobby. T. G. Chambers, writing in 1907 about the technique of driving the Electromobile, listed as one of its disadvantages the fact that the electric vehicle required virtually no attention:

"Apart altogether from its limitations of range and speed, it is certain that there is not much sport in driving an electric carriage. It is far too simple and too unexciting to be attractive. The fascination of the petrol engine to the man who is born with an engineering instinct is largely due to its imperfections and its eccentricities. In these respects, it possesses a soul that has much in common with the human, and one may safely prophesy that when the day arrives that every motor-car shall run with monotonous certainty, the main attraction of driving will have departed, and the amateur will turn his attention to balloons or airships,

The driver of a car like this 1903 Fiat did much more than merely steer it and work the pedals. He might have to pump oil to the engine at frequent intervals if the lubrication was not automatic, or pump air into the petrol tank to maintain the fuel supply.

seeking for further difficulties to overcome."

Some cars demanded more attention than others, of course, but in general it can be said that the driver was making frequent, almost continual, small adjustments to the mechanism all the time he motored along. There was, as already indicated, the problem of keeping the engine running as smoothly as possible despite frequent changes in load (due to changing gradient) and road speed (because of corners, other traffic, etc.), so there were controls for adjusting the engine speed in any one of half-a-dozen different ways, or even a combination of some of them: altering the ignition timing, the opening of the inlet or exhaust valve, the throttle opening or the mixture strength at the carburettor. Some cars had what was called a "surface carburettor," which was not much more than a container of petrol from the surface of which the vapour was collected, or a similar device incorporating a wick from which the petrol would evaporate. On rough roads the petrol was joggled about, and more vapour came off than on smooth roads. So the mixture strength varied with the road surface, and the driver making his way through city traffic, say, had to allow for the fact that his engine would respond one way on tarmac, another way on cobblestones.

There were the repeated gear changes, often calling for not one gear lever, but two, to be moved each time to engage the appropriate pinions—or, in the case of belt drive, to bring different-sized pulleys into operation. At intervals the driver would have to use a hand pump to keep up the fuel supply to the engine, if this was by air pressure in the tank and there was no automatic pump to maintain it. Sometimes the lubricating oil was delivered in the same way; sometimes, every few miles, it had to be pumped up from the supply tank and directed by means of a tap to the engine or transmission. When sight-feed lubricators were provided, these had to be watched to make sure they were passing oil through, and doing so at the correct number of drops per minute to each component served by them. If there was no coolant radiator (and often, in the case of the earliest cars, there was not), the water tank had to be checked at fairly frequent intervals and topped up as necessary.

Steam cars were in a class by themselves. It is a curious fact that the steam enthusiast of today, in his ardent championship of the cause, denies the very expertise that he possesses, insisting that any child could drive one. Certainly their controls were greatly simplified as time went by, and brought into line with the conventional layout adopted for petrol cars, but early steam cars, at least, were only at their best when driven by a trained engineer with a pocketful of spanners. J. Broughton Dugdale's instructions on driving the Franco-American Gardner-Serpollet run to 6½ pages of a 1903 publication, but a small excerpt gives some idea of the difficulties its driver had to take in his stride:

"Always have with you a stick with a small quantity of beeswax stuck into a cavity at the end. Occasionally, when driving, test the tightness of the [relief] valve by opening the testcock. If you think your pumps at any time are not throwing their proper quantity of water, and yet you can feel them distinctly beating when you grip the hand-pump handle, suspect the valve. If you find it is leaking, and thus you are by-passing a considerable quantity of the water which should be going to the boiler, and you cannot make the valve close tightly by lifting it several times and letting it fall suddenly, unscrew the plug on the top, pick out the ball

with the aid of the waxed stick, and with the reverse end of the same stick, slightly pointed, clean the seat of the valve in the steel plug. If the ball appears to be pitted or damaged replace it with a new one. This will probably remedy the defect, and will not cause a stop of more than a couple of minutes.

"It is well to know that by means of the relief valve you can form an opinion whether you have a good superheat or not. Thus, when running, lift the valve for a moment and close it again. If you have a good superheat your steam pressure will fall when the valve is open, and will rise rapidly again on closing it. If you have but a poor superheat, and, consequently, too much water in the boiler—in other words, if your boiler is becoming what is known as drowned—the changes of pressure on lifting and closing the valve will take place slowly. Another trick worth knowing, when driving up a very long hill (an occasion on which one is very liable to draw on the stored heat of the boiler and so gradually cool it down), is to alter the relative proportions of oil and water fed to the boiler by occasionally, say two or three times a minute, for the space of two or three seconds only at a time, lifting the relief valve and so by-passing a certain quantity of the water which would otherwise pass to the boiler. Thus the boiler will have an excess of fuel supplied to it above the proportion of water."

The controls of many vehicles called for the paradoxical combination of strength and a delicate touch. The steering of most early motorcars was heavy, and to ease the effort involved, steering wheels grew large in diameter over a period of decades. But before that, and especially on solid-tyred wheels, it was a matter of hanging on grimly to a twitching wheel or tiller and remaining continually alert to prevent it being snatched from one's grasp altogether, possibly with disastrous results. Braking, too, was a manoeuvre demanding care. Usually there were two systems, and on a long downgrade the careful driver used them alternately—first one, then the other—to make sure that neither would overheat and become useless.

Nothing was more unwise than merely "slamming on the brakes"—partly because the result might well be to spin the car around if the brakes worked on the rear wheels only, but also to avoid applying undue strain to the wheels and tyres. Lord Brabazon of Tara was only a schoolboy when he witnessed the effect of such an action, as told in his autobiography, *The Brabazon Story*: "I saw my first accident at Harrow. I was coming back from the station after a visit to my parents when to my joy I saw a motor wagonette coming down Grove Hill. The driver, one Sewell, put his brakes on too quickly and the spokes ripped out of the wheels and the car capsized, right beside me, killing the driver and knocking the four other occupants about very badly."

Not all the problems that a driver faced were mechanical, as Lord Brabazon also recalled. His father shared the dislike and disapproval that most of his generation felt for motorcars, but one day, at the age of 80, he overcame them sufficiently to ask his son to drive him to Bushey Park, on the outskirts of London. Brabazon was naturally anxious to please his father (the age differential was enormous, he being only 20 at the time), but circumstances dictated otherwise:

"This was a tremendous honour. I had the loan of a 14 hp Renault two-seater. We were living in Cranley Gardens at the time, and off we went down the Fulham Road. We hadn't gone a quarter of a mile when a hansom cab pulled across the road from behind a bus which was overtaking something, straight across my path, to go down a side turning. With an adroitness which I still admire I swerved, crouched under the horse's head as it loomed above me, drove between a lamp-post and the railings of a house, and eventually got back on the road again. An interval of five minutes passed during which we drove on. Then my father turned to me and said: 'Ivon, will there be many incidents like that? Frankly, I find them very alarming.' "

That was in 1904. It was to be some time before horses came to accept the motorcar, and accounts of early motoring are filled with stories of encounters between motorists and horsemen, some of them revealing little consideration on either side. It was a serious matter, for of course there were horses everywhere, and they could well become terrified when such a strange, noisy, evil-smelling device appeared in their path. They still can, as anyone who drives an early car in country districts will soon find out for himself, and it is a moot point who finds such an encounter more alarming: the driver who is trying to manoeuvre his chuntering, fuming vehicle as unobtrusively as possible past this large, wild-eyed and trembling animal, or the rider who is doing what he can to control and soothe his mount. Relations between the two were not helped by some motorists who would dash by without slackening speed, or some horsemen who expressed their opinion of motorists by lashing out with a well-aimed whip.

So the motorist, while having to "play" the mechanism of his vehicle like a theatre organ with all its knobs and pedals, was at the same time guiding it through a hostile world filled

*Taking the bull by the horns, so to speak, a lady
owner of 1904 makes quite sure her carriage
horses grow accustomed to the sight and sound
of her new Panhard.*

RADIO TIMES HULTON PICTURE LIBRARY

JACQUES LARTIGUE

LONDON TRANSPORT EXECUTIVE

Animals were among the commonest hazards the early motorist had to deal with, and might be encountered anywhere—from cows in the depths of the European countryside to a flock of sheep in the very middle of London.

with unpredictable hazards. It was only during the earliest days that his passage aroused such ungovernable fury in his fellow humans as to make them throw stones at him, but he had still to contend with many another danger. If we may accept the views voiced in 1907 by W. Poynter Adams, even the humble cyclist was one of them:

"It is a curious physiological fact, and one ever to be remembered by a motor-car driver, that to novices and those who have not acquired confidence in cycle riding, the approach of a large, rapidly moving vehicle actually induces a feeling of attraction and a desire to fall off the machine in front of the approaching monster; of course, such nervous people should not ride on roads where motor-cars are likely to be met with, but then, unfortunately, motor-cars do not confine their attention to specified roads, and are quite as likely to be met in country lanes as on the high roads."

The alternative solution—that any cyclist afflicted with such a moth-and-candle compulsion would be well advised to sell his bicycle and stay at home—apparently did not suggest itself to Mr. Poynter Adams.

One way and another, boredom was not really a problem that troubled the early motorist, and he certainly enjoyed the actual operation of driving, despite its difficulties. Yet many of those who could afford to do so (and most of them could) also employed a chauffeur, or at the least a "man" who accompanied them on journeys to do the donkey work of starting the engine, mending punctured tyres, and cleaning the car down when the day's trip had ended. Without their help few women would have been able to take up motoring as early as they did, when much of the work was physically beyond them. An article in *Veteran and Vintage*

Magazine records that although the late Duchess of Bedford was a most enthusiastic driver, using two Rolls-Royces—a 1913 landaulette for weekdays and a 1920 model for Sundays, nevertheless "the Duchess always had three chauffeurs at her disposal, plus an extra one to look after her two aeroplanes." This was unlikely to inconvenience the eleventh Duke because her requirements accounted for less than a quarter of his motoring staff: he had sixteen chauffeurs altogether, working under the direction of a "motor superintendent":

"He was in charge of cars and men alike, acting as intermediary between them and the Duke. If His Grace wished to reprimand a chauffeur, the rebuke would be entrusted to the superintendent. Also on the staff was a foreman who looked after the workshop where the cars were serviced and repaired. Single chauffeurs 'lived in,' and did their own catering; married men lived in rent-free cottages. Of course, if a single man wanted to marry in service, the Duke's permission had to be obtained.

"Duties were on a rota system. Normal hours were 8 am to 6 pm on weekdays, 8 am to 1 pm on Saturdays, and Sundays free. We were organised into squads of four, and every third day we worked a 24-hour shift. On these occasions we slept at the Abbey, and were available to serve as firemen should the need arise."

The writer of the article, a former chauffeur of the Duke, remembered his employer's Rolls-Royces (there were four of them) as fairly easy to handle, but the early Napiers were another matter:

"Even with the aid of a half-compression lever it was well-nigh impossible to swing the big Napiers. . . . Pistons were about the size of a tea-plate. The wood-rimmed steering wheels had a diameter only slightly greater, and the

AUTOCAR
RADIO TIMES HULTON PICTURE LIBRARY

In the days when a certain class of car owner always employed a chauffeur, the vehicle he owned was equipped accordingly. This 1927 Jarvis-bodied Buick, intended for the British market, has a stout partition between front seats and rear, so the interior fittings include a speaking tube for giving instructions to the driver.

effort required for clutch and footbrake was nothing short of Herculean. The engines were a mass of copper pipes and polished aluminium —even the make-and-break cover of the magneto was polished brass. A trembler coil was provided as a standby for starting only. Footboards were covered in aluminium edged with brass, while the dashboards were solid aluminium. What with such items as radiators, lamps, door handles, bonnet hinges and hub caps, no wonder lashings of Brasso was needed to keep everything smart.''

The fleet of cars—twenty altogether—had to be maintained in perfect order, but they were actually used very little, so the unfortunate chauffeurs spent most of their time either cleaning and polishing, or merely hanging about waiting for orders:

"The longest road journey the Duke ever made was from Exeter station to his estate near Tavistock, a matter of 44 miles. He travelled by train from Bletchley to Exeter [about 170 miles], but two cars (his Rolls-Royce and a 1910 60 hp Napier) had to be driven down from Woburn the day before. . . . On arrival at Exeter, the chauffeur in charge had to send a telegram to Woburn to advise that the cars had made it safely.

"On his rare visits to London he was driven to Hendon [7 miles out], where he changed cars. Two vehicles (a Wolseley and a Cadillac) were kept at his town house in Belgrave Square, with two chauffeurs, an arrangement adopted because it was felt that the country chauffeurs were not competent to drive in town. The country crew had to garage their car at the Hendon Central Garage, and were given the cryptic instruction, 'Wait'; if the Duke intended to stay in London overnight he would order the car back to Woburn. The standard reply was a smart salute and a 'Very good, Your Grace.' ''

Though undoubtedly a martinet, the Duke was remembered by his former chauffeur as "a good employer who looked after his staff well.'' Some of the cars, maintained and driven with such care, lasted an incredible thirty years and more, so that several of the oldest were still in regular use when World War II broke out in 1939. A year later the eleventh Duke of Bedford died, the chauffeurs were dismissed, and every car—apart from one almost-new Rolls-Royce— was sold to a scrap dealer. His unique motoring establishment was no more.

A good chauffeur, like a good butler, was greatly valued, and in the late 1920s a first-class man could command as much as £5 a week— more than twice the wages of a factory worker, and about as much as a housemaid earned in four to six months. A contemporary motoring guide urges employers to treat their men with consideration, reminding them that ''A driver who is 'fussed' during driving cannot drive safely or well,'' and that time must be allowed for washing, maintenance and leisure: ''When the car is out until two or three o'clock in the morning, a clean car and wakeful chauffeur cannot be expected at nine o'clock.'' The same publication summarizes relevant provisions of English law, one of which was that if the driver should have a fatal accident in the course of his employment, his employer was required to compensate his dependent relatives (including illegitimate children).

Tuition in driving was an obvious carrot to dangle before the potential customer in earlier days, as soon as those who sold motorcars began vying with each other for business. The new car would be delivered to a country buyer, say, by a chauffeur/salesman who worked for the manufacturer, concessionaire or dealer.

An English dealer offers a right-hand-drive Ford Model T for £115, a pair of number plates for five shillings (£0.25), a tin of petrol for a shilling (£0.05), a gallon of oil for one-and-ninepence (less than £0.09), and throws in a two-hour driving lesson for another five shillings! These prices would be twenty to thirty times as high nowadays.

This individual would remain in the neighbourhood for a short time to initiate the new owner and his "man," if any, into the mysteries of driving and maintenance. As Hugh Tracey tells us in *Father's First Car*, this is what the London concessionaires did in 1907 when Dr. Tracey of Devonshire bought a 10/12 hp Peugeot. A letter to the doctor's wife (who was visiting friends at the time) reveals that car salesmen have changed remarkably little in seventy years:

"I believe I have the right chauffeur in the house at the present moment, a young fellow called Brane. He is very smart and most intelligent. I am sure we couldn't have a better coach. . . . Brane says he knows no small car like this for magnificent workmanship, everything is solid, genuine and of the very best. He does not see why we should ever have a breakdown, but advises that once in 8 or 9 months it should be overhauled so that if any pins or other gear are wearing or working loose they may be replaced. He says the corresponding English cars, Swift, Singer, etc., are all built quite flimsily in comparison with ours, all for show and great speed, and they all constantly break down. He says he has taken out several of these Peugeot cars now to purchasers and they have every one of them proved big successes."

The smooth-talking chauffeur's course of instruction lasted only four days, at the end of which, says Hugh Tracey: "Brane, the perfect driver, with a golden sovereign in his pocket, took the car back to Bridgwater. . . . He took with him Gunner, the coachman, to be transmogrified within three short days into motor mechanic and chauffeur." The disasters and vicissitudes that followed, as poor Gunner cannoned off dogs, cows and gateposts in the inter-

vals of trying to mend the Peugeot or keep it running, make stirring reading indeed.

One year after Dr. Tracey's purchase another doctor's son, Stanley Roberts of London, was approached by a coachman who feared dismissal—like many of his kind—because his master was going in for motorcars. He would gladly pay, he said, to be taught how to handle one of the new breed of vehicles. So young Roberts, then only 19, gave him lessons, and two years later established in his father's garage what was to become, in less than a decade, the world's biggest motoring school. At the outbreak of World War I in 1914 the British Army owned not one single motor vehicle of any kind—not so much as a motorcycle. They had to requisition cars and lorries wherever they could, and in desperation they turned to Roberts' still-young British School of Motoring so that soldiers could be turned into drivers—which they were, in two weeks, at 5½ guineas a time.

The commonest way of learning, though, was by means of practice with the help of a friend or a local garageman, and this was ideal if the instructor knew what he was about, like Bellamy Partridge's Tom Hunter:

"I had changed my mind about driving to the office that morning and had decided that it might be the better part of valour to take a cranking and driving lesson from Tom before trusting myself out on the road. As it turned out, it is just as well that I did, for I found that there were a number of starting precautions that I had forgotten.

"Tom insisted that I must go through the motions several times, and then, just to be on the safe side, he wrote out a list and tacked it on the wall of the shed. He also insisted that I should be the one to handle the crank, saying that the only way to get over being afraid of it was to get used to it. He had me start the engine and stop it at least half-a-dozen times before we backed out of the shed—and he made me do the backing. As soon as we were on the road I headed for the country, intending to keep to the byways where few conveyances were likely to be met. But Tom vetoed the plan and kept me on the main-traveled roads. His idea was that I might just as well get used to meeting teams, since I was going to meet plenty of them every time I went out in the car.''

During the 1920s one of the most exclusive of all driving schools was formed—the Rolls-Royce Chauffeurs' School. Originally set up at the Company's Derbyshire factory, it is still in existence today as part of a larger establishment at the main London service depot with, nowadays, courses for dealers' service staff and lorry drivers. Pupils are accepted only after three years or 30,000 miles with the same employer, and with a letter of recommendation. When the chauffeur has successfully completed a two-week course, a Rolls-Royce representative carefully checks over the car that he maintains and drives. If the inspection is satisfactory, there follows the ceremonial presentation of a silver Rolls-Royce cap badge—the ultimate symbol of success in the world of the professional driver.

Officialdom's interest in the motorist, once his presence had been accepted rather grudgingly by the governments of one country after another, was largely confined to extracting money from him and ensuring that he, or at the least his car, was identifiable. Whilst a licence to drive was usually required, and a fee was charged for its issue, very few authorities cared anything about his *competence* to drive.

In Britain, for instance, the main provision of the 1903 Motor Car Act was that the vehicle should be registered (a registration fee being charged, of course) and carry number plates so that if its owner committed an offence he could be traced and suitably punished. It also required that the vehicle should be licensed annually, on payment of a separate and additional fee. On top of that, it demanded that motorists should obtain an annual driving licence (on payment of yet another fee) from their local county council. John Montagu played a prominent role in shepherding the bill through, being one of the handful of Members of Parliament who actually knew anything about the subject under discussion. He considered it essential for road safety, as well as being altogether more equitable, that licences should be issued only to those whose ability to drive had first been tested and proved satisfactory.

However, the final debate in the House of Commons opened on August 11, the day before the opening of the grouse-shooting season, and it soon became clear that neither safety nor fairness would be given any consideration if they seemed likely to delay the passage of the bill. The whole question of driving tests was swept smartly under the mat, and the debate ended at 2 am. For thirty-two years the British resident who wanted a driving licence had only to pay five shillings (£0.25) to his local county council, and that was that. So long as the fee was paid, nobody seemed to mind in the least if the applicant was utterly incapable of driving. Indeed, *Autocar*, the leading British motoring magazine, once tried to shame the authorities into changing the regulations by successfully obtaining a driving licence for a blind beggar.

The French, on the other hand, having taken the lead in the development of motoring, also appreciated that the motorist's driving ability was not something that should be taken for granted. This meant that visitors from countries such as England were required to undergo a driving test when they landed in France if they wanted to use their cars there, even if they were on holiday. After World War I, however, it was arranged that the leading motoring organizations of other countries (in Britain it was the Royal Automobile Club) could carry out driving tests without reference to any government department and issue recognized certificates of competence for use wherever they were needed. But within the British Isles the situation remained anomalous even after driving tests began in 1935. Tests were compulsory in England, Scotland and Wales, but not in Ireland, north or south, until the middle 1950s.

In America, too, the situation was confusing because in this case—as in many others—the regulations varied enormously from state to state, and even within some of them. Some places demanded a written examination and a medical test before issuing a driving licence, as described in an article that appeared in the women's page of *The Car* in 1902:

"In Chicago, where a public examination and a licence are required of automobile drivers, most women who come to take the examination are accompanied by male escorts. The applicant for a licence goes first to the Health Department, where the health test is imposed. This examination is to determine chiefly whether the applicant has a weak heart, and whether she may be colour blind. Colour blindness may be a most serious defect after dark, when a swung bridge showing a red light might be mistaken for the green safety light and bring disaster. As for a weak heart, every automobile driver can testify as to the shock that may come to the most unsuspecting and iron-nerved of men who drive these machines through the crush and jam of down-town. The disposition of women in an emergency to faint and let a machine run where it will is one of the serious aspects of a weak heart, and this in women has made the heart test of first importance.

"When a woman has passed the Health Department's test she appears at the office of the City Electrician at the appointed hour to take the mechanical examination. In such case she gives in the type of automobile which she is to run, whether it is to be steam, gasoline or electrical. Perhaps she may take the examination for all classes of machines, but it will be required of her that she name the kind of machine that she is to run and a licence will be issued for that kind of machine only. If for any reason she chooses to change to any other style of automobile she may have another licence on application, at which time she will surrender the old one.

"Of the 35 women who hold automobile licences in Chicago, about half are single women and almost without exception all are young. The majority of these conduct electric and steam vehicles. In New York, however, a strong tendency has been indicated of late towards the gasoline machine. The Oldsmobile is frequently seen driven by women, the Packard counts more than one devoted *chauffeuse* among its admirers, and recently the large imported French machines have found a genial reception after it was realised that their snorting sounds at low speed are no indication of ferocity."

But Bellamy Partridge, in *Excuse My Dust*, presents a different picture when writing of New York State only a few years later; probably about 1906, for the car in question is a second-hand twin-cylinder Rambler:

"We parked the car in front of our house, and as Tom was leaving to go over to Mrs. Bannister's he reminded me to write to the Secretary of State in Albany and send two dollars as a licence fee. 'Will they send me a number?' I asked, anxious to have something to hang on my new motor vehicle. 'They'll send you a little brass seal like a dog tax number, but you'll have to get your own tag to hang on the back of the machine.' 'Anything else?' Tom smiled. 'Well, there's an operator's licence, but that doesn't cost anything and they'll send it to you without your even asking for it.' "

A 1909 document issued by the state of Ohio was called a "Chauffeur's Certificate of Registration," and specified the type of vehicle the holder was permitted to operate. A nation-wide survey carried out that same year quoted New York as one of the few eastern states that did not require all operators to be licensed; in common with Ohio, Illinois and California it merely called for chauffeurs to be licensed—but the distinction between "operator" and "chauffeur" in this context is by no means clear. So far as most other states were concerned, there was either no licensing requirement included in the motoring laws, or there were no motoring laws at all. Some states applied their regulations to the vehicle, some to the driver, and some to both. Occasionally a town or city would produce regulations of its own in addition to those of the state, which sometimes resulted in the motorist having to drape several different plates on his vehicle. But whereas British regulations demanded number plates to be fitted front and rear, in America the plate was normally required only at the rear.

One aspect of driving we have barely touched on is performance at the advanced level—whether it be the skilled handling of a "vintage" sports car, a masterly passage through teeming metropolitan traffic, a fast cross-country journey in difficult conditions, or any other manifestation of the art. It is a subject that is, perhaps, best avoided. It arouses widely divergent reactions, some of them curiously violent. At one end of the scale stand the people who will admire such a demonstration unreservedly, feeling no urge to emulate what they know to be beyond the limits of their own ability. At the other, there are those who will condemn it out of hand as a menace to mankind, and hurl abuse at anyone who dares suggest that some people can and do drive better than others. There is a vast gulf between the two extremes of view, far too wide to be bridged in any way. The protagonists cannot communicate with each other, for they have no common language.

Not only is the reaction a highly individual one—it can also be unexpected, and one cannot always predict who is most likely to understand the nature of virtuosity behind the wheel. This is what the Anglo-Irish author Joyce Cary wrote concerning a display of driving he experienced at first hand during a visit to the United States in 1951:

"Four businessmen and myself, all with urgent affairs in Plattsburg, proposed to hire a car. We phoned to various numbers, but had refusals everywhere—the weather was too bad that afternoon to risk a car along the lake road [from Burlington, Vermont, around Lake Champlain]. At last we went out in a body to try persuasion at the garages. The first refused flat. At the second, where we caught the foreman in the doorway staring at the snow and surround-

DETROIT PUBLIC LIBRARY

ed him, we had at first the same head-shake. But when we pressed him, saying how important it was for us to get to Plattsburg before the roads were blocked with drifts, he said that he would go and ask his boss.

"This depressed us very much, for we recognized a formula for getting rid of our importunity. But after five minutes the boss himself appeared, a large and prosperous-looking man who would have passed anywhere for the President of a Wall Street bank, and said that he would take us himself. He then put on his sober Bank President's overcoat and hat, lit a cigar, and brought us out a car. This was the beginning of an experience that I would not have missed for anything in the world. What is more enchanting than the highest skill combined with perfect nerves? The boss was a master at this sort of winter driving. And he needed to be. No chains would hold on that road which was solid hard ice, ice which was full of ruts and large smooth bumps on which the car skated this way and that, sideways and even backwards. In enormous slides. And all the way the storm was beating, or rather exploding, against the wind screen, so fast that the wipers could not clear it before it was again blurred. . . . But the driver, sitting upright and intent, never made a mistake. He seemed to know by instinct just how much to accelerate when we slithered, and where. I have never forgotten those skids. They were the largest, the most cockeyed, and strangely, the most deliberate, that I have ever felt. . . .

"Our average speed throughout was under fifteen miles an hour; we were more than six hours on the road and arrived long after dark. The driver's concentrated attention did not falter throughout, but the only mark of tension I saw in him was his absolute immobility as he sat straight up holding the wheel, and his smoking—he smoked cigars the whole way without pause. The price for this unforgettable affair, to me, was five dollars."

Malcolm Foster, who quoted this passage in his biography of Joyce Cary, commented that the writer "enjoyed the trip as he always enjoyed danger. Danger made him feel wholly alive and pushed all his senses to their extremes. And he always enjoyed seeing someone do anything really well, utilizing skill and concentration and achieving success with what seemed absolute ease. He hated the slipshod, the unprofessional, the indifferent. . . ."

PUNCH

ECCENTRIC DRESS

"*This very morning . . . another new and exceptionally powerful motorcar will arrive at Toad Hall on approval or return. At this very moment, perhaps, Toad is busily arraying himself in those singularly hideous habiliments so dear to him, which transform him from a (comparatively) good-looking Toad into an Object which throws any decent animal that comes across it into a violent fit.*"

KENNETH GRAHAME,
The Wind in the Willows (1908)

Aman who goes for a walk in the rain wears a mackintosh if he wants to avoid getting wet. By the same elementary reasoning, a horseman or coachman donned protective clothing of one kind or another for travelling in weather that was wet or cold. The discomfort and inconvenience of a winter journey had to be accepted; there was, after all, no alternative—except to stay at home. In recent times we have even managed to romanticize the situation, and at Christmas the shops sell colourful pictures of bluff Dickensian characters, their ruddy faces beaming above mountains of capes, greatcoats and scarves as their coaches bowl merrily along through the snow-covered landscape.

The real thing was somewhat less romantic, of course. In the winter of 1812, the year that Charles Dickens was born, the Bath coach arrived at Chippenham one morning after travelling all night from London, a distance of ninety-four miles. At the staging inn one of the outside passengers was observed to be unconscious from the cold. Closer inspection revealed that two of the others were actually dead.

So nobody thought it peculiar that an early motorcar protected its occupants up to the middle of their shins—no more. If horse-drawn carriages were built that way, why not horseless carriages? What designers quite failed to appreciate—because it was something entirely new, as surely as if they had landed on the surface of another planet—was the effect of travelling through the air at two or three times the speed of a horse-drawn vehicle. In cold weather the wind seemed to cut straight through the heavy box-cloth coats and woollen mufflers that had sufficed in the days of the horse, but in good weather the sensation was so novel, and so exhilarating, that it is remarked on again and again in the writings of the period. It is doubtful,

though, if anyone will ever equal Sir Osbert Sitwell's description of the experience as he recalled it in his autobiography, *Left Hand, Right Hand*:

"They would sit together, the two of them, the man at the wheel, the girl beside him, their hair blown back from their temples, their features sculptured by the wind, their bodies and limbs shaped and carved by it continually under their clothes, so that they enjoyed a new physical sensation, comparable to swimming; except that here the element was speed, not water. The winds—and their bodies—were warm that summer. During these drives, they acquired a whole range of physical consciousness, the knowledge of scents, passing one into another with an undreamt-of rapidity, the fragrance of the countless flowers of the lime trees, hung like bells on pagodas for the breeze to shake, changing into that of sweetbriar, the scent of the early mornings, and of their darkness, of hills and valleys outlined and tinged by memory; there was the awareness of speed itself, and the rapid thinking that must accompany it, a new alertness, and the typical effects, the sense, it might be, of the racing of every machine as dusk approaches, or the sudden access on a hot evening of cool waves of air under tall trees; —all these physical impressions, so small in themselves, went to form a sum of feeling new in its kind and never before experienced. Even the wind of the winter, at this pace snatching tears from their eyes, and piercing through layers of clothes, was something their fathers had not known."

Elsewhere and less poetically, the use of goggles was strongly advised to prevent possible eye trouble developing from the cold wind, dust or flies—even, perhaps, small pieces of flint thrown up by an unguarded tyre—and ladies were recommended to wear a mask to protect the complexion; a healthy tan or glowing skin was not at all fashionable in the early twentieth century. John Montagu was one of several pioneer motorists who considered goggles preferable to windscreens, because "on cars capable of any speed it is far better to enable the human body to withstand the vagaries of climate than to indulge in glass frames fixed on the car itself, which always tend to work loose and rattle, and may in the case of accident be the means of cutting your face with broken glass." The possibility of appalling injury was a very real one, for windscreens were made of thick plate glass. Safety glass was not invented until 1905 and did not come into general use for a further decade, at least.

Then again, the front splashboard or "dashboard" of the car was so low—below knee height, as already mentioned—that a windscreen had to be of positively enormous proportions if it was to serve any useful purpose; as much as five feet wide and maybe three feet or four feet high in many cases. So it was immensely heavy, very difficult to keep secure and free from rattles in its wooden frame, and to force this huge, vertical sheet of glass through the air had a ruinous effect on speed and fuel consumption. Given a stiff headwind and a fair gradient, a large windscreen would bring many an underpowered car to a standstill. Consequently, it was usually omitted— even, indeed, when the car had been fitted with a towering "Cape cart hood" to protect the occupants from rain, and the effectiveness of the hood was minimal at anything above a walking pace.

Some shared the sentiments of Mrs. Edward Kennard, who in 1905 wrote: "One hunts in cold, damp weather, and when it is dry and hot

McCOMB COLLECTION

Weather protection was nil on early racing cars like this 1903 Star. Joseph Lisle, the son of its designer, wears a full-length rubber poncho, gloves, boots, goggles, and a cap with peak at the back.

The menfolk of this 1902 motoring party at Beaulieu wear heavy overcoats and, without exception, the yachting cap favoured by almost every motorist at that time. The deerstalker now popular with old-car enthusiasts may keep the ears warm, but it was very seldom worn by early motorists. The car is a British-built Brush, much rarer than the American vehicle of the same name.

one motors. To each its appropriate time." Others were prepared to go motoring whatever the weather, so they were compelled to amass an extensive (and expensive) wardrobe for the purpose, and the motoring publications were filled with advice on clothes.

Harry Lawson, whose schemes for the promotion of the infant British motor industry eventually landed him behind bars, was one of the earliest leaders of motoring fashion. He devised a costume complete with yachting cap for members of the Motor Car Club (which he founded), and wore it on the original London to Brighton Run (which he organized) of 1896. According to one reporter, he looked like a Swiss admiral. However, the headgear survived as the chauffeur's cap of later days, and his taste in caps was followed by more illustrious persons, as recorded in *The Car* of June 4, 1902:

"*What the King Wears*: For motoring His Majesty is usually garbed in dark blue with a yachting cap built for him by Morgan. He wore a similar suit when motoring lately in the Isle of Wight and through the New Forest. To wrap around him, for on that day although the sun was warm the air was rather keen, the King had a neat rug of dark blue cloth lined with check, and by the way this is another hint, always provide two rugs for the chauffeur and one sitting by his side. This gives sufficient length to wrap the rug securely around each person and prevents any accident which might be brought about by the material hanging over the side and interfering with the wheels."

That no less a person than Edward VII should go motoring was of the greatest importance to the movement in England, where so many people detested the motorcar and everything to do with it. Unfortunately they included some of the most influential men in the country, from those who made the laws down to those who administered them, and as many a hapless motorist discovered when heavily fined for some alleged offence—sometimes blatantly trumped up on false evidence—they readily gave vent to their prejudice. Nobody had a clearer understanding of this than John Montagu, a Member of Parliament and representative of one of the most respected families in England, when he chose to lend his active support to the cause, for as he wrote in later years, "many persons would hardly speak to a well-known motorist like myself. Indeed, I was considered by some of my own relations to be a dangerous revolutionary."

In April 1902, the year of his coronation, Edward VII interrupted a yachting holiday to come ashore at Buckler's Hard, near Beaulieu, and go for a drive with John Montagu. This was not his first drive with his host—he had been driven by John Montagu three years before, also in the New Forest—but it was his first as the reigning monarch of England. It was important, then, that this occasion should be very fully recorded, and John Montagu made sure of doing so in the weekly motoring magazine he had just founded. As editor, he planned the contents of *The Car* astutely so that it would be read with interest in what his advertisement manager referred to as "the best houses in the land." There were well-illustrated features about the landed gentry, their mansions, their estates, their motorcars—and, of course, the clothes that they wore when they were motoring. The condemnation of motoring apparel that Kenneth Grahame later put into the mouth of Mr. Badger in *The Wind in the Willows* may be petty, but it is a good indication of the way many people felt about cars for many years,

JOCASTA (WITH AN AXE OF HER OWN TO GRIND,
INGRATIATINGLY)—*"Oh yes, papa, it does suit you.
I never saw you look so nice in anything before!"*

and John Montagu recognized this prejudice as one of several that had to be opposed. In *The Car* it was frequently emphasized that the fashionable motorist, at least when in London, had no need to affect peculiar garb. J. E. Hutton, the young motoring enthusiast who was to make a name for himself by racing Mercédès cars, made just such a plea in one of the earliest issues:

"It must have been a great source of wonder to many why some people who own motorcars should think it necessary to endeavour to make themselves as conspicuous as possible by means of their eccentric dress and appearance.

"I have often noticed when discussing cars with strangers, especially ladies, that the first question is 'Oh, do you dress up in india-rubber suits and masks?', and then they usually conclude with such a withering oration upon the appearance of motorists in general, and oneself in particular, that one is constrained to change the subject. I am quite aware that for touring purposes, and long runs in fast cars in bad weather, something like leather is the only material that will keep driving rain out, while if you are following other cars in a race or driving through paths in the country, goggles are a necessity to keep dust and flies from the eyes, but I cannot see the necessity of making oneself appear ridiculous in the streets of London, where the very people we wish to convert to automobilism will observe us in garments that are only fit to explore the sewers in.

"We want Society to take up motoring, then trouble will automatically cease with the country magistrates, but Society will not sacrifice its appearance of smartness for any novelty, however fascinating it may be, and if Society thinks that to motor and to look like a coal-heaver or burglar are identical, Society will not take it up —and then goodbye to further hopes of liberty. Eccentric clothes and goggles are quite unnecessary in ordinary circumstances, in ordinary practice, and are only required under very exceptional circumstances."

There were fashion articles contributed at different times by John Montagu's first wife, the former Lady Cecil Kerr, by Lady Olga Montagu, and by Lady Troubridge, the famous writer on etiquette. In the first issue of *The Car* Muriel Beaumont, later Lady du Maurier, modelled "a new motor hat with removable hood," and subsequently the Hon. Florence Amherst was commissioned to design a special motor cap for the ladies, which could be bought from leading milliners. It was obvious that some of the contributors revelled in such opportunities to discuss all manner of new clothes, and displayed a truly feminine delight in doing so:

"And now listen to the description of some absolutely irresistible creations from Jay's in the line of coats and muffs suitable for motoring, and do not look at the bright sunshine of June and wonder when I break to you gently that they are mostly of fur. Remember, as I said before, that when rushing through the air at well beyond say what pace, out of deference to the law, nearly all thin wraps afford no protection whatever and nothing but cloth, serge or fur seems really comfortable. I was first shown a coat of silver baboon, a very rare skin from the west coast of Africa. So rare indeed is it that, although this one is obtainable for the modest sum of £11, it would be a matter of some difficulty for the firm to obtain another to order. The collar and reveres are made of lynx, a fur which is more becoming near the face. This is a coat which could be worn for ordinary carriage driving as well as motoring, and there are very

EXPECTATION —*The Browns welcoming the Robinsons (awfully jolly people, don't you know), from whom they have had a letter saying that they will arrive early in the day by motor.*

REALISATION—*The Browns, when the arrivals have removed their motor glasses, etc., disclosing not the Robinsons, but those awful bores, the Smiths.*

Examples of motoring wear from Harrod's catalogue of 1904

few days in chilly England when a light wrap of this kind is not enjoyable.

"A fetching long coat of wild catskin was being made for Lady Algernon Gordon-Lennox. It was adorned with a large collar of raccoon cloth. Yet another useful coat of grey cloth had a roll collar of astrakhan to match. But this is not all, and as I know you like an infinite variety of choice let me tell you of a costume of Russian coltskin which I saw made in the evergreen blouse, bodice and skirt style, the latter being completed round the feet with leather to match the shade of the costume. This trimming was also repeated on the bolero, and on the small cape which formed a part of the collar. The sleeves were slightly fulled into bands round the wrist, and the whole effect was indescribably smart and unique.

"As for headgear, here are two pretty toques of Jay's, both eminently suitable for summer motoring, being both practical and becoming, a combination only too seldom found in motor headgear. One, which is most serviceable for country wear, is entirely composed of straw, soft, crumpled black straw below and burnt straw above, and has two smart quills of the same ornamented with steel buttons. The other, which is perhaps more suitable for town wear, is a coarse straw, sailor shape, bound with black velvet and made very becoming by the decoration on one side of a closely arranged bird and twists of blue soft silk ribbon."

For the male motorist, of course, there were no such delights as hats of burnt or crumpled straw, with or without closely arranged birds; he was expected to stick to his yachting caps. And the very columnist who waxed ecstatic over silver baboon and wild catskin answered a reader's letter thus:

"BELGRAVE."

Two views of a **New Serviceable Coat** for Motoring and Driving.

	Full Length.	Three-quarter Length.
Full length—In Heptonette Mixtures	59/6	49/6
,, ,, Alpaca, White, Black, Navy	69 6	59/6
,, ,, Silk Gloria, Showerproof	79/6	69/6
,, ,, Silk Mackintosh	£5 15 6	£5 5 0

PIPINGS, SELF OR CONTRASTING SHADES.

"*Coats for Automobilists*: The coat you tell me your husband has ordered sounds very smart, but forgive me for saying it is not quite practical to have the fur lining outside, although a great many motorists affect this fashion. Like Redfern I incline to the belief that a coat of leather outside and lined with fur is far more sensible, as the dust and rain alike fall off a smooth surface and adhere to the fur."

No wild cats or Russian colts for the menfolk, either. The Dublin-published 1908 *Encyclopaedia of Motoring*, however, expressed different views on the use of leather, apparently having a Celtic axe of its own to grind:

"Complete leather garments are not essential, neither are they healthy, owing to the fact that they confine the body's exhalations. It is really only the front portion of the trunk that requires special protection, and therefore a waistcoat with leather front is sufficient for summer. This waistcoat should have closely-fitting sleeves, and the back should be of woollen material. Of course, an overcoat should be worn also except in the very warm weather, and it should be made to lap completely over the chest for greater protection, and also to prevent the rain from driving in. It is advisable to line the portion covering the chest with kid or light leather. The coat should also be long and full at the bottom, so as to sit over the knees comfortably.

"A mackintosh coat should be carried to put on over the ordinary cloth coat in actual rain. The habitual use of mackintosh, however, is most unhygienic. It can be altogether avoided by getting a coat made of Galtee cloth, manufactured by Messrs Mulcahy, Redmond and Co., of Ardfinnan, Co. Tipperary, Ireland, and patronised by His Royal Majesty [sic] King Edward VII. We have used one of these coats for several years, and find it perfect from every point of view. It is made of three layers of different materials. The outside is mohair; woven with the mohair is pure merino, and the inside consists of warm Irish freize. The combined material is porous to air, and therefore hygienic. When it rains, however, the moisture causes the merino to contract, and brings the individual hairs of the mohair so close together that a hose can be turned on the coat without any moisture penetrating. In use we have never known the coat even to get damp except at the point of the right elbow, which had rested on the side of the car during a continuous day's rain."

The writer nevertheless went on to explain that he always wore a long mackintosh skirt under his Galtee coat, reaching from waist to ankles!

Scarcely two people had the same ideas about ideal motoring wear, it seemed, the leather fanciers disagreeing with the champions of a rubber poncho or coats made of a wide variety of fabrics. The *Motor Manual* of 1912 got right down to the bottom of the problem by advising drivers to wear a woollen undervest *made to button down the side* and preferably double-breasted because "the upper part of the chest is rarely sufficiently protected either by men or women, and most attacks of cold and bronchitis can be traced to want of proper protection for this sensitive part." The same publication approved of breeches and leather gaiters "for professional drivers," adding a warning for other motorists:

"The amateur, however, who drives in ordinary costume, should be careful that the lower part of his legs is properly protected. His trousers should not be too loose and should be of substantial thickness, and his undergarments

MOTOR ACCESSORIES DEPARTMENT.

GOGGLES, HOODS, ETC.

The Aluminium Cup Goggles.

No. 531½ Leather, unlined ... 2/9
„ 531 „ White Kid
lining 6/6
„ 533 Leather, White Kid
lining, with nosepiece ... 7/6

Goggles with Silk Mask.

In Silk, colours : Fawn, Dark Grey,
Silver Grey &c.

No. 301 Lady's size ... 1/11
„ 401 Gent's „ ... 2/6
„ 501 With folding nose-
bridge 3/0

Lady's Goggles.

No. 304. Silk, with Chenille edging
in Fawn, Dark Grey and Silver
Grey. 3/6

Do. do. in White Kid, 4/6

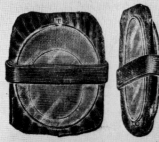

The Patent Folding Goggles.

Complete in case 9/6
Paris Vienna 11/6
„ with rain protector 14/6
Horn Goggles 8/6
Mica Eye Shields... ... 2/0

Leather Goggles for Winter.

No. 513. Folding nose bridge
in Fawn, Brown, Grey or Black.
Suede, lined White Chamois.
5/6

No. 423. Do. do. Non-folding
nose piece and with elastic. 4/6

The Speed Goggles.

No. 530. Light metal frame, lined Leather,
edged Chenille. 3/6
No. 530A. Do. do. with Aluminium
frame. 4/6
No. 532. Do. do. with Aluminium frame
and hinged nose. 5/6

The " Coverall " Wrap.

In soft Silk or Chiffon. With
attached Veil to cover face, which can
be thrown back without disarranging
Wrap. 7/6

New Lined Hood and Mask.

With Fur lining for Winter. 16/6
With Silk lining and Mica Shield. · 16/6

The " Desirée."

Combined Mica Mask, Veil, Wrap
and Hood. Completely envelopes
hat and hair. In soft Silk, all
leading shades. Clear Mica front
let into net veiling. 12/6
Waterproof, 16/6

and socks of stout wool and well fitted, and his boots considerably thicker than those he would wear to walk down Bond Street in the season. Shoes are a mistake; the ankles would get terribly cold in winter.''

By the time that information had been published it was out of date; scarcely any motorcar of 1912 left the occupants' legs exposed, bodywork afforded much more protection, and windscreens were coming into general use. As a basis for articles in motoring magazines, the subject of clothes hardly survived World War I, and the only motorists who found it necessary to dress up were those who drove cyclecars or sports cars. The sports car addict, indeed, continued to favour cars so lacking in weather protection that throughout the 1930s he was very likely to be mistaken for a motorcyclist. One accessory company marketed a cylinder of waterproof material, elasticized at each end, which was bought by those who drove midget British sports cars with the right elbow outside the door.

To put it another way, special circumstances called for special measures. One of the most special, surely, is recorded in L.T.C. Rolt's autobiography, *Landscape with Machines*:

''At that time my uncle Kyrle was using a 1906 6hp single-cylinder Rover to commute between his house and the works at Northampton, a choice of vehicle which even in 1924 was considered a trifle eccentric since it possessed neither hood nor windscreen. It was a brilliant summer's day with a sky of cloudless blue when my uncle first invited me to accompany him to the works in the Rover. I was therefore somewhat surprised when he attired himself for so short a journey in a seaman's oilskin and sou'wester. It was a precaution which I thought excessive.

''But I soon discovered the reason for it. Ascending the hill on the approach to Northampton in bottom gear, the Rover began to boil so violently that we were liberally sprayed with hot water, and so enveloped in steam that it became difficult to see the road ahead.''

BITS AND PIECES

"*Of late, electrical horns have come into use, in which a harsh sound is produced by a series of raps upon a metal disc, and mechanical devices have been brought out to produce a noise in the same way. The exhaust has been applied to blow whistles, and so on in endless variety every device for producing a noise has been offered the motorist for use as a road warning. These mechanical and electrical devices are based on the same principle as the old clappers used in the fields by boys hired to scare away crows. The only advantage they seem to possess is that the driver is saved the trouble of squeezing the rubber bulb, and has only to press a button.*"

RANKIN KENNEDY,
The Book of the Motor Car (1913)

Just over twenty years ago a mysterious phenomenon was observed among the motorcars of the world. On the front ends of their bonnets they began to sprout curiously shaped devices. The disease spread fast wherever motorcars existed. It had only to appear in one otherwise healthy vehicle, and in no time at all, it seemed, all the other cars in the district would display the same symptoms.

The device that sprouted from the bonnet was known as a bug deflector, and its purpose, one understood, was to divert the airstream flowing over the front of the car and thus keep the windscreen clear of squashed insects. Now there had been no sudden, worldwide plague of locusts. The fly and mosquito population had, with the usual seasonal fluctuations, remained at about its normal level. Yet the fact remains that one motorist after another, from Seattle to Saigon, went out and bought a bug deflector.

Accessory manufacturers latched hungrily on to this heaven-sent bonanza. They made bug deflectors in every shape they could think of: a fan, a butterfly, a stylized bird, a peacock with outspread tail. They made them in flat plastic, moulded plastic, clear plastic, in various offensive colours and in die-cast metal. They charged as much as they dared, and still the motorist went on buying. Even the world of motor sport, which is normally completely immune to this sort of thing, flirted with specially made deflectors on cars that took part in long-distance road races, or fitted them on rally cars to keep the windscreens clear of snow on the long trek to Monte Carlo.

And then one day we looked around, and lo! there was not a bug deflector to be seen—not anywhere. It was very, very strange. Hundreds of thousands of presumably sane individuals had spent hundreds of thousands of dollars and pounds on a small gadget which they had fitted to their cars, kept there for a few months, then unscrewed and thrown away. The inevitable question is—why? If bug deflectors didn't work, why did people buy them? If they did work, why did people not go on using them?

The Great Bug Deflector Mystery was more widespread than most, but it is by no means an isolated example of the curious urge to bedeck one's vehicle with gewgaws: one has only to look around at the wiper blades festooned with multiple plastic thingumajigs which are alleged to prevent the blades from lifting off at high speed. At least one respected technical journal has shown that they are almost completely useless for this purpose, but it did not halt the sale of plastic thingumajigs—especially for use on vehicles that are incapable of high speed.

So the motivation of the motorist is clearly something very deep-seated which deserves to be studied more closely. The car of today is not lacking in items that would once have been considered "extras," for the manufacturers vie with each other to claim that theirs is the most fully equipped vehicle of its kind on the market. Virtually everything the driver *really* needs has been fitted at the factory, and he can use his car for years without adding the smallest knob or switch to the equipment he will find already on or in it. He does not go out shopping for a screen washer, an ashtray or a demister; his car has been provided with all these already, and more besides.

The accessory dealer has therefore had to adopt different tactics, and the name of his game is no longer addition, but substitution. He succeeds in persuading a significant proportion of car owners that the factory-designed

BELOW: *Most early turn signals took the form of semaphore arms. This strangely anthropomorphic version is fitted to a Hispano-Suiza.*
BOTTOM: *The Bullnose Morris did not really have two gear levers; the control to the right of the driver actually dipped the headlamps.*

steering wheel, road wheels or seats should be discarded altogether and replaced by an alternative which can be bought from (where else?) the accessory shop. Sometimes such a substitution is entirely justified, and the accessory makes good the shortcomings of a poor original design, or meets the specialized requirements of a driver who is more particular than most. But sometimes it is difficult to avoid the uncomfortable conclusion that when it comes to buying expensive rubbish, there's no sucker like a motorist.

However misdirected it may be on occasion, though, the urge to improve one's lot is surely a very basic one, without which the human animal would still be wearing skins and living in a cave. It found full expression in the early days of motoring, when that experience could be damp, draughty, uncomfortable to a degree, and sometimes downright dangerous. The novice driver of seventy-five years ago must have been thrilled, through and through, when he first beheld his new and fascinating vehicle with its lustrous paintwork, gleaming brass and rich leather upholstery. But before it had been in his possession many months he was liable to become conscious of one or two shortcomings, if only because of the inconvenience they caused.

There were, for example, no doors. There was no hood, no windscreen, and of course nothing in the way of sidescreens, either. There was no rear-view mirror. There was no spare wheel. There might well be no lamps fitted to the car when he bought it, or even a horn, and almost certainly no instruments whatsoever.

Each item was considered an extra to be bought and fitted—if thought necessary—after the car had been purchased. The choice might

BELOW: *This 1897 Daimler has a folding hood, which affords little real protection when under way because there is no windscreen.*
BOTTOM: *Even a large car like the Mercédès had no provision for carrying oddments of luggage and personal belongings, so it was often necessary to fix baskets to the outside.*

be dictated by personal preference in some cases, simple prudence in others. Some owners, for example, would be spartan enough to make do without additional weather protection, but few could overlook the considerable advantages of a "Stepney" or similar spare rim when the wheels of the car were not detachable and punctures an almost daily occurrence; it saved so much of the time that would otherwise have to be spent repairing tyres at the roadside, perhaps in filthy weather. The initial simplicity of the entire under-bonnet mechanism left a speedometer as virtually the only instrument that could be fitted to a car, since there was usually nothing else to indicate but its speed and the distance covered. Until these became a legal requirement in some countries, however, speedometers scarcely rated as more than a rather expensive gadget to amuse (or perhaps terrify) the occupants. The rear-view mirror, too, came late on the scene, since it served no useful purpose when—the vehicle one drove being the fastest thing for miles around—nothing was ever likely to appear in it. Most (though not all) countries called for the vehicle to show at least one lamp at night and be equipped at all times with a bell, horn or other means of giving "audible warning of approach." But in any case it was folly to be without lamps when breakdowns were so common that no driver could be sure of reaching home before dark. As for horns, these were for some reason considered immensely important, not infrequently duplicated, mounted as close to the driver's hand as possible, and often manufactured in a variety of fierce, reptilian shapes.

So the extra components or accessories—it is not always easy to distinguish between the two—were acquired and mounted on the motor-

The motorist seemed obsessed by the need to give "audible warning of approach" during the early part of the century. There were bulb horns, electric horns, horns with their own air pump driven from the flywheel, and horns operated by winding a handle, not to mention bells, gongs and exhaust whistles. The devices here illustrated were advertised between 1906 and 1911.

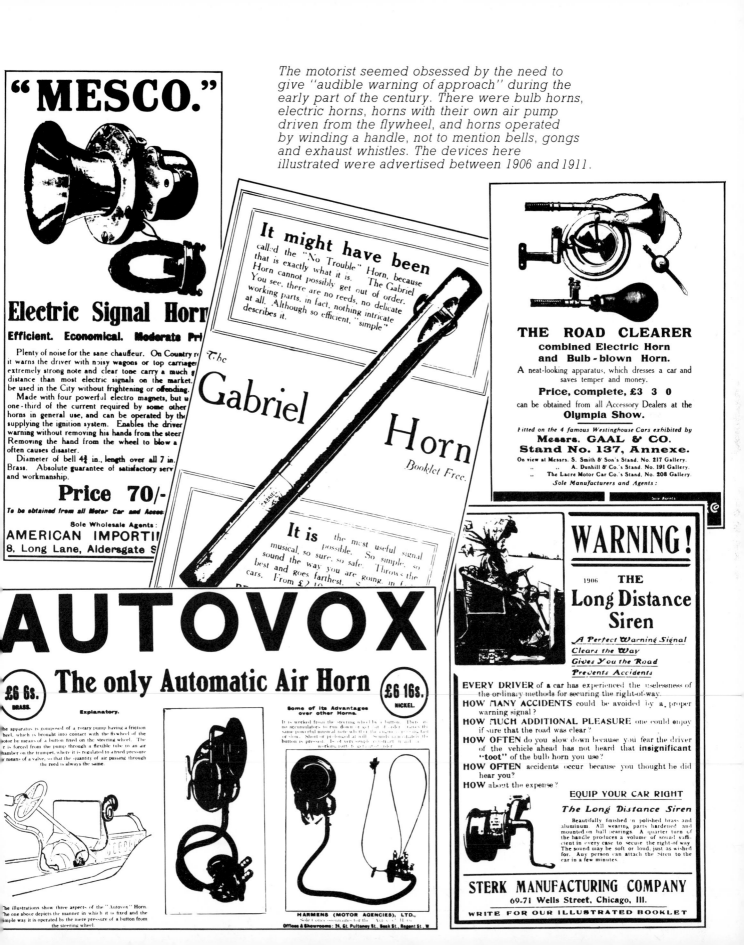

"MESCO."

Electric Signal Horn

Efficient. Economical. Moderate Price.

Plenty of noise for the sane chauffeur. On Country roads it warns the driver with noisy wagons or top carriages extremely strong note and clear tone carry a much greater distance than most electric signals on the market. be used in the City without frightening or offending.

Made with four powerful electro magnets, but uses one-third of the current required by some other horns in general use, and can be operated by the supplying the ignition system. Enables the driver warning without removing his hands from the steering. Removing the hand from the wheel to blow a often causes disaster.

Diameter of bell 4½ in., length over all 7 in. Brass. Absolute guarantee of satisfactory service and workmanship.

Price 70/-

To be obtained from all Motor Car and Accessories

Sole Wholesale Agents:
AMERICAN IMPORTING
8, Long Lane, Aldersgate S

It might have been

called the "No Trouble" Horn, because that is exactly what it is. The Gabriel Horn cannot possibly get out of order. You see, there are no reeds, no delicate working parts, in fact, nothing intricate at all. Although so efficient, "simple" describes it.

The **Gabriel Horn**

Booklet Free.

It is the most useful signal possible. So simple, so musical, so sure, so safe. Throws the sound the way you are going, in front best and goes farthest. cars. From £2 10

THE ROAD CLEARER

combined Electric Horn and Bulb-blown Horn.

A neat-looking apparatus, which dresses a car and saves temper and money.

Price, complete, £3 3 0

can be obtained from all Accessory Dealers at the
Olympia Show.

Fitted on the 4 famous Westinghouse Cars exhibited by
Messrs. GAAL & CO.
Stand No. 137, Annexe.

On view at Messrs. S. Smith & Son's Stand, No. 217 Gallery.
" A. Dunhill & Co.'s Stand. No. 191 Gallery.
" The Lacre Motor Car Co.'s Stand, No. 208 Gallery.
Sole Manufacturers and Agents:

Sole Agents

AUTOVOX

The only Automatic Air Horn

£6 6s. BRASS.   **£6 16s.** NICKEL.

Explanatory.

The apparatus is composed of a rotary pump having a friction wheel, which is brought into contact with the flywheel of the motor by means of a button fixed on the steering wheel. The air is forced from the pump through a flexible tube to an air chamber on the trumpet, where it is regulated to a fixed pressure by means of a valve, so that the quantity of air passing through the reed is always the same.

Some of its Advantages over other Horns.

It is worked from the steering wheel by a button. There are no accumulators to run down or get out of order, gives the same powerful musical note whether the engine runs fast or slow. Short or prolonged at will. Sounds immediately the button is pressed. Is of very simple construction and no working parts to get out of order.

The illustrations show three aspects of the "Autovox" Horn. The one above depicts the manner in which it is fixed and the simple way it is operated by the mere pressure of a button from the steering wheel.

HARMENS (MOTOR AGENCIES), LTD.,
Sole Concessionaires for the "Autovox" Horn
Offices & Showrooms: 24, Gt. Pulteney St., Beak St., Regent St., W.

WARNING!

1906   THE
Long Distance Siren

A Perfect Warning Signal
Clears the Way
Gives You the Road
Prevents Accidents

EVERY DRIVER of a car has experienced the uselessness of the ordinary methods for securing the right-of-way.

HOW MANY ACCIDENTS could be avoided by a proper warning signal?

HOW MUCH ADDITIONAL PLEASURE one could enjoy if sure that the road was clear?

HOW OFTEN do you slow down because you fear the driver of the vehicle ahead has not heard that **insignificant "toot"** of the bulb horn you use?

HOW OFTEN accidents occur because you thought he did hear you?

HOW about the expense?

EQUIP YOUR CAR RIGHT

The Long Distance Siren

Beautifully finished in polished brass and aluminum. All wearing parts hardened and mounted on ball bearings. A quarter turn of the handle produces a volume of sound sufficient in every case to secure the right-of-way. The sound may be soft or loud, just as wished for. Any person can attach the Siren to the car in a few minutes.

STERK MANUFACTURING COMPANY
69-71 Wells Street, Chicago, Ill.

WRITE FOR OUR ILLUSTRATED BOOKLET

car. But of course the process of improvement did not stop there. It continued all the time, at first with the simplest alterations and additions to the vehicle, of the kind that suggested themselves to any experienced motorist. In *The Car*, for example, several tips were put forward by John Montagu in 1902 under the heading "Little Things that Matter." Some are worth repeating by virtue of their very simplicity:

"In these days, when motorists are continually being confronted with unreliable police evidence, it is most valuable to have a watch with a comparatively big second hand, so that the times over well-known distances can be correctly checked. The dial should be sufficiently large to be easily read, and at night a little glow-lamp above worked from the accumulators is very handy. One or two firms make excellent watches for this purpose. They can be screwed onto the dashboard and when so fixed cannot be stolen. Those which are fixed on by means of leather flaps are a temptation to every thief, and many motorists have suffered in this way.

"Another advantage of a watch on the dashboard is that in cold or rainy weather one has not to fumble about in an inaccessible pocket for a watch with numbed fingers while anxiously regarding the road, steering or changing gear. You can also avoid undue haste when train catching, as the clock will often show that you have plenty of time in hand, and 'train fever' need not, therefore, beset you."

Improving the seats was a matter that engaged the motorist's attention, as indeed it does to this day:

"The comfort of the driver on the front seat and also of the passengers is a matter of the first importance. The driver's seat should not lean too far back, and there should be good support for the small of the back. The strain of driving a long distance, especially if the roads are bad or the steering is not working very well, is very great, and a comfortable seat is a *sine qua non*. The most comfortable seats are those built with sufficient support for the back, and if room can be spared in the width there should also be an arm, or two arms, padded and covered with leather. Side shocks will then be found to matter but little.

"For your lady passengers, a small cushion covered with leather should be provided. This will be found to be a great comfort, for men are apt to forget that when a woman sits in a chair she needs support for the middle of her back far more than a man, there being an indentation between the shoulders and the waist in modern costume to which a cushion gives not only support but helps to keep the dress and figure in good shape. Your lady friends will enjoy drives with you much more if this little matter is attended to. The cushion should be hung from the back of the seat by two straps, one from each corner, and can then be lowered or raised as wanted."

A similar addition would be worth trying with some car seats even now, three-quarters of a century later. Then there was a fitment for the dashboard which could be described as the forerunner of today's glove compartment:

"It will be found worth while to have a little box screwed on to the dashboard in which you can keep a box of matches, a map, small compass, a table of distances, or notes. These will be found to be extremely handy, especially when touring. The box should be constructed so that in wet weather it is waterproof."

An early form of inspection lamp was recommended for use on those cars which, having electric ignition (by no means universal in

1902), would be provided with a source of power:

"If your car carries accumulators, a small 4cp incandescent lamp with a flexible wire will be found most useful at night in case of breakdowns or punctures. You can then fully examine any defects with the greatest ease, and should anything happen to the petrol tank or its pipes there will be no danger of fire or explosion. The current required is very small, and the lamp should be covered with a strong network of brass wire, as it is apt to get broken. Also, if you do not wish to light a big acetylene lamp for a run of five or ten minutes the little electric light will conform with the law, besides being handy for manipulating the vehicle in the garage at night."

And finally, some extremely sound advice on the use of leather to protect chassis joints, just as synthetic rubber "boots" serve a similar purpose on some parts of a modern car:

"During muddy or dusty weather it is very important that there should be leather protections placed on the joints of the steering connections underneath your car. The continual working of oil and fine grit from the road produces an action on the joints similar to that of being rubbed with fine emery paper, and eventually produces undue play. . . . Leather is often used on French cars for protecting the joints on the end of the springs where they meet the scrolls which project from the frame. There is a good deal of continual play on these, especially over a rough road, and mud working on the pins tends to wear them, and in time the pin may give way and let the body down on the axle. These leather protections to the steering connections can be made by any intelligent saddler, and should be closed with a strap at each end so that they can be firmly fastened,

otherwise they may work loose, and so become a source of danger."

At the time when these suggestions were published, the motorcar was only just beginning to assume its traditional form as pioneered by Panhard, Renault and Mercédès. There was a chassis frame of approximately ladder shape carried by two axles through the medium of long, laminated "leaf" springs which took the brunt of shocks from uneven road surfaces. Designers were in the process of realizing that it was better for the chassis to be fairly close to the ground, but it was taking time to achieve this. The road wheels no longer followed slavishly the practice of the equine world by being small at the front and large at the rear; they were now more likely to be the same diameter at each end, and in almost every case they were fitted with pneumatic tyres because the advantages of these—which were many—outweighed their disadvantages. The engine, which might have two, four or even more cylinders, was mounted vertically at the front end, between the two sides of the "ladder," and transmitted its power through a friction clutch, probably of shallow cone shape and lined with leather, to a gearbox usually mounted separately a little behind, with one or perhaps two gear levers mounted on the right side of the chassis frame; this arrangement was followed almost without exception, whether the car was built in England, America, or continental Europe. The final drive from the gearbox was either by shaft or chain to the back axle.

Ahead of the vertically mounted engine was the radiator, its gilled tubes (like some labyrinthine furry caterpillar) gradually giving way to the honeycomb construction which was not only more efficient, but allowed the development of a distinctive and handsome shape

At first there seemed every likelihood that the automobile would develop along the lines of the original Benz or the 1896 Peugeot (TOP) with its rear engine, tiller or handlebar steering, and spindly solid-tyred wheels of different diameters. But the 1899 Panhard (BOTTOM) had its engine at the front under a "bonnet," wheel steering, and sturdy wooden road wheels of almost the same size, with pneumatic tyres. This was followed by ...

profoundly influenced the appearance of the entire car. Incidentally it conveniently served to support the front end of the bonnet which covered the engine, running back to that relic of the horsedrawn carriage, the splashboard or dashboard. This was acquiring a new role in life, for the front side of it offered a convenient mounting for oil tanks and other ancillaries to the mechanism, while the driver's side was the obvious place for sight-feed lubricators, hand pumps, and the various instruments which began to appear. Through the floor at first, then (as it became more steeply raked) the dashboard, passed the steering column, topped by a thick-rimmed wheel. Only a few eccentric manufacturers clung to steering by tiller or lever, motor-racing experience having proved the superiority of the wheel beyond doubt.

Brakes, however, still varied considerably from car to car. The spoon brake or tyre brake was fortunately disappearing, as was the external contracting or band brake which acted on the rear wheels, these giving way to Renault's simple but highly efficient internal expanding or drum brake. This, too, acted on the rear wheels. The front wheels were unbraked for two reasons: as they had to turn with the steering, it was difficult to arrange a linkage to them; also it was thought that front brakes would make the car skid and perhaps overturn. Usually — but not always — the rear-wheel brakes were operated by a lever on the right side of the chassis, close to the gear lever, and there was also a pedal which often brought into operation a brake that acted on the transmission line, just behind the gearbox. This was an effective brake which remained in use for two or three decades, but it could be fierce in action and tended to wear the transmission.

Frame, springs, axles, wheels, brakes,

steering, engine, transmission, radiator and dashboard were all lumped together under the label "chassis" (which, to the French, originally meant something you kept in the garden for growing cucumbers in). The bodywork was a separate item commonly made by coachbuilders, who at first knew nothing about motorcars and therefore produced a structure ill-adapted to its purpose. The gap between chassis and bodywork was not only symbolic, but real: the front seats were so far behind the dashboard that at first it was scarcely possible to fit front doors at all. (And what that space does to the shins on a wintry day has to be experienced to be believed.) Yet the same coachbuilders would cram the rear seats so close to the front ones that there was not *enough* space for rear doors. Sometimes the back seats were placed fore-and-aft, one on each side so that the rear passengers faced each other, and these could easily be reached through a little door at the back. The rear-entrance tonneau, as it was called, was a comparatively snug and convenient body style, but the door at the back brought problems of its own when it came to fitting a folding hood of some kind.

Mudguards were at first rather delicately shaped and made of curved wood or reinforced leather. Gradually it was appreciated that the higher rotational speeds of the road wheels fitted to a horseless carriage, and the greater thickness of their tyres, called for more extensive mudguarding. Running boards united the front and rear mudguards on each side, and came to serve many useful purposes. They provided additional protection from the mud thrown up by the front wheels, took the place of the early step-irons used by passengers when getting into the car, and offered a con-

McCOMB COLLECTION

. . . the much lower-built Mercédès of 1901 (BELOW) with bonnet closely following the lines of the honeycomb radiator, and an altogether more unified body shape. The process is continued in the 1907 Rover (BOTTOM), which has the beginnings of a scuttle dash behind the bonnet, embryonic front doors, full doors to the rear part of the body, a windscreen, and road wheels of the same size front and rear. Now, if the passenger compartment . . .

MERCEDES

BRITISH LEYLAND

. . . is enclosed completely along the sides, as in the 1912 Fiat Tipo Zero (BELOW), the shape begins to look familiar, despite the curious windscreen and mudguards. It is a short step, really, to the well-known open touring car—like the 1925 Fiat 509 (BOTTOM)—in which the body runs horizontally in a straight line from the shoulders of the radiator to the very back. The doors are big, mudguarding is ample, and the much smaller wheels carry comfortable "balloon" tyres. Eventually . . .

FIAT

. . . by 1932 the open car had become almost a rarity. Most chassis carried completely closed bodywork like this Chrysler Six, with only a sliding roof to let in the air and sunshine.

venient mounting for the battery, a fitted tool-box and a spare petrol can. Last but not least, as many a vintage car enthusiast has discovered, they were the perfect place to put tankards of beer without marking the paintwork.

The first major step towards greater comfort was taken when bodybuilders covered the legs of the front occupants with a "scuttle dash," later abbreviated merely to "scuttle," extending rearwards from the dashboard to a point just forward of the steering wheel. Once the scuttle appeared it became a simple matter to provide doors on each side to protect the occupants still more, and the top of the scuttle also proved the ideal position for a highly efficient windscreen of quite modest proportions. The only disadvantage of the new design was that instruments mounted on the dashboard were now lost from sight, shielded altogether from the daylight. And so, as described in "Knobs and Levers," they were moved further back and mounted on another board which inherited the name of dashboard—although some preferred to call it the instrument panel, and eventually the stylists of the motoring world, delving into architectural terminology, came up with the name of fascia or facia. The new dashboard was fixed just below the rear edge of the scuttle. Its forerunner came to be known as the bulkhead in Britain, firewall in America.

By the outbreak of World War I this chassis layout was well established as that of the typical motorcar, and a flush-sided open body was the norm. It remained so until the late 1920s, when the cheap pressed-steel saloon car gradually displaced it. In detail, however, the motorcar changed a great deal during that period. In America, where production expanded faster than anywhere else in the world, cars were

Even in 1900 there were closed cars, of course. But with bodywork such as this, a low-powered machine like the de Dion could scarcely pull itself along against a contrary wind.

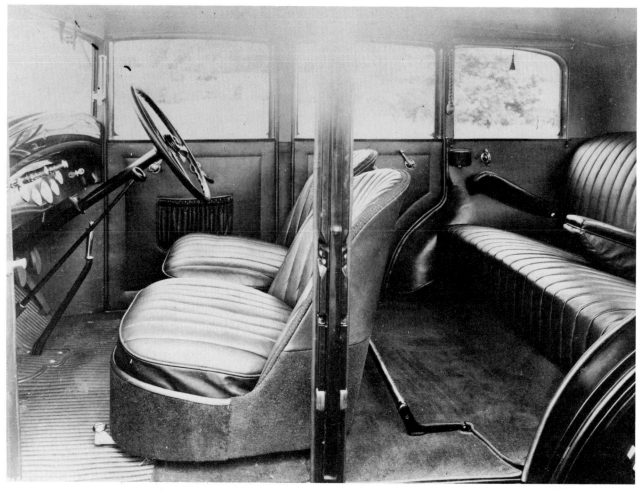

Car makers still had much to learn about
suspension systems in the "vintage" years, but
their shortcomings could be masked considerably
by fitting immensely deep, well-sprung seats of
the type seen in this six-light 1929 Chrysler.

bought as a means of transport for use in fair weather or foul. They had to be easier to start, and their various controls arranged in such a way that they could be driven easily by somebody who was not a professional driver or even a keen motorist. They needed better lights so that they could be driven after dark without undue strain. Although tyres had improved enormously, they needed to be better still. And as the numbers of cars increased, better brakes became another necessity.

In Europe, too, sales began to boom, and those involved in the motor trade discovered that things had changed since earlier, more leisurely days. Cars were no longer bought by those who were wealthy, or at least comfortably off. The man who went out to buy a car after the war was somebody who would never in his life have aspired to a horse and carriage. He was an owner-driver who would have to take the wheel himself, whatever the conditions, because he could not afford a man to do it for him. For the same reason he would wash the car himself, and mend the punctures, and do at least the basic maintenance work.

So the pressure on the manufacturer to change and improve his product was considerable. Competition was intense, with more and more new companies moving into the motor business, and anybody who wanted to survive had to think of novel selling features to outdo his competitors. Items previously regarded as extras were incorporated in the standard specification, while the accessory manufacturers, for their part, tried to dream up new gadgets to sell to the eager motorist.

Only the most expensive chassis were now fitted with special bodies made by coachbuilders to the requirements of individual buyers. The car manufacturer now offered a

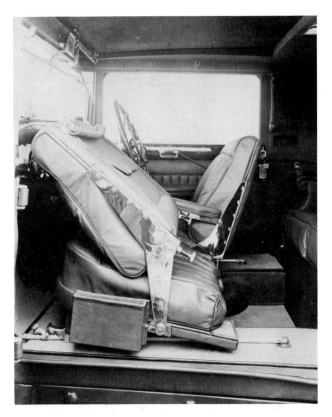

Folding seats give access to the rear compartment of a 1929 Daimler Sportsman's Coupé by Weymann. The model's title is justified by its curious blend of massive luxury and cramped discomfort; the body weight must have made the performance minimal.

McCOMB COLLECTION

TOP: *This 1913 de Dion carries such decorations as a rear windscreen, multiple exhaust whistle, travelling trunk, and a massive searchlight mounted on the scuttle.*
ABOVE: *A full-size hood and sidescreens provide good weather protection on this rare 1924 M.G. 14/28 tourer.*

range of standard designs which were built in quantity, either in his own factory or by one of his suppliers. The fact that most bodywork was still of the open tourer type was not, of itself, considered a disadvantage at first, for a typical touring speed was only about 30 to 40 mph (in Britain there was an overall speed limit of 20 mph until the end of 1930, though it was widely and very understandably disregarded). If they felt cold, those who went motoring were content to don gloves and overcoats. Even in rain a driver and his passenger could stay surprisingly dry, sheltered only by the windscreen, if they were able to keep going at a reasonable pace—something far easier to do in those days, when there was so much less traffic about.

For the larger touring cars, a popular accessory was a separate windscreen to protect the rear-seat passengers. Some coachbuilders also took this up, especially in the United States, where the "dual cowl phaeton" was considered an ultra-smart body style.

In bad weather the occupants of a typical tourer would erect the large, folding hood which was made of stout canvas or thin leather fixed to a framework of wood and metal. It was firmly secured to the top edge of the windscreen frame, and at the sides they would fix in place a set of screens, made of talc or celluloid mount-

ed in canvas frames, to fill the gap between
hood and bodywork. Admittedly all this took
time, but it certainly protected the interior of
the car from rain and made it comparatively
snug in winter.

On the other hand, it demonstrated all too
clearly how the solving of one problem leads
to the posing of another. The growing tendency to enclose the occupants immediately
placed greater emphasis on the importance of
the windscreen, which played such a crucial
role in the driver's view of the outside world
and presented a considerable hazard if it became obscured. Some manufacturers tried to
solve the problem by—almost literally—putting
it aside; the screen was made in two halves,
split horizontally with the upper half pivoted at
the top, so that the driver could flip it up in bad
weather and see straight out. Naturally, it was
a chilly way to drive in wintertime, but on the
whole preferable to fiddling about with some
of the various hand-operated wipers sold by
the accessory companies. Moreover, it provided unrivalled visibility in fog, and for this
reason alone many experienced drivers re-
gretted the passing of the opening windscreen.
When fixed screens became more common,
better wipers were a necessity, and different
methods were tried to operate them automatically. One of the less intelligent was to drive
the wiper by cable from the gearbox, thus ensuring that the windscreen blurred over with
rain as soon as a car came to a halt in town
traffic. The suction-type wiper, connected by a
rubber tube to the inlet manifold, lasted a surprisingly long time despite its one overwhelm-
ing weakness: when the driver accelerated to
overtake another vehicle, the inlet manifold
depression was reduced and the wiper would
slow down or even stop, blurring the screen

*A double-fold windscreen like the one fitted to
this 1910 Berliet could be swung closer to the
occupants in an attempt to provide better
protection, or out of the way completely when it
was raining (as there were no effective wipers
in the early days).*

The windscreen wiper has arrived, but the windscreen of this 1931 Austin 12 is still pivoted along the top of the frame so that the driver can swing it open if he wishes—an arrangement that was extremely useful in foggy weather.

with rain at the worst possible moment. Eventually the electric wiper—invented by a Hawaiian dentist in 1917—replaced all the others, finally becoming available in multi-speed versions for heavy rain, with intermittent operation for light rain.

The first "safety" windscreen consisted of two sheets of glass cemented on each side of a sheet of celluloid. Invented early in the twentieth century, it was not generally adopted until the mid-1920s, and even then many cars were still sold with ordinary plate-glass screens and side windows; in Britain, safety glass was not legally required until 1937. During the 1940s laminated glass started to give way to toughened glass, which was manufactured in such a way that it shattered into small particles when broken. This new material had certain advantages: it was less likely to inflict serious cuts than the sharp slivers of broken laminated glass, less likely to break when a bending strain was transmitted through the frame, and did not discolour with age as laminated glass sometimes did. Above all, it was cheaper to make, especially in the curved shapes demanded by body stylists in later years. This led to its widespread use after World War II, despite its tendency to shatter when hit by a flying stone, causing an immediate loss of visibility, instead of merely cracking as a laminated screen does in the same circumstances. Various attempts have been made to alleviate this, but toughened glass windscreens are still banned in the motor racing world, and the manufacturers of high-performance cars prefer to use laminated glass.

Modern styling also caused the windscreen to be moved forward and steeply raked, a combination which greatly accentuates the obscuring effect of dead insects or dirt particles on the surface, and helped to make screenwashers a necessity rather than a luxury. Manually operated or automatic washers had existed for years, but the early motorist felt little need for them. His lofty, vertical windscreen stayed much cleaner than those of today, and although the roads were often dirty, he was not condemned by traffic conditions, as we so often are, to drive for miles behind a slow lorry that is flinging up a steady spray of muddy water. He could scarcely have imagined a time when the screenwasher would be not merely desirable but actually required by law in some countries; still less that it would sometimes be accompanied by a similar device for washing the headlamp glasses. On the other hand, there was far less compulsion to keep on going when traffic was lighter; even on a narrow road one could pull up to clean the windscreen, the lamps or the windows without causing serious inconvenience to others on the roads.

The car of the 1920s—open or closed—was so far from being air-tight that the driver was not much troubled by condensation on the screen, especially if he knew the old trick of rubbing half a potato over the inside of the glass. In very cold weather some ice might form on it, but the hardened motorist knew how to deal with that, too: a little piece of packing between bonnet-top and scuttle—a folded duster, say, or some cardboard—would make a gap through which warm air flowed from the engine compartment as he drove along, striking the windscreen and defrosting it most effectively. Years later, he would buy from the accessory shops an electric heating element which was fixed to the bottom of the screen by means of two rubber suction cups. It worked, after a fashion, and for lack of anything better it was still in use a decade and more after World War II. At that time Rolls Royce pioneered the use of a rear window with a built-in heating element, which is now to be found on some of the cheapest cars.

The young motorist of today might imagine that the unheated open touring car of fifty or more years ago was bitterly cold to drive in winter. Bracing it was, assuredly, but nowhere near as cold as a modern convertible with the heater switched off. There was always a certain amount of heat coming off the engine—quite a lot, if it was a big one—and the bulkhead did virtually nothing to stop it soaking through to the driver and passenger. Some welcome heat came from the gearbox, and one might even feel a little through the wooden floor from the exhaust pipe, running just below. So the car played its part in keeping its occupants warm in mid-winter. Unfortunately it also did so in mid-summer, when it was the last thing one wanted.

It was different for passengers in the rear seats, of course. They wrapped themselves in thick rugs and resorted to portable footwarmers filled with boiling water or hot charcoal. Various experiments were tried with interior heaters that used hot air ducted from the engine or the exhaust, but they were never really successful. For two decades or so the commonest type of interior heater was the recirculatory (known with well-deserved contempt as the "fug stirrer"), which used an electric fan to pass air over finned tubes heated by the radiator water. Eventually the functions of heating, ventilating, demisting and defrosting were designed into the car from the start. In those parts of the world where it was required, the same policy was followed with regard to air conditioning. Unfortunately some manufacturers believed that air-conditioning equipment could be regarded as an accessory, even for small cars which had barely enough power available to operate it, with the remarkable result that switching on the air conditioning had much the same effect as applying the brakes.

Ride comfort was another facet of the passengers' well-being that accessory manufacturers once claimed to improve—with but little justification. Pneumatic tyres made the nineteenth-century car more comfortable than solid rubber tyres did, and in the early 1920s balloon tyres proved more comfortable than beaded-edge. The shortcomings of a suspension system could be masked to some extent by efficient dampers, and during the 1930s a British manufacturer sold a set with remote-control adjustment so that the driver could stiffen up the suspension as he increased his speed. Leaf springs were certainly more consistent in their behaviour if fitted with a good set of leather gaiters, complete with grease nipples. But the real problem was that few designers fully understood the complex and conflicting requirements of a first-class suspension system. American car manufacturers plumped for comfort, with disastrous effects on the controllability of their mid-1930s models. The British achieved good handling with their sports cars, if not their saloons, but sacrificed comfort in doing so. It was left to the Continental designers to produce the first sophisticated suspension systems, pointing the way to the modern car which combines a smooth ride with the ability to out-corner the best pre-war sports car that money could buy.

To accomplish this, however, they needed the help of the tyre manufacturers, who for a long time offered little in the way of new developments. After the introduction of the balloon tyre there was no significant step forward until 1948, when Michelin first began to market radial-ply covers. From Dunlop, a few years later, came the tubeless tyre, which reduced the likelihood of sudden deflation following a puncture, but somewhat increased the possibility that the cover would leave the wheel rim when deflation did occur. This led, in turn, to the so-called "safety wheel" which could be driven on safely, though of course at reduced speed, when the tyre had deflated. The most remarkable progress in recent years, however, and one to which most tyre manufacturers have contributed, has been in the development of new rubber mixes, which have combined with wider treads and generally improved carcass construction to provide a level of road adhesion that would once have been dismissed as impossible to attain. It is only a couple of decades ago that the experienced driver reduced his speed and used considerable discretion when he saw ahead of him the sheen of a damp road surface, knowing how much the grip of his tyres would be reduced. Present-day tyre adhesion, wet or dry, is such that many motorists will go right through life without ever experiencing a skid, and in some cases the confidence displayed approaches overconfidence.

Closely allied to the question of tyre adhesion is that of efficient braking, since it is impossible to achieve one without the other. Unfortunately for the motorist, brake manufacturers spent years barking up entirely the wrong tree, for they were obsessed by the notion that the front wheels must never lock under any circumstances. So long as they fitted brakes that worked only on the rear wheels, either directly or through the transmission, it was not possible to make them efficient. The greater the force applied to those wheels—by whatever means—the sooner *they* locked up,

Safety First !

One of the big virtues of the
DUNLOP
CORD BALLOON TYRE
(Wired or straight side type)

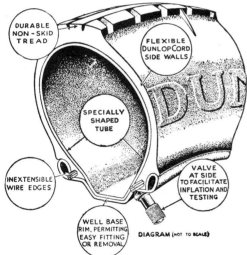

DURABLE NON-SKID TREAD

FLEXIBLE DUNLOP CORD SIDE WALLS

SPECIALLY SHAPED TUBE

INEXTENSIBLE WIRE EDGES

VALVE AT SIDE TO FACILITATE INFLATION AND TESTING

WELL BASE RIM, PERMITTING EASY FITTING OR REMOVAL

DIAGRAM (NOT TO SCALE)

is that it is absolutely *safe*. In principle, it is a *Straight Side Tyre*, and cannot accidentally leave the rim—even when the inflation pressure falls. It is independent of air pressure for its hold upon the rim and is the *safest* Balloon tyre in the world—just as pre-eminent as the normal pressure Dunlop Cord.

'fit Dunlop and be satisfied'

If you wish to convert your car to 'Balloons,' write to SERVICE MANAGER, FORT DUNLOP for a quotation.

DUNLOP RUBBER CO. LTD., FORT DUNLOP, BIRMINGHAM. Branches throughout the World.

DUNLOP—THE STANDARD *by which* ALL TYRES *are* JUDGED

C.F H.73*

Fitting brakes to the front wheels as well as the rear improved stopping power so much that drivers, like the owner of this 1925 Buick Light Six, would often display a warning triangle at the rear. Reading FRONT WHEEL BRAKES *or* FOUR WHEEL BRAKES, *it was meant to discourage other drivers from following too close behind.*

and it was sheer luck if the driver did not find himself admiring the view in the opposite direction. Quite apart from the danger of skidding, which was very real, there was the simple fact that a locked wheel slows a car much less effectively than one which is still turning.

What the brake designers had overlooked was something of fundamental importance. When the brakes of a car are applied, its weight is thrown *forwards*, transferring a greater proportion of it from the rear wheels to the front ones. So the rear wheels, having become lightly loaded, are extremely prone to lock. Even when the increasing speeds of the 1920s at last forced manufacturers to fit four-wheel brakes, some of them stuck firmly to their old belief—even Rolls-Royce, who arranged the linkage so that the rear wheels were braked harder than the front ones and thus ensured that the system was most inefficient.

Although hydraulically operated brakes were introduced by Duesenberg as early as 1921, thus dispensing with the various shafts, levers, rods and cables demanded by mechanical systems, there was the niggling possibility that a burst pipe, or even a tiny piece of grit lodging in a valve, could cause total brake failure without the slightest warning. This was perhaps one reason why mechanical brakes lingered on for another fifteen years or so despite their various shortcomings. These, however, the accessory manufacturers helped to cure, or at least alleviate. The piercing squeal that was emitted by the brakes of a ''Bullnose'' Morris, and one or two other makes as well, could be reduced by fitting ''brake mufflers'' around the drums. If a heavy car was hard to stop, a vacuum servo unit worked wonders to minimize the pedal effort.

Unfortunately the greater effectiveness of

hydraulic brakes began to be largely nullified when body stylists insisted on hiding the road wheels behind so much sheet metal that the brake drums, deprived of their normal flow of cooling air, tended to overheat. For the driver, the result was the terrifying phenomenon known as brake fade, which was to remain a major motoring hazard for many years, although the makers of brake linings and brake fluids did what they could to reduce its effects. Eventually it was overcome completely with the introduction of the disc brake in the early 1950s. Yet this, too, brought its problems. One was the difficulty of providing an efficient handbrake, which was overcome in most cases by retaining drum brakes at the rear. Most leading brake manufacturers also devised a valve or other arrangement to prevent wheel locking, at either the front or the rear, and the possibility of complete failure was countered by providing either a dual master cylinder or two completely separate braking systems.

A study of the motoring press half-a-century ago reveals all manner of gadgets which were marketed in the late 1920s to meet the considerable demand existing at that time. There were not nearly so many before World War I, some had disappeared before World War II, and such items as still exist nowadays have mostly taken their place as part of the standard specification—which is why it becomes virtually impossible to draw a firm line between accessories and components in the very characteristic list published in a 1929 motoring encyclopaedia:

"Accumulators, air cleaners, all-weather equipment and rear screens, etc., anti-dazzle devices, brake linings, brake mufflers, brake systems, bumpers, carburettors, carburation controls, clocks, covers (dust and waterproof), direction indicators and stop lights, etc., electrical equipment, engine heaters, engine temperature indicators, fire extinguishers, free-wheel devices, glass (safety), gradient meters, grease guns, heaters and foot warmers, horns, ignition systems (magneto and coil), interior fittings, jacks, locks (ignition, gear, etc.), loose covers (seat), mascots, number plates, oil filters, petrol filters, petrol gauges, radiator muffs, radiator shutters, seat adjusters, shock absorbers, spare wheel and tyre covers, sparking-plug testers, speedometers, spotlights, spring gaiters, synchronometers, thermostats, tools, trunks and luncheon cases, tyre gauges, tyre pumps, valve tools, wheels and wheel discs, wheel chains, windscreen wipers." A notable absentee is the car radio, which had been tried out in Britain as early as 1921 (and would then have been called a "wireless set," of course). By the time this list was published in Britain, however, the car radio was already a listed option on some American cars.

An "engine heater" was not intended to keep the car's occupants warm, but to prevent the radiator water from freezing overnight in winter, and it could be anything from a simple oil heater on the garage floor to an electric heating element fitted permanently to the car. The "gradient meter," usually called a "Tapley" after its best-known manufacturers, was a very popular device to tell the driver how steep a hill his car was climbing; it could also be used to test acceleration or brake efficiency, and a modified version is still used for the latter purpose nowadays.

But the king of them all was Chinn's Patent Synchronometer, a sort of combined speedometer and tachometer connected to the gearbox by a cat's-cradle of cables. It had no less than four needles indicating either mph or rpm on

various scales, not to mention counters that read trip and total mileage, and with this it was claimed that the driver could make perfect gear changes every time; all he had to do was to synchronize the road-speed needle with the needle indicating the speed of the gear he wanted to engage. An independent reviewer made the dead-pan comment that: "Some drivers, however, prefer to keep their eyes on the road, and make changes by the old method." As the synchronometer cost 15 guineas (£15.75, equal to about £150 nowadays) this is hardly surprising.

Not that the old-style "crash" gearbox was easy to handle. A contemporary manual devotes five pages to giving instructions for changing up, and a further thirteen pages to the technique for changing down, but despite the efforts of the motoring writers to explain it all with diagrams and directions, not everyone succeeded in acquiring the knack of double-declutching and slowing down or speeding up the various gears to ensure their silent engagement.

Many, indeed, had no intention of trying; they took the view that it was the designer's job to devise a transmission system that was easier to use, as Henry Ford had done for the Model T in 1908 (and Lanchester, de Dion and others before him). Simplified gear changing was the aim of several manufacturers during the late 1920s, and General Motors did extensive research in this direction. But it was one thing to design a simple planetary gearbox with only two speeds, low and high. It was quite another to provide three or even four forward gears in the same way. The Wilson preselector gearbox was offered by Vauxhall in 1927 and Armstrong Siddeley the following year; it was inclined to be heavy and cumbersome, but it was improved and adopted by other British manufacturers over the next few years, without ever gaining widespread approval from drivers. France produced the Cotal electrically engaged transmission, which also failed to find favour generally. General Motors came up with the best compromise in 1928 when they listed synchromesh transmission for the Cadillac, and developed versions of this system have remained the most widely used in Europe.

Meanwhile the central gear-lever position spread across the Atlantic from the States, forcing Britons to change gear with the left hand instead of the right, but also making it easier for manufacturers to provide the driver with a door of his own. By 1938, however, General Motors had switched to a steering-column gear lever for Cadillac and produced an optional automatic gear change for the Oldsmobile. Two years later this had been developed into the "Hydramatic," the world's most successful fully automatic transmission system. Since that time, accessory manufacturers have at intervals attempted to simplify normal gear changing by arranging for automatic clutch operation, as in the British "Manumatic" and French "Ferlec" systems, but none has met with success.

Many pioneer motorists have commented feelingly on the difficulty and danger of driving at night, their way illuminated by what Algernon Berriman remembered as "smouldering lamps that blinked their compliance with the law through sooty glasses." The typical nineteenth-century carriage lamp was an impressive-looking object with its bevelled and perhaps engraved glasses, its silver reflectors, pagoda-like ventilators above and graceful stalk beneath—but the light it gave was that of a single tallow candle (held in place by a long coil spring). And it was not pleasant to try and guide

a motorcar along a dark country road by the dim light of two candles, as Charles Jarrott discovered for himself one night in 1897:

"Then did I realize the great difference between driving a fierce racing car in broad daylight and handling the same car in the dark. Unlighted carts, wandering villagers and dawdling lovers presented fresh terrors at every yard of the road, until at last I got on to the low speed, and there remained. The expostulations of Wellington were useless. When he goaded me to 'let her go' I replied that so far as I was concerned I was not going to travel any faster. . . ."

Almost a decade later, J. E. Vincent found night motoring no more enjoyable when touring with friends in Norfolk:

"[The road] ran first for five miles straight as an arrow; the straightness was apparent at the time, but the five miles seemed like twenty. A fine mist was frozen over the watery land, nothing was visible at one side except, at stated intervals, a towering telegraph pole, and on both sides, at shorter intervals, were puny and poor trees which may have been poplars or willows. It became my duty, seated beside the man at the wheel, to peer into the darkness, trying to distinguish any possible obstacle or turn, to make out the character of any light that might be seen, and to watch for the bend which, after another straight run of some three miles, would take us to Acle. As a rule I could just see the outline of one telegraph post as we passed its predecessor; there was, in all probability, a deep dyke on either side, and it was an ideal night for running into a country vehicle travelling without a tail light. . . . It was, in short, a trying experience to the nerves and to the eyes, and we resolved to avoid night journeys as much as might be in the future. The resolution was renewed when we looked at our strained and bloodshot eyes the next morning. . . . Night travelling by motorcar in winter is not to be recommended unless the moon is strong."

At anything more than a walking pace the carriage lamp was almost completely useless, and oil lamps were at first little better. These, however, were in time greatly improved and could even be used fairly satisfactorily as headlamps. They were also less trouble to maintain than acetylene lamps, which continually suffered from blocked jets and filters. But a good acetylene lamp gave a brilliant white light—better than early electric lamps, in fact, and bright enough to call for the use of cowls or shutters as dimming devices.

The acetylene gas was generated by simply bringing water into contact with solid calcium carbide in the base of the lamp, and various designs were evolved to ensure a steady flow. If the lamp was a small one, the motorist who undertook a long night journey had to take care not to let it run short of carbide. Nor, of course, could it be allowed to run out of water, but if this happened the driver could usually make good the deficiency, one way or another. Soon it was found more convenient to generate the gas in a large separate container mounted on the running board, with pipes leading to the lamps. The generator, like the lamps themselves and their attendant piping, had to be cleaned at frequent intervals. It was just one more trial for the early motorist that when he was cleaning out the acetylene system it quite often exploded. But the early motorist was nothing if not stouthearted: in the words of a contemporary manual, "the resulting explosion is not by any means alarming."

With remarkable prescience Berriman commented in 1914: "By the time that electric light has become a standard fitting on cars, very few people will stop to remember that there has been any difficulty associated with its introduction.'' When he wrote that, Cadillac and others had already standardized electric lighting and starting, but it had certainly not been easy to overcome the many problems encountered in arranging for an electrical generator to operate satisfactorily at a speed that was far from constant. Some, indeed, had not been entirely overcome fifty years later. From quite an early period motorists had tried using small electric sidelamps or tail lamps, simply connecting them to an accumulator which was recharged at home whenever it was convenient, but they could not use electric headlamps, as these would have taken far too much current and the battery would have quickly gone flat. Once a reasonably efficient recharging system had been developed, however, the situation was different, and the accessory dealers were not long in selling adaptors so that acetylene headlamps could be converted to take electric bulbs.

Inevitably, when electric headlamps became more powerful the dazzle problem arose once more, to become an evergreen topic for the correspondence columns of most motoring magazines, and suggested cures ranged from the improbable to the absurd. One of the simplest, the Barker Dipping System, was also one of the most effective: the two headlamps were mounted on a common bar which could be rotated, tilting both lamps downwards, by merely moving what looked like an extra gear lever at the right-hand side of the driver. Later the reflectors alone were swivelled by a mechanism mounted inside the lamp body: either pneumatically, using small vacuum cylinders connected to the inlet manifold, or elec-

The extraordinary-looking headlamps on this Ford are "Woodlites," which were quite popular in America for a while during the late 1920s despite their strange appearance.

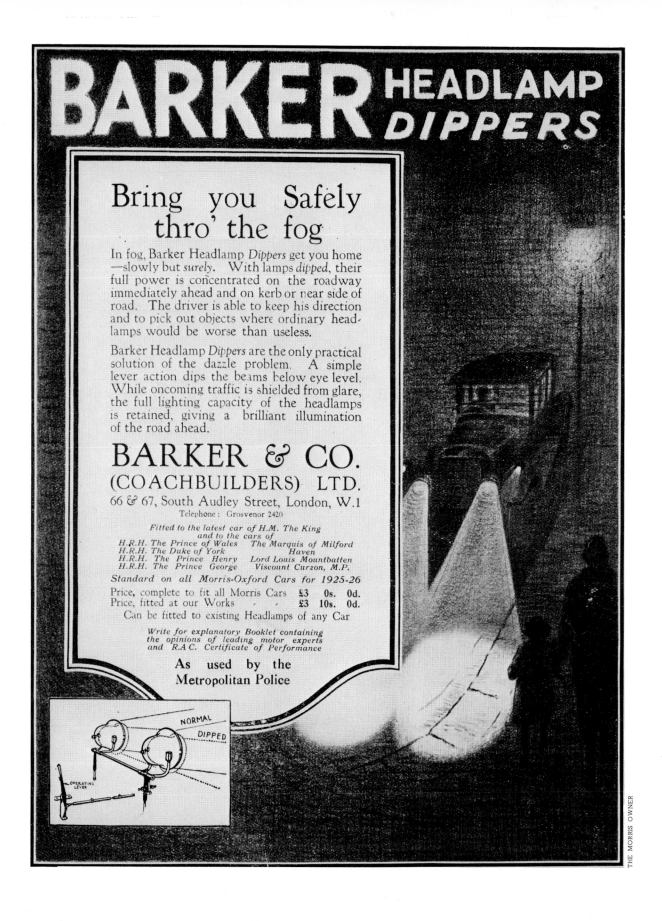

BARKER HEADLAMP DIPPERS

Bring you Safely thro' the fog

In fog, Barker Headlamp *Dippers* get you home —slowly but *surely*. With lamps *dipped*, their full power is concentrated on the roadway immediately ahead and on kerb or near side of road. The driver is able to keep his direction and to pick out objects where ordinary head-lamps would be worse than useless.

Barker Headlamp *Dippers* are the only practical solution of the dazzle problem. A simple lever action dips the beams below eye level. While oncoming traffic is shielded from glare, the full lighting capacity of the headlamps is retained, giving a brilliant illumination of the road ahead.

BARKER & CO.
(COACHBUILDERS) LTD.
66 & 67, South Audley Street, London, W.1

Telephone: Grosvenor 2420

*Fitted to the latest car of H.M. The King
and to the cars of*
H.R.H. The Prince of Wales   The Marquis of Milford
H.R.H. The Duke of York   Haven
H.R.H. The Prince Henry   Lord Louis Mountbatten
H.R.H. The Prince George   Viscount Curzon, M.P.

Standard on all Morris-Oxford Cars for 1925-26

Price, complete to fit all Morris Cars   **£3   0s.   0d.**
Price, fitted at our Works   - -   **£3 10s.   0d.**
Can be fitted to existing Headlamps of any Car

*Write for explanatory Booklet containing
the opinions of leading motor experts
and R.A.C. Certificate of Performance*

As used by the Metropolitan Police

NORMAL
DIPPED
OPERATING LEVER

THE MORRIS OWNER

trically by means of magnetic solenoids. As bulb manufacturers improved their methods they were able to incorporate two filaments in each bulb, one of them offset, so that the beam could be deflected by switching from one filament to the other. To this day the leading manufacturers are still developing new systems. Some of them will, no doubt, make present methods seem as outdated as the charming little roller blind which the driver of the 1920s would raise to blank off his rear window (by pulling a knob attached to it by a long piece of string) if the motorist close behind was so discourteous as not to dip *his* headlamps.

In 1915 a handbook published by *Autocar* offered a warning to those who had treated themselves to one of the new lighting sets:

"After electric light has been fitted to a car, extra attachments, such as an electrically operated horn, cigar lighter, etc., should not be added too recklessly, as, if this is done, they may overtax the system, and lead to trouble with the accumulators. If it is desired to add many extra electrical fittings, the makers of the lighting set should be asked whether the original equipment will stand additional duty."

One wonders what the man who wrote those words would think of a car whose original equipment included not merely an electric horn and a cigar lighter, but four high-intensity quartz halogen headlamps, parking lamps, stoplamps, signalling lights, reversing lamps, hazard warning lights, an electric clock, electrically actuated instruments, panel lighting, more than a dozen warning lights (including one to indicate brake-pad wear), interior lighting, under-bonnet lighting, luggage compartment lighting, glove compartment lighting, a light over the ashtray, a map-reading light, electric wipers front *and* rear, electric screen-

Attempts to solve the dazzle problem took many forms over the years before manufacturers learned how to make lights with a sharp cut-off. The Barker dipper of the middle 1920s (OPPOSITE) simply tilted the headlamps downwards mechanically, just by moving a lever (see also p. 143). Another popular arrangement was to switch to a pair of "pass lamps" mounted below the headlamps, as on the 1930 Cord L.29 shown above.

"When a patrol does not salute, stop and ask the reason why.'
(With apologies to the Automobile Association.)

"STOP!"

—said Mr. York, Motoring, "Have you got your Motoring Chocolate?"

"Of course I have," said the driver, "I never go out for a run without some. It's a very good 'meal at the wheel,' and it doesn't make you thirsty."

"You're right," said Mr. York. "Motoring Chocolate is made specially nourishing for motorists so that they can lunch in the healthy open air and enjoy every minute of the glorious sunshine."

ROWNTREE'S
MOTORING
CHOCOLATE
WITH ALMONDS AND RAISINS

½-lb. cakes: 6d. cakes and same quality in 2d. bars.
Plain or Milk.

The owner of a 1922 Cadillac demonstrates the electric cigarette-lighter which is one of an array of fitted accessories and tools.

McCOMB COLLECTION

washer, electric wash/wipe for the headlamps, electric starting, electric ignition, electric engine-cooling fan, electric fuel pump, an electric fan to cool the battery, electric fans for interior heating, ventilating, demisting and defrosting, air conditioning, electrically heated rear window, electrically operated sun roof, electrically operated windows all round, electrically operated door locks all round, electrically adjusted seats, a radio installation incorporating four speakers, a cassette player and an electrically operated aerial, a radio telephone, and an exterior rear-view mirror which is provided with an electric motor (so that its position can be adjusted from inside the car) and a built-in electric element to demist or defrost its surface in winter.

It has not been all progress, though. The driver of a magnificently equipped vehicle such as this cannot buy—as his father could, half a century ago—a tuppenny bar of Rowntree's Motoring Chocolate, which, said the advertisements, was "made specially nourishing for motorists so that they can lunch in the open air and enjoy every minute of the glorious sunshine."

RADIO TIMES HULTON PICTURE LIBRARY

AT HOME AND ABROAD

"*There's nothing in the world to equal travelling on a motorcar. You can go fast or slow; you can stop where you like and as long as you like; with a little luggage on your car you're as independent as a bird; and like a bird you float through the air, with no thought for timetables.*"

CHARLES AND ALICE WILLIAMSON,
The Lightning Conductor (1902)

Whatever pleasure anyone derived from overland travel before the middle of the nineteenth century, it was fairly effectively outweighed by the inconvenience, discomfort and expense which attended the process. To be transported by horse, whether on top of the beast or behind it, cannot be considered the acme of luxury even when one can afford the costliest of trappings. With the coming of the railway, however, travellers could cover long distances cheaply, quickly, and in conditions that seemed a bed of roses by comparison with the cramped interior of the average coach. Holiday-makers of quite modest income were able to explore their own and other lands for the first time. And explore they most certainly did, the extent of their travels bounded only by the shallowness of their purses and the limited amount of leisure at their disposal.

But the railway, like every other form of public transport, is hopelessly inflexible. A man in a train is a man in a straitjacket, unable to decide his own starting time, route, the pace at which he travels, frequency of his meals, or even the company he keeps. For anybody who really values freedom, this is the very negation of enjoyment, and the time taken up by travelling to such a rigid routine must be deducted from one's holiday instead of forming one of the best parts of it.

So it is scarcely surprising that from the moment when motorists could reasonably trust in the reliability of their vehicles, they started using them for what governments refer to, with increasing disapproval, as "pleasure motoring." Motoring, they discovered, was entirely different from travel by rail because the enjoyment began as soon as they left the familiar surroundings of their own homes. J. E. Vincent, author of a series of English travel books, put his finger on it when summing up a journey made early in 1906 in a White steam car:

". . . but in truth, distance really hardly counts within limits which grow wider every year, when one is motoring for pleasure. The essential things were that we took breakfast at a reasonable time and at leisure in Felixstowe, went by characteristic cross-country routes to Woodbridge and to Ipswich, strolled through Ipswich and shopped and lingered over luncheon, took tea at ease in Great Dunmow, explored many pleasant byways between it and London, and were back in London in plenty of time to dine and to go to a first night at the theatre, and not in the least too tired to do both with enjoyment. That is the new kind of pleasure which the motorcar has rendered possible, and it is a very real and genuine one."

The distance covered by Vincent's party was a little over one hundred miles, in fact. Their pleasure lay not in that accomplishment, but in being able to go from one place to another exactly as they wished and at their own speed, sometimes hurrying on to their next destination, sometimes dawdling to admire their present surroundings, but always in control of their means of transport instead of being controlled by it. This is what travellers found so novel and enjoyable when they started touring by car more than seventy years ago, and although the experience has long lost its novelty, the real enjoyment of motoring might be defined in precisely the same terms today.

At first there was only one part of the world where motorists could go touring rather than trailblazing. Only in western Europe were there sufficient good roads to permit of a tour being made—and even there, the only country that had mile after mile of long, straight roads to

Getting the car on or off a ship by crane, like this Rolls-Royce 40/50 hp here being unloaded at Boulogne in the early 1920s, was anything but convenient, but as soon as cars became reasonably reliable there was a steady flow of British motorists across the Channel to holiday in Continental Europe.

RADIO TIMES HULTON PICTURE LIBRARY

BRITISH MUSEUM

As early as 1904 the London, Brighton and South Coast Railway, bowing to the inevitable, was advertising a twice-daily steamer service from Newhaven to Dieppe, which was described as "the best and most popular starting point for Cycling and Motoring Tours in Normandy."

offer was France. When the 19-year-old Charles Rolls decided to drive from Cambridge to the family home in Wales to celebrate the Christmas of 1896, his Peugeot took most of three days to complete this cross-country journey of 140 miles. A few months later, Alexander Winton had to devote nine days' driving and two of rest to a trip from Cleveland to New York, some 400 miles on the roads of today. *Two years* before Winton's journey, in the summer of 1895, Emile Levassor had completed the 732-mile race from Paris to Bordeaux and back in a few minutes over two days, driving virtually nonstop.

As late as May 1901, Winton had to abandon an attempt to cross the United States from coast to coast, starting from San Francisco. After eleven days of struggling through black adobe mud and loose desert sand, he had got no further than northwest Nevada.

But early in 1902, undisturbed by Winton's failure (or, more probably, unaware of it), a certain D. E. E. Lehwess announced that he was going to drive right round the world. A naturalized German living in England, he proposed going from London to Paris, Brussels, Cologne, Berlin, Posen, Warsaw, St. Petersburg (Leningrad), Moscow, Omask and Tomsk, then across China by an undisclosed route to Japan, to Hawaii, San Francisco, then down into Mexico, eastwards again to New Orleans, then north to Chicago and Niagara (with a drive around part of Canada), and back to New York so as to sail for Liverpool and finally drive through England to complete his journey at London.

His chosen vehicle for this highly ambitious itinerary was a bright yellow conveyance named, for obvious reasons, the *Passe-Partout*. Specially built for him on a strengthened Pan-

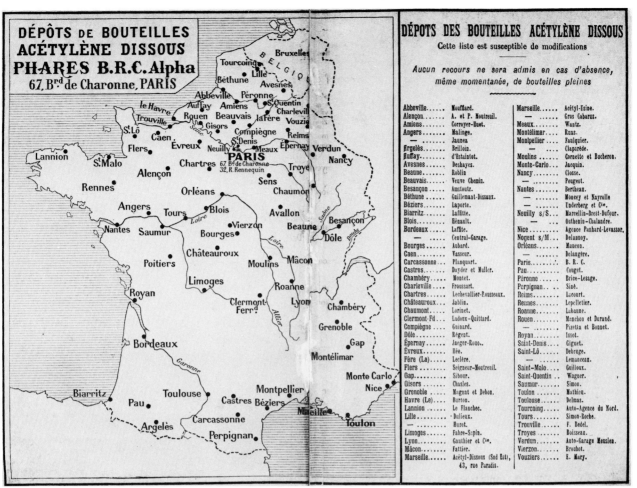

DÉPÔTS DE BOUTEILLES ACÉTYLÈNE DISSOUS PHARES B.R.C. Alpha
67, Bᵈ de Charonne, PARIS

DÉPÔTS DES BOUTEILLES ACÉTYLÈNE DISSOUS

Cette liste est susceptible de modifications

*Aucun recours ne sera admis en cas d'absence,
même momentanée, de bouteilles pleines*

Town	Depot	Town	Depot
Abbeville.....	Mouffard.	Marseille.....	Acétyl-Usine.
Alençon.......	A. et P. Moutreuil.	—	Grus Cabarus.
Amiens........	Corroyer-Huet.	Meaux........	Wantz.
Angers........	Malinge.	Montélimar....	Ruas.
—	Jaunea	Montpellier....	Faulquier.
Argelès.......	Brilloin.	—	Claparède.
Auffay........	d'Estaintot.	Moulins	Cornette et Bucheron.
Avesnes.......	Deshayes.	Monte-Carlo ..	Jacquin.
Beaune........	Roblin.	Nancy	Closse.
Beauvais......	Veuve Chemin.	—	Peugeot.
Besançon.....	Amstoutz.	Nantes	Bertheau.
Béthune......	Guillemant-Dissaux.	—	Moncey et Kayrolle.
Béziers.......	Laporte.	—	Underberg et Cie.
Biarritz......	Laffitte.	Neuilly s/S...	Marcellin-Brest-Dufour.
Blois.........	Hénault.	—	Outhenin-Chalandre.
Bordeaux......	Laffte.	Nice	Agence Panhard-Levassor.
—	Central-Garage.	Nogent s/M...	Delannoy.
Bourges	Aubard.	Orléans......	Mancon.
Caen.........	Vasseur.	—	Delaugère.
Carcassonne...	Planquart.	Paris........	B. R. C.
Castres.......	Dayder et Muller.	Pau.........	Couget.
Chambéry....	Montet.	Péronne.....	Brice-Lesage.
Charleville...	Froussart.	Perpignan....	Siné.
Chartres.....	Lechevallier-Rousseaux.	Reims........	Lacourt.
Châteauroux...	Jablin.	Rennes.......	Lepelletier.
Chaumont.....	Lorinet.	Roanne.......	Labaune.
Clermont-Fd..	Ladoux-Quittard.	Rouen........	Manchon et Durand.
Compiègne...	Guinard.	—	Pizetta et Bonnet.
Dôle.........	Régent.	Royan........	Issot.
Épernay......	Jaeger-Roux..	Saint-Denis....	Giguet.
Évreux.......	Hée.	Saint-Lô.....	Debruge.
Père (La).....	Leclère.	—	Lemanceau.
Flers	Seigneur-Moutreuil.	Saint-Malo....	Guilloux.
Gap..........	Sibour.	Saint-Quentin ..	Wagner.
Gisors	Chasles.	Saumur......	Simon.
Grenoble	Magnat et Debon.	Toulon	Mathieu.
Havre (Le)...	Burton.	Toulouse.....	Delmas.
Lannion......	Le Flanchee.	Tourcoing....	Auto-Agence du Nord.
Lille........	Dulieux.	Tours........	Simon-Roche.
—	Huret.	Trouville.....	F. Bedel.
Limoges......	Fabre-Sapin.	Troyes.......	Boisseau.
Lyon.........	Gauthier et Cie.	Verdun......	Auto-Garage Meusien.
Mâcon........	Fattier.	Vierzon......	Brouhot.
Marseille.....	Acétyl-Dissous (Sud Est), 43, rue Paradis.	Vouziers......	E. Mary.

SUR ROUTE

hard chassis (at a cost of £3000), this provided stowage space in its bodywork for an assortment of shooting and fishing gear in addition to sleeping accommodation and other home comforts for the crew. It was only thirteen feet long, but more than made up for this by being approximately nine feet high and weighing almost three tons.

This mammoth device left London at the end of April with three other cars in attendance, and covered twenty-four of its planned 24,000-plus miles before a loud bang announced the first tyre burst. Dr. Lehwess and his companions adjourned to a nearby hotel for lunch while the mechanics mended the tyre, and as it was nearly dark when he returned, the party covered only fifteen miles more before deciding to stop for the night. In Paris, which was reached early in May, they stayed for six weeks before continuing their ponderous progress. In Berlin

Before the days of reliable electrical systems, most cars had headlamps which burned acetylene gas, conveniently bought as containers of "dissolved acetylene" in preference to carbide generators. The map in this Continental guide details nearly eighty towns where fresh supplies could be bought when on tour in France.

they did even better; they stayed nine weeks before leaving, quite suddenly, in the middle of a foggy September night. But although they remained barely a week in Warsaw, it was beginning to look a great deal like winter when they reached St.Petersburg.

It was, in fact, mid-October when the party got to Moscow, and—as Napoleon had learned only ninety years before—October is not a good time for travelling in Russia. Quite soon afterwards, any passing *moujik* might have observed the abandoned *Passe-Partout* sinking slowly into the snow just six miles east of Nijni-Novgorod; in the meantime Dr. Lehwess and his friends were heading back to civilization in a warm railway train.

In May of the following year, 1903, Dr. Nelson Jackson commenced the first successful crossing of the American continent by car, and it must have been a source of great satisfaction to its Scots-born, Cleveland-resident maker that he did it in a Winton. His time, sixty-four days, was cut to sixty-one days by a Packard enthusiast named Tom Fetch before the year was out.

But nobody had yet crossed Asia. In 1907 a French newspaper suggested such a crossing, starting from Pekin (now Peking) and finishing in Paris after an 8,000-mile marathon which everybody insisted on calling a "motor race" although it was nothing of the sort; indeed, participants were particularly asked to stay as close together as possible on the journey for their mutual protection and convenience. By stipulating a Pekin start the organizers ensured that nobody could follow the example of Dr. Lehwess; what they did not do, however, was to make any effective inquiry into the state of Chinese roads. When five entrants eventually reached Pekin with their cars, they found, of course, that there was nothing a motorist would describe as a road at all.

Nevertheless, after sixty days the Itala of Prince Scipione Borghese arrived in Paris to be hailed as the "winner," followed almost three weeks later by two de Dions and a Spyker. Only one entrant, who drove a completely unsuitable three-wheeler, had had to drop out. It was a magnificent achievement by the four finishers, whose cars had been laboriously transported across a continent, dragged by oxen and man-handled by their own crews with the assistance of sweating coolies and other peasants. On the other hand, as Prince Borghese tried vainly to point out, all they had proved was that motoring across Asia was, as yet, impossible. What they had accomplished was admirable, certainly, but it had very little to do with driving a motor-car—and this was inevitable, since the entrants had discovered that for almost three-quarters of the distance there was no road to drive on.

The Prince's shrewd comment fell on deaf ears, and the same French paper, *Le Matin*, now conceived an even more fantastic idea: a motor race around the world, no less. Competitors were to start from New York and cross the American continent to Seattle, then head up the western coast of Canada into Alaska as far as Dawson City. From there, they were to swing westwards along the Yukon River to the Bering Straits, where they were to drive *across the ice* into Siberia, then continue southwest almost to the Manchurian frontier, and so join up with the Pekin/Paris route. On arrival in Paris the competitors would have covered some 17,000 miles and virtually circled the globe, apart from crossing the Atlantic.

The proposed route was widely condemned as absurd. In 1908 the greater part of Alaska and Siberia was still unexplored and

A Ford Model T goes touring in what was then the British protectorate of Basutoland in Africa (now known as Lesotho).

RADIO TIMES HULTON PICTURE LIBRARY

A stranded motorist tries to dry out the ignition system of his Berliet tourer, stranded by the 1926 floods in the centre of Calcutta.

RADIO TIMES HULTON PICTURE LIBRARY

almost certainly impassable, especially in winter, when it was hoped that the ice would be thick enough to support the cars. As for the route across America, much of this lay well to the north of the only one that any car had yet succeeded in following. It was reluctantly agreed that instead of driving straight to Seattle, the competitors should head for San Francisco, where they would go on board ship for the journey up the western coast of the continent to Valdez, then disembark to drive across Alaska as far as Nome, take ship again across the Bering Sea, and proceed as before across Siberia.

This change, though a wise one, unfortunately made the event in some ways even more absurd; it could scarcely be described as a motor race, or even as just a drive around the world, if the contestants were to spend so much of their time on board ship.

The entrants were a motley crew, as were most of their vehicles. One car carried skis which could be fitted to the front wheels, and a mast and sail for use in favourable winds. Another, a Motobloc from France, was so lavishly equipped that in size it resembled the ill-fated *Passe-Partout*. It had fitted drawers filled with tools and spares, and carried quantities of champagne for celebrating special occasions.

Only six cars actually started from New York, and the Motobloc's first day's run ended at Peekskill, not fifty miles out. There the crew spent several hours digging it out of a snowdrift before discovering, as night fell, that they had brought no food with them; only champagne.

The conditions that competitors encountered as they drove—or attempted to drive— across the American continent, in mid-winter, made the previous year's journey through

DETROIT PUBLIC LIBRARY

Eventually acclaimed winner of the fantastic 1908 motor race westwards around the world from New York to Paris, the Buffalo-built Thomas Flyer was one of three cars to complete the distance (there were only six starters!). The car survives today in the Harrah Automobile Collection at Reno, Nevada.

Not only roads, but bridges, too, were scarce in the early days of motoring in America. Here, two pioneer parties ferry a river during a Good Roads Tour from New York to Atlanta, Georgia, a journey that must have totalled 1,000 miles as they sought out a suitable route from one city to the other.

DETROIT PUBLIC LIBRA

Most enthusiastic of early American motoring tourists was Charles J. Glidden, who covered more than 45,000 miles in 39 countries, starting in 1902. He always used British Napiers for his journeys, and fitted them with flanged wheels for driving along railway lines in places where there were no roads.

China seem like a picnic. Four of the six cars reached San Francisco, one way or another. Only one, the American-built Thomas Flyer, attempted the drive through Alaska, which was immediately found to be utterly impossible. The other three, when they got to Seattle, went straight off to Yokohama by ship, there to be joined by the Thomas Flyer. Realizing that if they disqualified everyone who had broken the rules, the event would collapse about their ears, the organizers hurriedly redrafted the regulations. Later, faced with the possibility that a German car might win—at a time when France was strongly anti-German—they changed the rules again.

Three cars did actually reach Paris some seven months after leaving New York: the German Protos, which arrived first but had covered about 1,000 miles in a railway truck; the American Thomas, later accepted as the winner although it was said to have been completely rebuilt at the factory during the early stages of the event; and the Italian Züst, whose crew's many adventures supplied enough material for a complete book. The competitors had unquestionably overcome almost insuperable obstacles in the course of their long journey, but as a sporting competition the great race from New York to Paris was a complete failure, tersely dismissed by one American reporter as "a howling farce."

Meanwhile there were other motorists, no less adventurous if less interested in publicity, who ranged far and wide in their choice of touring grounds. The classic example of these was that dauntless New Englander, Charles J. Glidden, whose name is preserved today in the series of Glidden Tours, as well-known in America as the London-to-Brighton Run is in Britain. Having made a fortune in the telephone business, Charles Glidden decided to dispose of some of it by driving 50,000 miles in fifty different countries. He started at the end of 1902, setting off with wife and chauffeur in a British-built Napier—which he seemed to like, for he followed it up with three more Napiers in the next six years. When he could find no roads to drive along, he fitted flanged wheels to his Napiers and drove along the railway lines instead. In 1908, when the Gliddens felt they had had enough of motoring, the score stood at 46,538 miles in thirty-nine countries.

Another indefatigable motorist was the Baroness Campbell von Laurentz, whose husband's Scottish ancestry was partially obscured by the title bestowed on him by Ernest II of Saxe-Coburg-Gotha (a brother-in-law of Queen Victoria) for his services in the Franco-German War of 1870. The Baroness took up motoring in 1900 and soon began to travel widely, contributing articles to such publications as *Car Illustrated*, *Autocar*, *Ladies' Field*, and *Hearth and Home*. These were followed in 1913 by a book, *My Motor Milestones*, devoted to the practical aspects of her travels (on which subject she had kept copious notes) and providing a wealth of useful information for other motoring tourists.

As an example of her attention to detail, there was her solution to that perennial problem of the early motorist—how to carry luggage in a car that provided accommodation for the passengers alone. She designed two square fibre boxes to fit on the luggage grid at the rear, and had these made up for her by one of the big London department stores (they cost 26 shillings, or £1.30, the pair). They went on the grid with a piece of canvas underneath and over the top a tailored cover in proofed canvas, leather-bound: .

"In these, with a holdall, I have taken enough for three people (a married couple and myself) for a month on the Continent. It is astonishing how much they hold. My friend's look of despair when first she was shown 'all she could take' changed when she began to pack. There was enough for an extra suit and dress clothes for her husband, and an evening dress and several day changes for her. . . . These boxes are as good as new, and have made many tours in England, and ten abroad. The heavy things go at the bottom, and all that is sure to be wanted every day. A holland case made to fit exactly, with extension on two sides and tapes to tie, is then placed on the top of these, and when dresses and blouses have been neatly laid therein the two flaps are carefully folded over and tied. This has only to be lifted bodily out, and no repacking is required if anything is wanted from the bottom, and it saves the weight of a tray."

The holdall referred to was another of her inventions: a large bag fixed with straps, top and bottom, behind the front seats, which was used for mackintoshes and oddments "wanted on the voyage." A small patent-leather case hooked to the dashboard was reserved for maps (each in a celluloid case to protect it from the rain), driving licence and other documents, a notebook to record purchases of fuel, etc., and route information previously noted down in "a halfpenny account book, irreverently called 'the washing book.'" Inside the spare tyres was strapped a circular container of the type once known as a "chauffeur's case." But that was reserved for the ladies' hats: the chauffeur was allowed the whole of the space beneath the rear seat for his own personal belongings, together with the car jack. The remaining tools and spares went under the running boards "in

*Finding space for luggage was always a problem for the motoring tourist in earlier times. This 1925 Lancia (*TOP*) offers little room for cases, even with the spare wheels fitted outside. The 1929 Ford Roadster (*ABOVE*) carries a handsome trunk on its luggage grid, but dust was always likely to penetrate such containers eventually.*

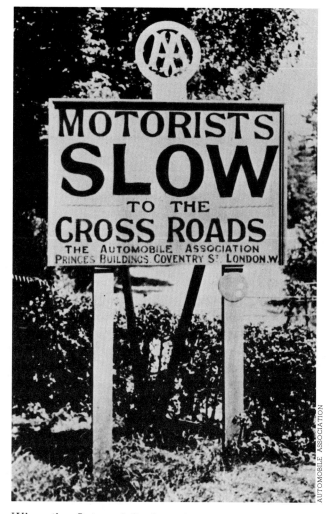

When the Automobile Association began erecting signs in Britain, the emphasis was on warning notices rather than direction signs, and a driver who was in unfamiliar country often had to stop to ask the way.

divided drawers, on one side the inner tubes; and levers, chalk and repair outfit on the other. Sparking plugs and other small things go in shallow drawers under the front seat, so I do not have to turn out my passengers for every little repair. A square box padded at the top makes a foot-stool, and contains the spare two-gallon can.''

Although the Baroness loved to drive, she had some difficulty in reaching the pedals. Even this was turned to advantage:

''I always drive with a wedge-shaped cushion, which matches the car, securely fastened to the back of my seat by straps. This was heavy, and a great waste of space, so I took out the stuffing, lined the interior with *tussoré* silk (in which I made little pockets), and had a flap made for the cushion which fastened down with glove-button clips on the side nearest the back of the seat. Into this I now pack all I want for the night. Night and dressing-gowns roll up at the bottom, flat brush and comb in case, slippers, etc., at the back and in front, my down pillow. All the little odds and ends in the pockets behind the pillow. Lastly, if the cushion is not full enough, my hot-water bottle can be inflated with air. What a joy on reaching my destination just to shake everything out on to the bed, and to have no unpacking to do! A handle along the top makes it easy to carry, and an air-cushion, made wedge-shape to fit, can be used when not touring and when staying in one place for a day.''

Another problem of the early motorist was how to find one's way in unfamiliar territory. There were very few signposts, for ordinary folk seldom moved outside the bounds of a ten-mile circle, even in the early part of this century. The turnpike trusts had largely ignored the duty placed upon them, by successive pieces of legislation, to put up direction posts at crossroads, and few of those that were erected survived the general neglect of the highways during the early years of the railways. In Britain and some other countries, the cycling clubs pooled their resources during the 1880s to erect notices warning their members of such hazards as steep hills, but they obviously could not afford direction posts. And the Motor Car Act of 1903 required local authorities in Britain to provide warning signs where hazards existed—but not directions.

One solution was to call on the services of a guide, though there was the chance that he might be too bewildered by the new sensations of motoring to make a good job of it, as J. E. Vincent observed in his 1907 book, *Through East Anglia in a Motor Car*:

"A new member was added to the party in the person of a resident at Norwich, desirous of reaching that ancient city in due course, who was supposed to know, and probably did know, every considerable turning of every high road in the two counties of Norfolk and Suffolk. He had not, however, enjoyed much experience as the pilot of an automobile, and he found, as I had in years gone by when I was new to the pastime, that eye and memory were not equal to moving together at a speed proportioned to that of the car. 'Which road?' the charioteer would cry—the new passenger was riding astern—when we were from fifty to seventy yards from a fork or turn, and hesitation would often be visible in the reply, so that it was necessary to slow down and sometimes, having invaded the wrong road, to back out again.

"This is not criticism, it is rather a matter of observation and experience. Only recently have the minds of driving and driven men been called upon to exercise their judgment, to choose a line, as a fox-hunter might say, while they are being carried through space much more rapidly than of yore, and the pace puzzles them at first. You are past a familiar turning in a car in less time than is consumed over approaching it in a dog-cart or on horseback, and the aspect of the turning itself has something strange about it; but you grow accustomed to the new conditions with experience. In fact, motor-cars sharpen the perceptions and spur the intelligence."

Towns, too, might confuse the motorist, as Henry Edmunds commented in an article written in 1902 for *Car Illustrated*:

"It is often easier to find one's way into a town than through it or out of it. It is curious that people have very limited ideas of the locality in which they reside, and often take it for granted that you know all the names of the streets, buildings, hotels and churches that they are familiar with, and try to direct you accordingly. When passing through a strange town I frequently take a pilot on board in the shape of a small boy, numbers of whom may be found, and who are only too pleased and willing to conduct you to an hotel or through the town you are passing. Let them stand on the step or sit on the footboard, and instruct them to give you plenty of notice as to turns and streets you may run through."

Within a few years direction signs were to be found more frequently in Europe, thanks to the efforts of many different organisations: highway or local authorities in some countries, and motoring clubs such as the Motor Union (which in 1910 merged with the Automobile Association), the AA itself, and the Automobile Club de France. In America they were slower to appear and at first owed their existence to commercial interests, being provided by local garages and

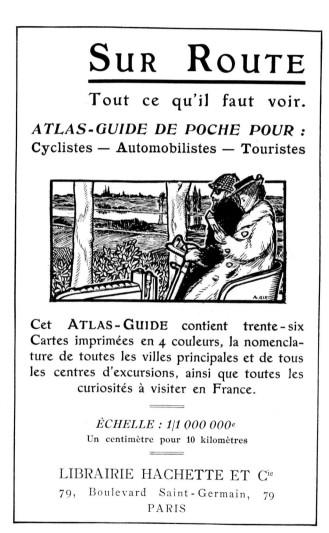

SUR ROUTE

Tout ce qu'il faut voir.

ATLAS-GUIDE DE POCHE POUR :
Cyclistes — Automobilistes — Touristes

Cet ATLAS-GUIDE contient trente-six
Cartes imprimées en 4 couleurs, la nomencla-
ture de toutes les villes principales et de tous
les centres d'excursions, ainsi que toutes les
curiosités à visiter en France.

ÉCHELLE : 1/1 000 000e
Un centimètre pour 10 kilomètres

LIBRAIRIE HACHETTE ET Cie
79, Boulevard Saint-Germain, 79
PARIS

*Earlier in the century when signposts were few,
a motorist who went on a touring holiday was
very dependent on maps and guides like this
Pocket Atlas-Guide which contained thirty-six
maps (printed in four colours), and apparently
detailed "all the curiosities to visit in France."*

one of the major tyre manufacturers. The inconvenience of doing without signs is well con-
veyed in *Excuse My Dust* by Bellamy Partridge:

"Nowadays the motorist can drive from
California to New York in less than a week
without once asking or losing his way. But on a
two weeks' tour through New England in 1910
I must have been off my road more than fifty
times, and I probably stopped to inquire my
way twenty or thirty times a day."

So the travelling motorist learned to plan
his tour in advance with the aid of whatever
maps he could obtain: the Taride and Jourdan
maps of Continental Europe and the various
publications based on the official Ordnance
Survey of the British Isles—Bartholomew's maps
of England and Wales, Johnston's maps of
Scotland, and Mecredy's maps of Ireland. Soon
he was able to refer to an enormous range of
road books and guides made available by the
publishers of motoring magazines, clubs, oil
and fuel companies, tyre manufacturers—even
by some of the motor manufacturers, too. By
1905 *The Car* advertised a set of maps of
England and Wales in a handsome leather case
(with lock, and a spring in the bottom to raise
the maps automatically when the lid was
opened), which could be mounted permanently
on the car; a guide-book entitled *Best Ways
Out of London*, which contained thirty route
maps, together with details of the ten steepest
hills in England; and a calf-bound *Road Book
and Guide*, incorporating a linen-mounted map
of the United Kingdom, touring-route information, a gazetteer and a concise encyclopaedia of
motoring. This was followed by a *Continental
Touring Guide*, a set of four routes from London
to the Riviera, and a series of books called
Roads Made Easy which gave detailed route instructions covering most parts of Britain, even

to the extent of providing photographs of major road junctions. In the days when many a popular car was barely capable of surmounting a 1-in-10 gradient without assistance, prudent motorists would also take account of the Contour road books when planning a tour.

In France there was the *Guide Taride* and, from as early as 1900, the great *Guide Michelin* begun by André Michelin himself, already famous for his early exploits as a racing driver. In America, from 1906 onwards, the makers of the White steam car published a series of free booklets giving routes for suggested motor tours. The Chadwick Company in Philadelphia went to even more trouble by placing on the market a curious device known as the Chadwick Automatic Road Guide, which was fixed to the dashboard and driven by cable from one front wheel. The buyer was provided with a set of perforated metal discs, rather like some types of early gramophone record. All he had to do was attach the appropriate disc for his journey, and route information was provided as he drove along; a bell rang out as he approached road junctions along the way, and he was able to read off route instructions in advance. It was an ingenious gadget (and has in fact reappeared in electronic form within the last few years), but most motorists who went touring in the USA put their faith in the leather-bound *Automobile Bluebooks* at $2.50 apiece, with their more conventional maps and route details—not to mention a very useful newsletter service which told subscribers the location of new speed traps.

With such a flood of information being poured out from so many sources, and this at a time when road systems were expanding at greatly increased speed and traffic regulations continually changing, inevitably the accuracy of the data was not always beyond question. Some motoring tourists, for example, must have had an unusually exciting holiday if they accepted the advice given in the 1912 edition of the *Motor Manual* that "The Rule of the Road in France now is to keep to the left, as in England, and overtake vehicles on the right."

Indeed, the rule of the road was confusing enough to the traveller, even without misinformation. It is a matter of fact that for many years one drove on the right in Rumania, on the left in Hungary, and on the left in all parts of Austria *except* the province of Vorarlberg, where one drove on the right. The motorist, having made his bewildered way through these adjoining countries, might perhaps proceed to Czechoslovakia (drive on the left) and thence through Germany (drive on the right) to Denmark (drive on the right), possibly continuing through Sweden (drive on the left) to Norway (drive on the right). Or he might, instead, cross from Austria into Italy, where everybody drove on the right until they came to the outskirts of Milan, Genoa, Rome and several other ancient cities where, in accordance with local custom, they would cross to the other side of the road and drive on the left.

Quite apart from guidebooks and touring information, the widespread interest in motoring travel also inspired a new form of fiction— the motoring romance. Charles and Alice Williamson, an English photographer-journalist and his American-born wife, set the fashion and established the formula for the genre in 1902 with *The Lightning Conductor*, a novelette which took its enthralled readers on an imaginary motoring tour across France to the Côte d'Azur (where elderly hotel guests were said to be complaining that the Riviera was "ruined" by the presence of so many motorcars!) and on to

Italy and Sicily. Alice Williamson wrote the book and was responsible for the highly romantic plot, while Charles supplied the photographic illustrations featuring the Williamsons' own elderly car, and presumably vetted (not always successfully) the technical references.

The Lightning Conductor was a best seller, even earning the approval of Edward VII, who called on the Williamsons to tell them how much he had enjoyed it. It was followed by more than a score of books, many of them based on the theme of a motoring holiday in Continental Europe, Britain or America: *My Friend the Chauffeur*; *The Car of Destiny*; *The Botor Chaperon*; *The Scarlet Runner*; *Set in Silver*; *The Motor Maid*; *The Heather Moon*; *The Lightning Conductress*; and more besides. There was little variation in plot or characters, however much the setting changed. A well-bred girl, often American, would meet and become fascinated by a tremendously handsome young man in the early stages of a motoring tour, but owing to some misunderstanding the heroine, not only well chaperoned but naive to the point of simple-mindedness, would mistake the hero for a mere chauffeur. There would be a great many more misunderstandings and a chase extending over several different countries, until usually about page 300 when the hero was revealed as the Honourable Somebody, and the heroine admitted to being hopelessly in love with him, thus leaving the way clear for a happy ending.

The motoring fiction of the Williamsons was echoed to some extent by Louise Closser Hale's *A Motor Car Divorce*, illustrated by the drawings of Walter Hale and published in 1906. This presented a romanticized account of a trip made by an American couple the previous year, when they had bought an 18 hp Northern,

shipped it to Naples, and driven through Italy and France before sailing back to the United States from Cherbourg. If Louise Hale was unable to claim a king as an enthusiastic reader, her book painted a much more convincing picture of the joys and sorrows of Continental motoring, and especially of the roads of Italy at a time when cars were so scarce that they encountered only six in the 350 miles from Naples to Rimini.

When the Hales landed at Naples, for example, their Northern refused to start because it had been filled with *petrolio* instead of *benzina*. This was exactly the fate that had befallen J. A. Koosen's Lutzmann in 1895, and Charles Jarrott's Panhard in 1898, and it happened to almost every early motorist at one time or another. The Baroness Campbell von Laurentz, too, complained that in 1901 the tank of her Locomobile was topped up with ''common lamp oil instead of petrol'' when she stopped in an English village. It was all the more exasperating for the Baroness, therefore, that when she made her first Continental tour in 1905, the same year as the Hales, she found the French had grown accustomed to the idea that cars ran on petrol (*essence*) instead of paraffin oil (*huile de pétrole*). Because by that time she had replaced her Locomobile by a Serpollet, and although both of these were steam cars, the Serpollet was that rare bird, a steamer fired by paraffin.

The Locomobile had been the Baroness' first car, delivered to her at Windsor in September 1900 and, she was told, the first of its kind to be imported from America. This may not have been strictly true, for it is known that Rudyard Kipling bought one in the summer of that same year, and later immortalized its frailties by dubbing it ''a wicker-willow lunch-

*Even in waterbound Venice the motor vehicle
was used extensively by tourists. In this picture a
party of holiday-makers is seen embarking at the
Lido.*

TIMES HULTON PICTURE LIBRARY

That enthusiastic lady motorist, the Baroness Campbell von Laurentz, aboard her 1905 Serpollet steam car. The Baron, who never drove and never wanted to, sits beside her, and the "small motor boy" occupies his usual position in the back seat.

basket" with its boiler "seated on four little paper-clips." It was allegedly capable of 25 mph, but the Baroness said hers would do no more than 18; not that this was of more than academic interest, one's cross-country average being much more profoundly governed by the fact that the water tank had to be refilled every twenty miles in any case. Despite this, the Baroness was soon embarking on tours of several hundred miles at a time, accompanied by her long-suffering husband and "our small motor boy," who spent most of his time jammed in the back seat along with the luggage. Unfortunately the small motor boy knew little about motors and the Baron knew even less, so the Baroness mended punctures with her own ladylike hands and cleared out clogged water gauges with a hatpin:

"Our difficulties became less and less. Things improved. The same kind of accident never happened twice; experience taught me. Notwithstanding all, very seldom did we fail to keep an engagement. . . . The 'Loco' ran continually, summer and winter, and had only one side slip. We went many delightful tours, and never found a hill which presented any difficulty."

Even when she engaged a competent chauffeur, this splendid woman continued to do most of the driving, and it became her normal practice to motor for long distances accompanied by the chauffeur and her personal maid, but only occasionally by the Baron, who did not share his wife's delight in making long journeys in open motorcars come hail, rain or snow. When a succession of engine troubles marooned them in rural France for two days, the poor man lost his temper and swore he would rather travel fourth-class by train. Thereafter, when his adventurous wife made one of her marathon trips across the Continent, he usually arranged to meet her at the other end.

The Baroness soon lost her early enthusiasm for steam cars, and within six months of returning from the first Continental tour in the Serpollet she had taken delivery of a 14/17 hp Dixi, an early predecessor of the BMW built at Eisenach. Two days later she was heading north for the English Lake District, on a three-week tour marred only by continual tyre trouble (because she had made the mistake of overloading the car with luggage and passengers). Ever resourceful, when she ran out of spare inner tubes she stuffed one cover with hay and tied it on to the wheel rim. Soon she was off again, touring in the Cotswolds, and there learned the trick of driving up a hill in reverse if it was too steep to climb in any of the forward gears. At the end of 1906 she took the Baron with her on a drive across France to Pau, and was delighted to find that the Dixi, unlike her steam cars, also provided enough space for the chauffeur, her maid and all the luggage. It was, they agreed, a most successful trip, for in almost eight hundred miles they had only one ignition fault and punctured only a few tyres. They did, though, run out of petrol in a remote area where none could be obtained, the Baroness having yet to grow accustomed to the needs of petrol cars.

In the summer of 1907, however, the Dixi—now almost two years old—was no longer at its best. A 2,000-mile tour from Brittany to the Alps and back was punctuated by a cracked chassis frame, a run big-end bearing, two broken timing wheels, a broken gear lever and a variety of other troubles. So the Dixi, which had never really been powerful enough for her needs, gave way to a fine big six-cylinder, 40 hp Minerva from Belgium, baptized the

following summer with a 1,500-mile trip to Baden-Baden and back.

February 1909 saw the big Minerva thundering across France with the Baroness at the wheel as usual, her faithful chauffeur at her side and both covered in a thick layer of frozen snow—for the Minerva had no windscreen; merely a celluloid device which could be erected *behind* the front seats. This, together with a Cape cart hood, sheltered the rear compartment only, and there cowered the maid, "coughing horribly."

The Baroness drove with an even more determined air than usual, for this was a journey with a mission. She had learned that Wilbur and Orville Wright were carrying out some of their aeronautical experiments in Pau, and she wanted to see them. More than that, she wanted a ride in their aeroplane, apparently undeterred by the fact that Orville had crashed only a few months before with fatal results for his passenger. On arrival at Pau she swept through all obstacles to meet and talk to the famous brothers, but they explained apologetically that they preferred not to take passengers if they could possibly avoid doing so; the only woman who ever went flying with them was their sister. Sadly the Baroness drove away again. A year later she visited Pau once more in the Minerva, this time in the hopes of flying with Louis Blériot, who had made the first flight across the English Channel the previous summer. Again she was unsuccessful, for Blériot was using a single-seater, but shortly afterwards she was able to have a short flight in one of Henry Farman's machines. The result was inevitable. The Baroness decided she must learn to fly.

But the Baron put his foot down. All this motoring was bad enough, heaven knows, but flying around in an aeroplane—that would be too much. The Baroness consoled herself with the purchase of a Rolls-Royce Silver Ghost, her pride and joy for future motoring tours, and got away to a grand start in January 1911 by shipping it to Algeria, where she drove a total of about 1,500 miles in the course of the next few weeks. This was followed, in the summer, by a trip to the Dolomites and back, the Baroness in her Rolls-Royce and her brother in his. It was noticeable how much more reliable cars and their tyres had become. In nearly two thousand miles her car had only one puncture, and the only real difficulty they experienced was in obtaining fuel in one part of Austria, where they had to buy benzine in large glass jars from the local chemist.

Early in 1912 came an even longer journey totalling 2,269 miles: to Nice and Monte Carlo, on into northern Italy, and back through Switzerland and across France. On the outward trip she put up a running average of 28 mph, covering the 821 miles from Boulogne to Nice in five days. So an average daily run was more than 160 miles; on one particular day, in fact, and despite a heavy snowfall, she completed 187 miles. A few months later, when driving back across France at the conclusion of her holiday, she achieved her longest run yet—218 miles in a day.

Yet there were signs of disenchantment at last. The Baroness complained that the Riviera was "no place for motoring, being quite spoilt by tramlines and overcrowded with motorcars." It was the same story the following August when she travelled with her brother and nephew, all three of them in Rolls-Royces, for a 1,000-mile tour in northern France: "We went on to Mont St. Michel—oh, so crowded, and such rows of cars! What a difference from the two former occasions on which I had visited it! Brittany is quite overrun now."

To prove her point she took a photograph —reproduced in *My Motor Milestones*—in which about twenty-five cars may be seen parked on the shore below the monastery. Poor Baroness; she really should have taken up flying before touring by motor became the pursuit of every Tom, Dick and Harry.

THE ROAD UNFOLDS

"But in order that the motor may cease to be injurious and become beneficent, we must build roads suited to its speed, roads which it cannot tear up with its ferocious tyres, and from which it will send no clouds of poisonous dust into human lungs."

ANATOLE FRANCE, Ile des Pingouins (1907)

In the days when Britain was thickly wooded, primitive man often travelled along the ridges of the hills, making pathways like this one which runs along the summit of the Malvern Hills in Worcestershire. Prehistoric remains are usually found nearby.

An archaeologist who has studied early highways more thoroughly than most, O. G. S. Crawford, believes that they were neither designed nor made, but simply evolved naturally as the result of primitive man's need to get from one place to another. It was a need more vital to him than to his immediate successors of historic times, who were static by comparison. He was a hunter rather than a farmer; he had to move about in order to pursue game.

Where the countryside was thickly wooded he travelled along the ridges of the hills, which allowed him to move with greater speed because the vegetation was less dense, and as the visibility was correspondingly better, he also avoided the danger of being himself surprised by a predator. In Britain these ridgeways, as they are called, are dotted with such man-made relics as flint mines and hill forts, indicating that they were in use during the Stone Age, Bronze Age and Iron Age, if not earlier. Their exact age is unknown. One writer has gone so far as to suggest that the Berkshire Ridgeway, with its nearby White Horse and Wayland Smithy (its name borrowed from Teutonic mythology, but actually a chambered burial place), is the oldest road in all Europe. He believes that man may have walked along it before Britain became detached from the Continental land mass to become an island. Crawford, however, considers that the oldest visible piece of road in Britain is a short track giving access to a flint mine near Cissbury Ring in Sussex. This is what is technically a hollow way—a hillside path worn deep into the Downlands chalk in the course of many centuries of use.

There are other classifications, too, belonging to various periods of history, and sometimes revealed to the amateur explorer by local place names. "Portway," for example, is not necessarily a road leading to a port (although some do), but to one of the gates (*porta*) of a walled town. Names like Saltford, Salters Hill or Saltergate suggest a saltway, along which the salt merchants carried their wares by packhorse from the coast or from an inland salt-making centre in the days before refrigeration, when meat had to be salted down for the winter. In some places one can pick out the line of a driftway or drove road, along which cattle and sheep were driven to market. Right through the eighteenth century the drovers continued to use their own traditional routes to avoid paying the heavy tolls charged on the main turnpike roads, and occasionally a simple inn or beerhouse set in isolated countryside is, in fact, on the line of a drove road, a bucolic equivalent to the well-appointed coaching inns of the main highways.

The different categories are not always clearcut. A drover urges his herd of beasts along part of a ridgeway, and it becomes a drove road. It may even become a modern highway. An ancient track falls into disuse, surviving as a mere country lane or, completely overgrown, just a dotted line on a large-scale map. Years later a highway engineer finds that line convenient for his purpose, and the giant earth-moving machines are set to work turning a Stone Age man's footpath into part of a six-lane motorway.

But whatever the significance of primitive tracks, it is the Romans who stand pre-eminent as road builders. Solid as the rock with which it was constructed, the Roman road acted as the foundation stone of Western civilization. This amazing network of highways stretched boldly out from the eternal city to the farthest limits of its influence, carrying the Imperial Post and allowing the Roman Army to reach a trouble

Two thousand years of weathering has broken up the surface of the Roman road at Wheeldale in the North Yorkshire Moors, some twenty miles from Scarborough. But it can be clearly seen for a distance of three miles. The line of the same road can still be traced to the north and south of this stretch, and there are remains of a Roman military camp only five miles away.

spot without delay to deal swiftly and ruthlessly with any uprising. Given an ample supply of fresh horses, a man could travel along those roads faster than anyone in the world had done before him. He could, indeed, travel faster than anyone until a couple of millennia afterwards, when the railway came to Victorian England. The whole basis of Rome's iron grip on its mighty empire lay in this unprecedented communications system.

The Romans realized the importance of good roads early in the period of the republic, when still struggling to annex the whole of Italy. Three centuries before the birth of Christ they had started work on the great Via Appia, the Appian Way, which was eventually to reach Brindisi, 350 miles away at the "heel" of Italy. To the north of Rome they built the Via Flaminia, the Via Salaria and the Via Caecilia, while the Via Aurelia ran up the west coast to Pisa (the strange aura of anachronism that now affects Roman history is the fault of the Lancia company, who borrowed ancient road names for their new models). Finally, with the establishment of the empire, the roads stretched out from the north of Italy to the Danube in the northeast, down through what is now Yugoslavia to penetrate Greece, and over some of the highest Alpine passes into France. The result was widespread movement and trading between countries, on a scale that makes present-day Europe's Common Market seem like a small get-together in a suburban backyard.

Roman roads were not just the physical manifestation of a line on a map, but part of a complex and rigidly controlled organization. There were normally post houses every five to fifteen miles where horses could be changed, and rest houses every twenty miles or so where travellers could rest or stay overnight. (Just in

the same way as caravan depots were built throughout the Middle East at a day's "camel distance" apart.) Granted these facilities, it was accepted that Imperial couriers should cover fifty miles a day when going about their duties, but twice that distance could be achieved if necessary. Edward Gibbon mentions that six days sufficed for a certain journey of some 650 miles—a distance that he himself, fourteen centuries later, took three weeks to cover by stagecoach. It is also recorded that the 1,140 Roman miles from Rheims to Rome were covered in nine days, a remarkable average of 160 miles a day.

The popular generalization is that Roman roads ran straight as a die from starting point to destination, ignoring and surmounting all obstacles. This is not strictly true. In flat country the Romans were certainly more disposed to take the shortest possible route, ignoring any existing tracks, but they were quite prepared to zigzag on occasion; across the Alps or the Apennines, for instance.

Normally the road was laid out in straight lines from one sighting point to the next, using beacon fires on the hilltops. When the course of the road was decided, two parallel ditches would be dug, and between these the bed of the road was first consolidated with firmly rammed or beaten earth. On top of this were placed, usually, four layers of road metal: one of large stones, preferably flat, laid in mortar; one of smaller stones or masonry rubble in mortar; one of finer concrete made up of lime, chalk, powdered brick or other available material mixed with clay; and finally the paved surface itself, ideally of hard stone blocks carefully matched and jointed. The total thickness of the various layers was often three feet or more.

The width of the paved surface varied con-

AA DRIVE PUBLICATIONS

siderably. It might be fourteen feet wide and edged with raised stone kerbs, plus a soft shoulder seven feet wide along each side, so that the ditches were twenty-eight feet apart; but there are even wider Roman roads in existence. Although local labour was pressed into service for maintenance in far-flung parts of the empire, the work was done to high standards, under strict supervision and using good materials. As comparatively little wheeled traffic was carried, attention was needed only at infrequent intervals.

For solidity and long life, no better method of road construction has ever been devised. After two thousand years and more, many a Roman road is still in use today, hidden from sight beneath a modern top dressing. In some parts of Italy even this has been dispensed with, and the original surface paving may still be seen. In our language, too, the Roman road survives, for it is the adjectival part of *via strata*, a paved way, that gives us our modern word *street*.

And in Britain, after the departure of the Romans, the Anglo-Saxons gave to the roads various names of their own which—like the roads themselves—have in some cases survived to the present day. From London to Chichester by the present A29 road (through Billingshurst and Pulborough) runs Stane Street, so called because it was paved with stone. The Fosse Way, from Cirencester to Leicester, then on to Lincoln by the A46, got its name from the *fosse*, or ditch, on each side of it. Some names are those of local tribes. The Waeclings of Hertfordshire gave theirs to Watling Street, the present A5 from London through Dunstable, Towcester, Hinckley, and on north of Birmingham to Shrewsbury. The Earnings of Cambridgeshire are commemorated in Ermine or

Ermin Street, now the A14 from Royston to Godmanchester and parts of the modern A1 and A15 northwards through Lincoln to the Humber. Aquae Sulis, the Roman city of Bath, became Urbs Achumanensis and gave its name to the now rather obscure Akeman Street, which makes its way to London by a roundabout northerly route that includes part of the A43 road from Oxford to Bicester.

Though the Anglo-Saxons thought up names for the Roman roads, they had little use for them except when waging major wars. Theirs was a small-town life, mostly confined to villages which lay apart from the highways. They had their own network of tortuous minor roads linking the villages and fields, which served for the short distances they wished to cover.

Naturally they did nothing to maintain the Roman roads. The whole superb system was neglected for more than a thousand years, and road building techniques learned under Roman rule were completely forgotten. This happened in every country once civilized by the Romans. Even in Italy itself the roads were left to disintegrate, or were robbed of their material, until only a small fraction of their original mileage survived. Without roads, life became localized and society was organized on a feudal basis. Indeed, overland communication almost ceased, and the only effective means of long-distance transportation was by water. It was quite literally easier for Columbus to discover America than it would have been for him to carry out a thorough exploration into the interior of Spain.

The first European country to build up a modern highway system was France. Towards the end of the sixteenth century, the Duc de Sully drew up a national programme of road building to aid Henry IV's campaign to establish prosperity in the land. His work was continued, some sixty years later, by Colbert, who arranged for the resurfacing of 15,000 miles of French roads under Louis XIV, but the most effective road programme was that of Turgot, whose "Six Edicts" of 1776 put an end to the *corvée* system by which roads were maintained—or rather, neglected—by unpaid labour. Because of Turgot's efforts, an excellent road system existed when Napoleon came to power, enabling him to prove the truth of his axiom that rapidity of movement is the secret of military success, and thus establish an empire as the Romans had done before him.

If Napoleon could have arranged for his *Grande Armée* to travel by motor, he would assuredly have done so; he actually did have Cugnot's steam tractor of 1771—the world's oldest self-propelled vehicle—brought out of storage for some tests which proved unsuccessful. By the middle of the nineteenth century France could boast some 46,000 miles of excellent national highways, a heritage that was soon to give her the advantage over all other nations in the establishment of the new motor manufacturing industry.

Britain at first lagged far behind, the need for roads on a national scale being at one time unrecognized. Farmers sold or bartered their produce at traditional fairs held in local market towns, a short distance away by packhorse or farm waggon. Over longer distances, trade was maintained largely by water, the shape of Britain being such that no part of the nation is more than seventy-five miles from the sea.

Only the monarch had a special interest in good highways, which would help him to control his kingdom, contain the power of sometimes overambitious nobility, and quell dissidence wherever it arose. It was because of this interest that Henry VIII felt some misgivings when he dissolved the monasteries, for the Church, as an act of piety, traditionally played a leading role in the building of bridges and maintenance of roads. It was thought wise to put aside some of the confiscated revenue "whereby valiant beggars may be set to work" to repair them. Henry's laws for better highway maintenance were largely ineffective, however. One edict merely served to condone the practice (already widespread in England) of beating out a new route to one side or other of a marshy piece of road, thus making a detour around a bad patch instead of taking the trouble to repair it. After this had been done a few times, the route became tortuous indeed. Chesterton's famous "rolling English road" was the work of people who were lazy, not drunk.

Britain, like France, had her *corvée* system, by which every parishioner had to devote four days a year to repairing local roads. The work was inspected by surveyors appointed under Mary Tudor's "Statute for the Mending of the Highways." This act, brought in as a stopgap measure in 1555, was intended for a trial period of seven years. It lasted 280—from three years before the accession of Elizabeth I to two years before that of Queen Victoria. Its ineffectiveness may be judged by the fact that James of Scotland spent six weeks travelling from Edinburgh to London in 1603, when he was taking over the English throne in succession to Elizabeth.

During the seventeenth century the situation grew worse as wheeled vehicles came to be used more widely. London, twenty-five times the size of Bristol, her nearest rival, became not only the administrative centre but the focal point of the nation's trade. The city had its own hackney coaches. The first regular mail service was established. Goods were trans-

Caution to Waggoners.

WHEREAS great INJURY has of late been done to the TURNPIKE-ROADS, owing to Waggons and other Carriages, with Narrow Wheels, being drawn by a greater Number of Horſes than the Law allows:

Notice is hereby given,

That from and after the 1ſt Day of April next, Informations will be laid, and the Penalties be levied on the Owner and Driver of every Waggon, Wain, Cart, or other heavy Carriage, which ſhall be found paſſing on any Turnpike-Road having the Wheels of leſs Breadth, and being drawn by a greater Number of Horſes than under-mentioned, or having a Middle Tire or Binding round the Wheels, contrary to Act of Parliament.

By the General Turnpike Act, 13 G. 3d, C. 84, No Waggon, Wain, Cart, or other Carriage, (except Coaches, &c.) ſhall paſs on any Turnpike-Road but with Wheels of ſuch a Breadth, and with ſuch a Number of Horſes drawing the ſame, as follows:

Breadth of Wheels.		No. of Horſes.
Four-Wheel Carriages 9 Inches		8 Horſes and no more.
6		6
Leſs than 6		4
Two-Wheel Carriages 9		5
6		4
Leſs than 6		3

And the Wheels to roll on a *Flat* Surface.

On Pain that the Owner of every ſuch Carriage ſhall forfeit 5l, and the Driver 20s.

Dated March 20th, 1800.

RADIO TIMES HULTON PICTURE LIBRARY

Most governments resorted to restrictive measures at one time or another (this notice is dated 1800) in an attempt to reduce the damage done to soft road surfaces by wheeled vehicles; especially those with narrow tyres.

ported increasingly by heavy carriers' waggons, frequently overloaded and dragged through the mud by teams of six or more straining horses. The effect on the road surface was disastrous. A London journal of 1692 records that in the early part of that year the Speaker of the House of Lords was unable to attend a conference in the House of Commons because of "the badness of the roads at this present." The Speaker lived at Kensington, little more than two miles from the Houses of Parliament. As well might a New Yorker say he couldn't make it from 23rd Street to City Hall.

Under James I, Charles I, and even under Oliver Cromwell, repeated attempts were made to restrict or suppress the use of waggons and coaches, on the basis that if the roads were inadequate for the traffic, it was the traffic that should suffer. This policy, which called for neither intelligence nor financial outlay, was adopted in preference to any measure that would have actually made the roads better. However, Cromwell's 1654 "Ordinance for Better Amending and Keeping in Repair the Common Highwaies within this Nation" contained a glimmer of light in the form of a road tax by which funds could be raised for maintenance work. The volume of traffic continued to increase during the Restoration period, so that by the end of the century one could travel by stagecoach from London to Plymouth (215 miles), Kendal (270 miles) or Newcastle-upon-Tyne (280 miles). The fastest service was a "flier" to Oxford (55 miles) in a day (13 hours) during the summer, two days in winter. Naturally the roads deteriorated even more, and on part of the Great North Road it was decided, in 1663, to levy a toll on travellers "whereas the ancient highway and post-road

leading from London to York and so into Scotland . . . is become so ruinous and almost impassable that the ordinary course . . . is not sufficient for the effective repairing of same."

This was the preamble to England's first Turnpike Act, a purely local measure intended to aid the inhabitants of three counties who had despaired of keeping pace with ever-increasing road repairs which were beyond their means. Eventually it was to transform the whole administration and financing of road maintenance; by the early part of the nineteenth century there were 1,100 turnpike trusts in existence controlling 23,000 miles of English roads and collecting £1.5 million a year in tolls. The system spread to America, where from 1795 onwards some of the first intercity highways were financed in this way.

Private enterprise came into the picture in 1706 when the English Parliament granted turnpike powers to independent trusts instead of to local magistrates acting on behalf of a parish or similar public body. The system had its shortcomings, and many trusts were undoubtedly corrupt or badly administered, but in the two hundred years of its existence British roads were better maintained than ever before, frequently widened and straightened, and sometimes lengthened considerably. The funds which the turnpike system attracted made it possible to seek expert advice for the first time, with spectacular results. Not since the Romans left had road making in Britain been entrusted to people who knew what they were doing.

The two most respected names in the history of road making are those of two Scots, Telford and McAdam. Telford, the son of a shepherd, was also a builder of bridges, canals and aqueducts. From 1803 onwards he built

MARY EVANS PICTURE LIBRARY

almost one thousand miles of new road in difficult terrain in his native Scotland, but even this achievement was eclipsed by his Holyhead Road, which linked the Welsh port with the old Roman road from Shrewsbury to London. The existing road through North Wales was so bad that in 1808 the Post Office had had to abandon their attempts to run a mail-coach service along it; it was, they said, too dangerous. One section of 194 miles was administered by no less than twenty-three different turnpike trusts when Telford started work in 1815, but he succeeded in gaining control over all of them. He insisted that the assistant surveyors who worked under him should be professionals, and that every barrowload of material should be of good quality and handled by a skilled labourer. He would have no dealings with incompetent or casual workers. When a House of Commons committee presented a progress report after his first few years of work on the Holyhead

Road, it was the sheer professionalism that was emphasized above all:

"The science which has been displayed in giving the general line of the road a proper inclination through a country whose whole surface consists of a succession of rocks, bogs, ravines, rivers, and precipices, reflects the greatest credit upon the engineer who has planned them; but perhaps a greater degree of professional skill has been shown in the construction, or rather the building, of the road itself. The great attention which Mr. Telford has bestowed to give to the surface of the road one uniform and moderately convex shape, free from the smallest inequality throughout its whole breadth; the numerous land drains and, when necessary, shores and tunnels of substantial masonry, with which all the water arising from springs or falling in rain is instantly carried off; the great care with which a sufficient foundation is established for the road,

Dubbed "The Colossus of Roads" by Robert Southey, the Poet Laureate, McAdam was a Scot who amassed a fortune in America and spent most of it on road-making experiments.

and the quality, solidity, and disposition of the materials that are put upon it, are matters quite new in the system of road-making in these countries."

This was perhaps not strictly true, if one looks back far enough, for one might say that Telford had extended a Roman road by methods which the Romans themselves would have found very acceptable—and not at all unfamiliar.

McAdam was born just eleven months before Telford, moved to New York at the age of fourteen, and was a rich man when he returned to Scotland at the age of twenty-seven. He came into road making as an amateur, carrying out experiments at his own expense after buying a share in a local turnpike trust, and prepared a memorandum on the subject which attracted considerable attention. It was time, he said, to ask if existing road making methods were satisfactory. The roads must be changed to suit the traffic, instead of restricting traffic to suit the roads. Road making and maintenance must be done by skilled people, and the labouring performed by labourers, not layabouts. To those who advocated nationalization as the way to develop a system of highways, McAdam replied that the government would be more likely to use roads as a source of revenue than to honour its duty to maintain them as an essential public asset.

The publicity given to McAdam's memorandum bore fruit in 1816 when he was appointed surveyor to thirty-four turnpike trusts, and in this capacity he supervised the repair of some seven hundred miles of road in fifteen counties. Later he moved to London as a consultant, and planned to bring all the many Metropolitan turnpike trusts under the control of a single body. McAdam was eventually reimbursed by the government for his experiments in road making and repairs, but declined a knighthood when it was offered to him. His son and grandson each in turn held the appointment of General Surveyor to the Metropolitan Turnpike Trust. Perhaps that is why the name of John Loudon McAdam, who died in near poverty in 1836, has passed into the English language—while Thomas Telford, who achieved world renown and was buried two years earlier in Westminster Abbey, is now almost forgotten as a road maker.

By the second or third decade of the nineteenth century, Telford and McAdam had made their mark on the British countryside, and travel overland was altered beyond recognition as the stagecoach era approached its bustling climax of activity. Journeys which had once taken four or five days were now reckoned in hours: 17½ from London to Exeter (170 miles); 18 to Manchester (185 miles), and 21 hours to York (200 miles). There were 1,500 stagecoaches leaving London every 24 hours, 50 of them to the popular south coast resort of Brighton. A big operator like Chaplin of London owned 64 coaches, 1,500 horses, several coaching inns, and had a turnover of half a million pounds a year.

This golden age of coaching lasted only a short time, from about 1820, when the roads became good enough for fast travel, to 1836, when the rapid growth of steam railways brought it to a sudden close. The coach operators tried to meet the new mechanical menace by reducing their fares, but travellers had found the railways faster and more comfortable as well as less expensive. Then the General Post Office started cancelling the stagecoach companies' mail contracts and transferring to rail: the last mail coach from London to Bir-

A mid-1920s encounter in a Sussex lane underlines the fact that motor traffic was fast outgrowing the capacity of most roads at that time.

mingham ran in 1839; the last to Bath and Brighton in 1841; the last to Bristol in 1843; the last to Plymouth in 1847. All over the country the stagecoach operators were selling off their horses to anyone who would buy, dismissing grooms and coachmen, and leaving the coaches to rot in their inn yards. In 1830, when the railway line from Liverpool to Manchester was opened, there were twenty-nine stagecoaches running between the two cities. Within five months there were only four.

The turnpike system soon felt the pinch, and a railway-minded government recommended its complete abolition as early as 1836. Within the next two decades, toll income fell by 30 percent in most areas, sometimes more; one turnpike was taking £369 from stagecoach tolls in 1846, a bare £73 in 1850. Toll charges were reduced, less money was available for maintenance work, and the road surfaces began to break up from neglect. Again in 1864 a Parliamentary committee advised the abolition of turnpike roads, but nothing was done, and the system simply faded away. It took a long time to do so. The last London tollhouse closed in 1871, but twelve years later there were still seventy-one toll roads in the country. In 1895 the British turnpike system came to an end when the last toll point of all (on Telford's Holyhead Road at Anglesey) was closed down.

What happened in Britain was repeated in many other countries. The rapid expansion of the railways stifled further development of the highway system, and roads fell into disuse by the ordinary traveller, serving merely for short journeys and, when he had to go further afield, for access to the nearest railway station. The road from London to Brighton, which had carried fifty stagecoaches a day, was almost bare of traffic, as recorded by S. F. Edge:

"I remember the Brighton Road so narrow that not more than a couple of carts could pass each other. It was a long, winding, narrow highway, used by farmers' carts and the Brighton coach on weekdays, and by large numbers of cyclists during weekends. . . . One could go for miles along the Brighton Road without seeing a living soul."

The first motorcars made their appearance on roads which had known little wheeled traffic for half a century, and whose surface had become loose and rough from lack of maintenance. In this condition it provided a better grip for the hooves of horses, which used the roads most, so there was no incentive to alter it although those who rode in carriages travelled in some discomfort. In the earliest days of the automobile the full disadvantages of such roads were not revealed, since the car of that time differed scarcely at all from the horse-drawn vehicles that preceded it, being high-built, slow-moving, and equipped with large-diameter wheels which were fitted with thin tyres of solid rubber or iron. But in less than a decade the shape of cars changed considerably, and everybody who had anything to do with them faced a new, apparently inescapable menace.

The trouble was dust. Accustomed as we are to sealed road surfaces, it is well-nigh impossible to imagine the amount of dust that arose in the early part of this century when an ordinary car made its way along an ordinary road at quite a moderate speed. It was appalling. People walking or standing at the roadside were enveloped in a choking cloud, their clothes coated all over in dust, when a motorcar went by. The same fate befell cyclists, horsemen, or anyone in a horse-drawn vehicle when overtaken by a car—as of course they all were,

RADIO TIMES HULTON PICTURE LIBRARY

sooner or later. Everybody who lived near a road suffered by the passage of motorcars. Their windows and the paintwork of their houses were covered in dust, and on busier roads it seemed able to get through every minute crevice and penetrate all the interior furnishings as well. Crops and gardens were ruined—flowers, fruit and vegetables alike. Washing was spoiled as it hung on the line to dry, and had to be done again. An English authoress complained that she had to buy new typewriters (apparently she had several) because "they got so gritty."

It was a very real problem, and one that grew worse as cars became faster, lower-built, and increasingly used thicker pneumatic tyres. Some early motorists believe it was dust, more than any other single factor, that aroused such intense antimotoring feelings among those who did not own cars. Drivers were themselves very conscious of it. For several years, dust was a topic of conversation wherever motorists met, and an evergreen subject in the correspondence columns of the motoring magazines. In Britain, it even took its place in the annals of motor sport: competitors in the 1000 Miles Trial of 1903 had to drive over a sixty-yard patch of white flour so that the dust-arousing propensities of their vehicles could be assessed by the judges.

Officialdom thought in terms of stopgap measures. On hot summer days it was usual to lay the dust in city streets by sending out a horse-drawn watering cart. The solution, it was believed, was to find some cheap material that could be applied in a similar way, but with more lasting results, and in some cases the side effects of such a treatment seem to have been

"The ? of the Day—Should there be a speed (and dust) limit?": So ran the caption to this Punch *cartoon of the early 1900s, though there was a speed limit already.*

largely ignored. One misguided individual advocated spraying the road with a highly corrosive acid which would literally dissolve the dust—and, indeed, anything else that came in contact with it, including dogs, cats, horses and people. Crude oil, first employed very successfully on dirt roads in California to protect fruit crops from damage by dust, long before motorcars were invented, was too expensive to use elsewhere, but wool grease and other animal fats were tried. So were calcium chloride, bittern, sodium silicate, molasses and furnace slag. There were patent preparations such as Herr van Westrum's Westrumite (mostly petroleum and ammonia), Sandisize (wool grease, potassium hydroxide and creosote), and Crempoid (animal glue, potassium bichromate and vegetable oils).

John Montagu inaugurated a Dust Fund to which the British Prime Minister, the Hon. A. J. Balfour, contributed £100, and *Car Illustrated* carried out tests of many materials between 1903 and 1905, the magazine's findings being presented to Parliament. Eventually the dust problem was solved by the use of coal tar to bind the surface dust together and form a sealed coating. Once the various road-repairing authorities had been persuaded that the only way to do the job was to do it properly, the strange assortment of experimental materials could be forgotten. But it took time, because British roads were still administered by a multiplicity of small local bodies, and when the first International Roads Congress was held in Paris in 1908, Britain had no national representative to send because there was no central highways authority; the two organizations represented there by John Montagu—the Royal Automobile Club and the Roads Improvement Association—were both private.

The dust problem caused such concern that all manner of strange gadgets were devised in an attempt to solve it, including screens, flaps, trays, and what amounted to portable vacuum-cleaners mounted on the car.

The tar-spraying boiler eventually solved the dust problem. This early example at Staines, west of London, is mounted on two tyreless wheels and drawn by a horse.

In 1908, however, Lloyd George—then Chancellor of the Exchequer—set up the Road Board to arrange for the improvement of existing roads in Britain and the construction of new ones, making use of revenue derived from recently increased motor licensing charges and a new fuel tax. John Montagu was one of the original five members of this body, which remained in existence until 1920, when it was absorbed by the Ministry of Transport. His views on highway development were remarkably advanced for the period. They are too comprehensive to quote at length here, but they were summed up very lucidly by one of his biographers, Archibald Marshall, in these terms:

"By the invention of the internal combustion engine, the most effective combination of speed and cheapness passed from the railway locomotive to the motor-car. Therefore, the road over which the motor-car must pass becomes of primary importance. The roads of England were not built to accommodate traffic of such weight and speed as the coming of the motor-car has introduced. So as regards foundations, surface, corners, gradients and direction they must be adjusted to conform to their new task, or where this is not possible fresh roads suitable to modern conditions must be constructed. Roads, like all other artificial constructions of man, depend for their ultimate resistance and longevity upon their foundations. Therefore foundations must everywhere be made of sufficient strength and of such a nature as to take existing and increasing future road traffic, and must never be scamped or cheesepared.

"Surfaces give scope for a wider range of material and for experiment, but, since the golden rule is that the roads must be adapted to the traffic and the traffic on the roads is 90

RADIO TIMES HULTON PICTURE LIBRARY

DETROIT PUBLIC LIBRARY
KANSAS HISTORICAL SOCIETY

SMITHSONIAN INSTITUTION

OVERLEAF, TOP LEFT: *Two enthusiasts in a 1921 Bianchi tackle the ancient track at Box Hill, Surrey.* TOP RIGHT: *The occupants of a handsome 1905 Pope-Toledo from Toledo, Ohio, pause to consider road conditions before going on their way.* BOTTOM *To the pair in this stripped machine at Osborne County, Kansas, it is all great fun despite the mud.*

When John Montagu crossed the Atlantic to study American roads in 1912, he found that most were unpaved. Like this dirt road in Dorrance, Kansas, they were merely smoothed over at intervals with a simple, horse-drawn grader.

percent motor traffic, they should be made of bituminous, i.e. resilient and dustless, material, and waterproofed. If these conditions render them slippery and unsuitable for the remaining 10 percent of horse traffic the remedy lies in the alteration of the horse's shoe.

"Bearing in mind the essential conditions of speed combined with cheapness, slow traffic must be kept to the kerb, or even banished from the road altogether during certain hours. Where the economic conditions guarantee an adequate volume of traffic, as between large cities, direct roads solely for fast traffic [i.e., motorways] must be constructed."

In 1912 John Montagu crossed the Atlantic to study American road making. He found little enough to study, for many of the shortcomings of British roads were to be found duplicated, even accentuated, in the United States. The only road that could be called a national highway— the only one built by the US government—was the National Old Trails Road, inspired by George Washington and approved by Congress three years after his death, when Ohio was admitted to the Union. This very impressive highway ran from Washington, D.C., through Columbus, Indianapolis, St. Louis, Kansas City, Great Bend and La Junta to Santa Fe (reached in 1825, when it was still in Mexico), then on to Socorro, St. Johns and San Bernardino to cover a total of 3,096 miles, linking Atlantic and Pacific oceans. There were also the remnants of the first state-financed roads, some 340 miles of highway constructed between 1821 and 1837 in Kentucky.

There were some broken-stone roads— the Old York Road, the Baltimore and the Lancaster turnpikes—which had spread out from Philadelphia when the turnpike system reached America, but these had been put out of business (just as they were in England) by the steam railroad, which in the United States made a more significant contribution to long-distance overland transportation than almost anywhere else in the world. In America as elsewhere, the rapid development of railways had for a time brought road building to a halt, and various organizations were active in advocating a change of policy; one of the first was a cycling club, the League of American Wheelmen, followed by literally hundreds of Trail Associations, most of which amalgamated in 1911 to form the National Highways Association. At the time of John Montagu's visit, forty-two states were helping to finance road construction, and interest in constructional techniques was beginning to grow. There were, for example, experiments with cement-concrete roads which had begun in Bellefontaine, Ohio, as early as 1893, and increasingly heavy truck traffic in the cities had led to the use of brick paving and a variety of bituminous surfaces.

But it was the urban areas that came in for almost all the attention. The city streets might have a modern finish, but beyond them the road would dwindle away to little more than a rutted stretch of dirt track, and apart from an occasional gravel road running westward from some of the bigger cities in the East, there were scarcely any interstate highways.

The first Federal Aid Act was not passed until 1915, and not until 1921 was this expanded into the Federal Highway Act, which led to a network of trunk roads being created over most of the country. By 1928 there were some 300,000 miles of excellent road, laid out and built with amazing speed by state highway commissions under the provisions of the Federal Aid system. One-third of this mileage qualified for the numbered shield denoting an official United

KANSAS HISTORICAL SOCIETY

States Highway. Even then, however, there were still 2½ million miles of unsurfaced roads against ½ million surfaced, and of the surfaced road, only 90,000 miles were actually paved; many thousands of miles were still being treated with crude oil to bind the surface, or merely· graded at intervals because there was insufficient traffic to justify spending time and money on them.

In Europe, the outbreak of World War I in 1914 prevented further improvement in highways, while the massive movements of supplies subjected them to greater loads than ever before in the first conflict waged with the aid of mechanized vehicles and weapons. In the aftermath of war, many nations were left too impoverished to embark on the building of roads, or even to repair them.

France, however, emerged as the European nation which still had more and better trunk roads than any other. By the middle 1920s

she had 385,000 miles of road, almost 35,000 of which were up to *Route Nationale* standard. Germany's total was 134,000 miles, but Italy had a mere 38,500 miles of poor-quality roads which were, in any case, mostly confined to the more prosperous northern part of the country, and her economy was gravely handicapped by poor communications. The differing French and Italian situations were reflected in different parts of North Africa. Under French administration, Tunisia, Algeria and most of Morocco had good roads. But Libya, Italian-controlled, had almost none; even in 1931, a motoring tourist there found that it took a week to drive the eight hundred miles from Tripoli to Benghazi.

Very few men had yet grasped the full potential of the motorcar, or appreciated the contribution it was capable of making to industrial and commercial expansion in those countries which provided suitable highways for it. One of the few, surprisingly enough, was

From the earliest years of the century John Montagu campaigned for the building of motorways; this impression of such a road between London and Birmingham was drawn in 1921. The London/Birmingham motorway was not actually opened until 1959.

Anatole France. His *Ile des Pingouins* of 1907—a time when cars were still scorned as a rich man's plaything—contained this remarkable passage:

"Without doubt the future belongs to the metal beast. We are no more likely to go back to cabs than we are to go back to the *diligence*. And the long martyrdom of the horse will come to an end. The motor, which the frenzied cupidity of manufacturers hurls like a Juggernaut's car upon the bewildered people and of which the idle and fashionable make a foolish though fatal elegance, will soon begin to perform its true function, and, putting its strength at the service of the entire people, will behave like a docile, toiling monster.

"But in order that the motor may cease to be injurious and become beneficent, we must build roads suited to its speed, roads which it cannot tear up with its ferocious tyres, and from which it will send no clouds of poisonous dust into human lungs. We ought not to allow slower vehicles or mere animals to go upon these roads, and we should establish garages upon them and footbridges over them, and so create order and harmony among the means of communication of the future. This is the wish of every good citizen."

It is astonishing that a literary figure should have grasped one of the most crucial points of highway planning, the need for segregation to prevent conflict between road users. In Britain, unfortunately, this need went unrecognized by successive administrations for half a century. It was in 1903, when the overall speed limit in Britain was still 12 mph, that the Anglo-American reformer, Ebenezer Howard, aroused widespread interest with his plans to found the world's first garden city at Letchworth, some thirty miles north of London. John Montagu advocated in *Car Magazine* the building of a special road (he called it a "motor way") to link the new settlement with London, pointing out that it could also be extended northwards to provide a much-needed new route to Birmingham and the industrial Midlands of England. Such roads, he said, would also allow city workers to live in pleasant rural surroundings some distance from their place of employment, but still close enough in terms of travelling time. For years he continued to campaign for such roads with the oft-repeated warning that "The longer we delay, the more we have to pay." The first significant stretch of the M1 London/Birmingham Motorway, whose construction he had suggested in 1903, was opened to the public in November 1959.

If a motorway be defined as a limited-access highway built specifically for the automobile, it would appear that the world's first was built in the state of New York. The wealthy William K. Vanderbilt conceived the idea of a fast motor road running eastwards from New York City through Long Island, where he owned an estate at Centerport. Apart from the obvious convenience of the road for travel to and from the city, by making it a privately owned toll road he could also arrange to close it annually for the Vanderbilt Cup Race, which he had started in 1904. With a number of friends he formed a syndicate to purchase a narrow strip of land from the eastern border of Queens County, near Elmont, all the way to Riverhead, and in October 1908 the Vanderbilt Motor Parkway was opened. At that time it stretched as far east as Lake Ronkonkoma, a distance of some thirty-five miles in all, and in 1910 a spur was added to the western end bringing it to Springfield Boulevard, only a few miles north of the present John F. Kennedy International Airport. Parts of the parkway may still be traced today, not entirely obliterated by subsequent road building, and at least one of the tollhouses survives as a family dwelling.

Europe's first stretch of motorway was laid out in 1909, but circumstances delayed its completion for many years. Like the Vanderbilt Parkway it was a toll road, occasionally used for motor racing, and intended as a fast route out of a capital city to a pleasant residential area—but it was a mere six miles in length, and did not open until 1921. The Avus *autostrasse* ran in a dead-straight line from the western side of Berlin through the attractive Grünewald, almost to the Havel lakes, and survives in its entirety as the first part of the main road from Berlin to Potsdam.

It remained Germany's nearest approach to a motorway for many years, despite pressure from commercial interests for the construction of more. In that, the initiative passed to the country which had led the world, centuries earlier, in the building of super-highways. The first of Italy's *autostrade* was opened in 1925

soon after Mussolini gained control. It covered a distance of about thirty miles from industrial Milan to Varese, in the Italian Lake District of Lombardy, and was followed by similar roads to Brescia in the east (passing just south of Bergamo) and by way of Galliate westwards to Turin. Mussolini had great faith in his motorway programme as a valuable way to ease unemployment and aid the country's economic recovery. During the 1930s he added further short sections near Florence, Venice, Rome and Naples.

In 1933 Hitler became Chancellor of Germany, and soon he launched a seven-year plan for the building of 7,000 kilometres (4,350 miles) of *Reichsautobahnen*, which would, he said, "Bring the German state together in a new unity, provide freedom of movement for motorists, and deal constructively with the unemployment problem." But in 1937 the British Road Federation noted another possible motive for the German Chancellor's action:

"Herr Hitler is concentrating on the building of strategic highways instead of strategic railways, since cars can detour round a bombed section of road, while trains cannot. The cars which are being put on the roads in such great numbers will be available for use in an emergency to carry men and essential materials over these highways."

Germany's new motorways soon became the envy of other countries although its planned extent was not achieved before World War II, and certain economies had to be practised, such as providing only two traffic lanes in each direction, and limiting clover-leaf crossings to their simplest form. Even Holland, despite her small size, was moved to build seventy miles of motorway. France at first continued to favour the *Route Nationale*, but started on an *auto-*

route which was to bypass Paris on the western side. Spain did not aspire to motorways, yet the main roads were improved out of all recognition after the fall of the monarchy; the best, some said, were even better than the roads of France.

In Britain one of the leading campaigners for better roads, Colonel O'Gorman, commented that "During the forty years of the motor era, not one-half of 1 percent has been added to the mileage of roads that was extant in England in the reign of Queen Victoria." The Great North Road, hopelessly inadequate for the volume of traffic it carried, was so narrow for half of its total length that one parked vehicle would reduce it to a single track—not a single lane of traffic running each way, but one single stream. The Trunk Roads Act of 1937 gave the Ministry of Transport control over 180,000 miles of highway which had previously been administered by local county councils, designating them as trunk roads. This was intended as the first step towards improving them, but in practice it appeared to be merely an exercise in semantics.

In America, Robert Moses was perhaps the most active early advocate of new motor roads which would make it easier for city workers to reach leisure centres out of town, such as Jones Beach in Nassau County, and during the late 1920s and early 1930s this policy led to the construction of the Northern and Southern State Parkways and Hutchinson River Parkway, all in New York, and the Garden State Parkway in New Jersey. After World War II it was the awareness of defence requirements that sparked off a massive campaign in the 1950s to build thousands of miles of United States federal interstate highways. These now combine with freeways, thruways, turnpikes and express-

ways to make the United States more comprehensively provided with major trunk routes than any other country; yet many of the local roads, paradoxically, have remained inadequate and badly maintained to this day.

Because of the war Germany lost almost half her motorway system by partition, but the remaining 1,300 miles still amounted to far more than in other European countries. Nationalized in 1950, the West German motorways were rapidly expanded from 1959 on until, a decade later, their length had been almost doubled. By the middle 1970s they had reached 6,000 kilometres (3,700 miles), and work was well under way to enlarge the outmoded original *autobahnen* from four lanes to six. The Federal Republic's eventual aim is to ensure that 98 percent of the population will live within 25 kilometres (15½ miles) of a motorway.

Italy's motorway system, second only to that of Germany before the last world war, has retained that position with an even more impressive programme of expansion to pass the 5,000-kilometre mark in 1973, despite the enormous difficulties imposed by the physical formation of the country; 500 kilometres passed through tunnels, and 1,000 kilometres were carried by bridges or viaducts. France also sought to achieve 5,000 kilometres of motorways, but at the time of writing is still almost 2,000 kilometres short of her target. The most remarkable performance in Continental Europe has been that of Holland, which had slightly less than 70 miles of motorway at the outbreak of World War II in 1939. By 1965, with 490 miles, she had a greater motorway mileage for her size than anywhere else in Europe. Since that time, the total mileage of Dutch motorways has been almost doubled.

And in Britain, for years, there were no

Motorway in the making: an aerial view of Junction 23 being constructed near Loughborough, on the northward extension of the London/Birmingham motorway, M1. It shows the area of land absorbed by a simple interchange point between two roads when motorway standards are maintained.

R ROBERT McALPINE & SONS LTD.

motorways at all. In 1948 the Ministry of Transport told the House of Commons: "We are hopelessly in arrears. Sooner or later we must tackle this problem unless we are to be choked to death by the motor vehicles on our roads."

The first requirement was an act of Parliament to substitute the principle of limited access for the ancient concept of Freedom of the King's Highway which allows full right of way to all persons, whether walking, riding or driving. This was achieved in 1949 when the Special Roads Act was approved, but instead of actually building motorways, or indeed any other new roads, the government again took refuge in restrictive legislation which limited private motoring. In this way the need for a proper road-construction programme was temporarily concealed, but it was an unfortunate reversion to the head-in-sand policy of the 1890s and the effects were markedly similar, the British motor industry being placed at a marked disadvantage by comparison with those of other nations. When British family cars were placed on overseas markets, many were found to be incapable of maintaining the high cruising speeds that had become normal in countries which did have up-to-date highways.

At the end of 1958, Britain's first motorway was opened to the public. It consisted of 8¼ miles of road, built to bypass Preston in Lancashire. Even this short length, however, showed what a motorway could do to aid road safety, for it relieved motorists in that area of the dangers presented by 1,898 junctions and intersections on the superseded portion of the old A6 road.

For years the construction of British motorways proceeded at a snail's pace, totalling only 635 miles by 1970. Then came a jump forward to 1,024 miles in 1973 as a number of projects reached completion at about the same time. After this the pace slackened once again, and by 1976 the motorway mileage had reached 1,300. Or, to put it another way, exactly the extent of motor roads that would have been found in war-torn Germany more than thirty years before. With sixty-three cars to every mile of available road surface—motorway, trunk road, minor roads and all—Britain is the most crowded country in the motoring world.

POSTSCRIPT

It was 1906, the year in which Rolls-Royce were to reveal their new Silver Ghost model at the London Motor Show, and construction of the world's first motor-racing track was to commence at Brooklands, Surrey. Even among the diehards of Britain it was beginning to be admitted, however reluctantly, that the motorcar had possibly come to stay, but the full extent of its influence was not even imagined—except by the very few who were gifted with sufficient imagination to judge its possibilities. In that same year, John Montagu wrote these words:

"What is the future of automobilism? That it will to a great extent replace nearly every other kind of traction upon the surface of the earth, I have but little doubt. That it will help to solve political and social problems but at the same time create others, is equally obvious. It will affect values of land, towns and houses by a redistribution of values. Town houses and sites of all kinds, whether for business or pleasure, are going to become less valuable because they largely depend for their value on concentrated humanity, in other words, on inferior transit facilities. On the other hand, land in the country and on the outskirts of towns and in villages remote from railways will become more valuable because of the greater ease of access.

"Population will gradually tend to become less concentrated and be diffused over wider areas. Travelling in the broad sense will increase enormously, and dustless motor ways will be constructed between principal towns to carry the ceaseless traffic which will use them by night and by day. The workmen employed by the new method of transit will in twenty years overshadow in numbers and importance those employed by railways and tramways added together.

"Large towns will have special arterial

roads to connect their centres with main roads outside. There will be but little noise, no smell, and, with dustless roads, no dust in the traction of the future. No bacteria will breed in fermenting horse-manure, and the water-cart will be unknown. Produce will come direct from the country to the consumer, and necessaries and luxuries of life will be alike cheapened.

"The cultivation of farming in all countries in which the motor-car eventually prevails will gradually alter; the foods raised for the horse, partly or exclusively, will tend to disappear, for oats, for instance, will not be wanted to feed horses, and more foodstuffs for cattle will be grown, and a greater amount of land will be devoted to the raising of foodstuffs for mankind.

"Another great change which the motor-car will bring about will be the creation of a new kind of internationalism. To this influence the one preliminary condition will be the existence of passable roads. Europe in a few years' time will become for the motorist one vast holiday area, whether he is seeking health, change of scenery, a warmer or a colder climate as the case may be. Hotels, even in anti-motorist countries such as Switzerland, will find the motorist not only the most profitable but the most common source of revenue.

"The country which has the best roads will in future tend to become more and more prosperous, given that its natural advantages are not inferior to the countries which surround it. New countries which are being opened up will no longer build railways, but roads—as was the custom till seventy years ago, before the coming of the railway, and roads will be justly regarded as the necessary hallmark of civilization. Enormous sums will be invested in new road-making and new vehicles all over the world.

"Is this an exaggerated picture, the result of a vivid imagination only, or a prophecy to be fulfilled? Time alone can show."

More than seventy years later, the reader may judge the answer to that question for himself.

ACKNOWLEDGEMENTS

Unless otherwise specified, all photographs are
from the National Motor Museum, Beaulieu, England.

The authors acknowledge with thanks the assistance
provided by the following organizations and individuals
during the preparation of this book:

Douglas Armstrong
Automobile Association of Great Britain
William Boddy
Robert Bosch Ltd.
B.P. Oil Ltd.
British Road Federation
British School of Motoring
Burmah-Castol Co.
Chrysler UK Ltd.
Citroën Cars Ltd.
Tim Davidson
H. J. Davies
Design Council, London
Firestone Tyre & Rubber Co. Ltd.
Peter Flowers
Dr. Ernst Fuhrmann
Bernard Garrett
G. N. Georgano
Goodyear Tyre & Rubber Co. Ltd.
Shirley Henshaw
Institute of Petroleum, London
Russell Lowry
Joseph Lucas Industries Ltd.
Prince Marshall
Bill Mason
Michelin Tyre Co. Ltd.
A. J. Mothersele
Frederick M'packa
National Benzole Co. Ltd.
National Motor Museum, Beaulieu, England
Don Pinhorn
Pirelli Ltd.
Porsche Cars GB Ltd.
Cyril Posthumus
Royal Automobile Club, London
Smith's Industries Ltd.
Patricia Spencer
Volkswagen GB Ltd.
Woolf, Laing, Christie & Partners

BIBLIOGRAPHY

W. Poynter Adams, *Motor Car Mechanism and
Management*. London, 1907.
Autocar Handbook (8th edition). London, 1915.
Arnold Bennett, *Journal 1899*.
A. E. Berriman, *Motoring*. London, 1914.
Anthony Bird and Ian Hallows, *The Rolls-Royce
Motor-Car*. London, 1964.
W. Boddy, *The History of the Brooklands Motor Course*.
London, 1957.
John Bolster, *Motoring Is My Business*. London, 1958.
Lord Brabazon of Tara, *The Brabazon Story*. London, 1956.
Colin Buchanan, *Mixed Blessings: The Motor-Car in
Britain*. London, 1958.
Baroness Campbell von Laurentz, *My Motor Milestones*.
London, 1913.
Floyd Clymer, *Those Wonderful Old Automobiles*.
New York, 1953.
John Copeland, *Roads and Their Traffic, 1750/1850*.
Newton Abbott, Devon, 1968.
The Earl of Cottenham, *Steering Wheel Papers*.
London, 1932.
S. C. H. Davis, *Car Driving as an Art*. London, 1952.
John Day, *The Bosch Book of the Motor Car*. Glasgow
and London, 1975.
H. J. Dyos and D. H. Aldcroft, *British Transport*.
Leicester, 1969.
S. F. Edge, *My Motoring Reminiscences*. London, 1934.
Malcolm Foster, *Joyce Cary: A Biography*. London, 1969.
Anatole France, *Ile des Pingouins*. Paris, 1907.
J. L. Garvin (ed.), *Encyclopaedia Britannica* (14th edition).
London and New York, 1929.
G. N. Georgano (ed.), *The Complete Encyclopaedia of
Motorcars*. London, 1968.
———, *The Encyclopaedia of Motor Sport*. London, 1971.
Kenneth Grahame, *The Wind in the Willows*. London,
1908.
Louise Closser Hale, *A Motor Car Divorce*. New York,
1906.
Anthony Harding (ed.), *Car Profiles*. Leatherhead,
Surrey, 1966/7.
———, *The Guinness Book of Car Facts and Feats*.
London, 1971.
Stanley Harris, *Old Coaching Days*. London, 1882.
C. H. Hartmann, *The Story of the Roads*. London, 1927.
David Hodges and David Burgess-Wise, *The Story of
the Car*. London, 1974.

Charles Jarrott, *Ten Years of Motors and Motor Racing*. London, 1906.

Claude Johnson, *The Early History of Motoring*. London, 1927.

———, *Roads Made Easy*. London, 1907.

Rankin Kennedy, *The Book of the Motor Car* (3 vols.). London, 1913.

Richard M. Langworth, *Last Onslaught on Detroit*. Princeton, N.J., 1975.

Saint Loup, *Renault de Billancourt*. Paris, 1955.

F. Wilson McComb, *Veteran Cars*. London, 1974.

Ivan Margery, *Roman Roads in Britain*. London, 1955.

R. J. Mecredy, *The Encyclopaedia of Motoring*. Dublin, 1908.

G. R. N. Minchin, *Under My Bonnet*. London, 1950.

Edward, Lord Montagu of Beaulieu, *Lost Causes of Motoring*. London, 1960.

———, *The Motoring Montagus*. London, 1959.

The Hon. John Scott Montagu, *Cars and How to Drive Them* (4 vols.). London, 1902/1907.

H. F. Morriss, *Two Brave Brothers*. London, ca. 1918.

Motor staff, *How to Drive a Motor Car* (7th edition). London, ca. 1920.

———, *How to Drive a Motor Car* (11th edition). London, 1929.

———, *Motor Manual* (14th edition). London, 1912.

Elizabeth Nagle, *Veterans of the Road*. London, 1955.

T. R. Nicholson, *Adventurers' Road*. London, 1957.

St John C. Nixon, *Daimler 1896–1946*. London, 1946.

Dudley Noble, *Fifty Years of Motoring*. London, 1960.

Harold Nockolds, *The Magic of a Name*. London, 1945.

George A. Oliver, *A History of Coachbuilding*. London, 1962.

Bellamy Partridge, *Excuse My Dust*. New York, 1943.

William Plowden, *The Motor Car and Politics in Great Britain*. London, 1971.

Cyril Posthumus, *Period Cars*. London, 1973.

———, *Vintage Cars*. London, 1973.

John Prioleau, *The Motorist's Companion*. London, 1936.

L. T. C. Rolt, *Horseless Carriage*. London, 1950.

———, *Landscape with Machines*. London, 1971.

Gerald Rose, *A Record of Motor Racing*. London, 1909.

Michael Sedgwick, *Fiat*. London, 1974.

Sir Osbert Sitwell, *Left Hand, Right Hand*. London, 1946.

Ralph Stein, *The Automobile Book*. London, 1961.

———, *The Great Cars*. New York, 1967.

Hugh Tracey, *Father's First Car*. London, 1966.

Lady Troubridge and A. Marshall, *John, Lord Montagu of Beaulieu*. London, 1930.

Major F. E. Verney (ed.), *The Motorist's Reference and Yearbook*. London, 1928.

J. E. Vincent, *Through East Anglia in a Motor Car*. London, 1907.

Richard Wagner, *Golden Wheels*. Cleveland, Ohio, 1975.

Rodney Walkerley, *Motoring Abroad*. London, 1950.

John Welcome, *Best Motoring Stories*. London, 1959.

C. and A. Williamson, *The Lightning Conductor*. London, 1902.

Keith Winser, *The Story of Australian Motoring*. Sydney, 1955.

Edward Young, *Forty Years of Motoring*. London, 1955.

PERIODICALS: *Autocar, Autosport, The Car Illustrated, The Motor Car Magazine, Motor Sport, Pronto, Veteran & Vintage Magazine*.

INDEX